THE MORAL IMAGINATION AND THE LEGAL LIFE

Emerging Legal Education

Series Editors:
Paul Maharg, *University of Northumbria, Newcastle upon Tyne, UK*,
Caroline Maughan, *University of the West of England, Bristol, UK* and
Elizabeth Mertz, *University of Wisconsin-Madison/American Bar Foundation, USA*

Emerging Legal Education is a forum for analysing the discourse of legal education and creating innovative ways of learning the law. The series focuses on research, theory and practice within legal education, drawing attention to historical, interdisciplinary and international characteristics, and is based upon imaginative and sophisticated educational thinking. The series takes a broad view of theory and practice. Series books are written for an international audience and are sensitive to the diversity of contexts in which law is taught, learned and practised.

Other titles in this series:

Law and Leadership
Integrating Leadership Studies into the Law School Curriculum
Edited by Paula Monopoli and Susan McCarty

The Arts and the Legal Academy
Beyond Text in Legal Education
Edited by Zenon Bańkowski, Maksymilian Del Mar and Paul Maharg

Affect and Legal Education
Emotion in Learning and Teaching the Law
Edited by Paul Maharg and Caroline Maughan

The Moral Imagination and the Legal Life

Beyond Text in Legal Education

Edited by

ZENON BAŃKOWSKI
University of Edinburgh, UK

MAKSYMILIAN DEL MAR
Queen Mary, University of London, UK

Routledge
Taylor & Francis Group
LONDON AND NEW YORK

First published 2013 by Ashgate Publishing

Published 2016 by Routledge
2 Park Square, Milton Park, Abingdon, Oxfordshire OX14 4RN
711 Third Avenue, New York, NY 10017, USA

First issued in paperback 2016

Routledge is an imprint of the Taylor & Francis Group, an informa business

British Library Cataloguing in Publication Data
The moral imagination and the legal life : beyond text in
legal education. -- (Emerging legal education)
1. Legal ethics--Study and teaching (Higher)--
Methodology. 2. Lawyers--Education (Continuing education)
3. Lawyers--Professional ethics. 4. Arts in education.
I. Series II. Bańkowski, Zenon. III. Del Mar, Maksymilian,
1979-
174.3'0711-dc23

Library of Congress Cataloging-in-Publication Data
The moral imagination and the legal life : beyond text in legal education / by Zenon Bańkowski and Maksymilian Del Mar.
p. cm. -- (Emerging legal education)
Includes bibliographical references and index.
ISBN 978-1-4094-2808-4 (hardback) 1. Law--Study and teaching--Philosophy.
2. Law--Study and teaching--Methodology. 3. Law and ethics.
4. Art in education--Philosophy. I. Bańkowski, Zenon. II. Del Mar, Maksymilian, 1979-
K100.M67 2012
340.071--dc23

2012027615

ISBN 13: 978-1-138-27257-6 (pbk)
ISBN 13: 978-1-4094-2808-4 (hbk)

Contents

List of Figures and Tables

Figures

Tables

List of Contributors

Zenon Bańkowski is Emeritus Professor of Legal Theory at the School of Law, University of Edinburgh. He was Principal Investigator of the AHRC Beyond Text in Legal Education Project.

Anthony Bradney is Professor of Law at Keele University and was formerly Professor of Law at the University of Sheffield and the University of Leicester. He has published widely in, amongst others, the areas of legal education and law and religion. His publications include *Law and Faith in a Sceptical Age* (2009), *Conversations, Chances and Choices: The Liberal Law School in the Twenty-First Century* (2003) and *Living Without Law: An Ethnography of Dispute Avoidance and Resolution in the Society of Friends* (with Fiona Cownie) (2000).

Gillian Calder is an Associate Professor at the University of Victoria's Faculty of Law. Her current research interests include the relationship between women, work and family; the provision of social benefits through Canadian law; feminist, constitutional and equality theories; performance and law and the intersection of all of these questions with the goal of developing the ethical imagination of today's law student.

Maksymilian Del Mar is Lecturer in Legal and Social Philosophy at the Department of Law, Queen Mary, University of London. He was a Key Collaborator in the AHRC Beyond Text in Legal Education Project, based at the School of Law in Edinburgh.

Randy Gordon is an Adjunct Professor in the Dedman School of Law and a lecturer in English at Southern Methodist University. He is a partner in the Complex Litigation Group of Gardere Wynne Sewell LLP.

Paul Maharg is Professor of Legal Education at Northumbria University Law School and Adjunct Professor at the Australian National University College of Law. He has written extensively on legal education. He blogs at http://paulmaharg.com.

Thomas Wm. Mayo is Associate Professor at SMU's Dedman School of Law; Adjunct Associate Professor of Internal Medicine at the University of Texas – Southwestern Medical School; and Of Counsel, Haynes and Boone, all in Dallas, Texas. His courses include Election Law, Nonprofit Organizations, Health Care Law, and Bioethics and Law, as well as a literature course for fourth-year medical students and third-year law students entitled 'Law, Literature and Medicine'. He is a Fellow in the Dallas Institute of Humanities and Culture, a member of the Advisory Committee of the Program in Ethics in Science and Medicine at the University of Texas – Southwestern Medical Center and a former poetry columnist for the *Dallas Morning News*. He received his BA in philosophy from Amherst College and his JD from Syracuse University School of Law.

Clare Sandford-Couch joined the School of Law at Northumbria University in 1994, after having practised as a solicitor for several years in London and Newcastle, specializing in company and corporate matters. As a senior lecturer, Clare has specialized in business and company law, as well as contract and tort. Since 2008, she has been studying for a PhD in the History of Art at the University of Edinburgh; her research focuses on the use and depiction of images of justice in Italy c.1200–1400.

Julian Webb is Professor of Legal Education at the University of Warwick. From 2006 to 2011, he was Director of the UK Centre for Legal Education, based at Warwick. He is currently leading the team undertaking research for the Legal Education and Training Review (LETR), commissioned jointly by the Bar Standards Board, ILEX Professional Standards and the Solicitors Regulation Authority. He has published widely on matters of legal education policy and pedagogy, and his particular research interests at present focus on the history and regulation of legal education and the legal professions. He blogs, sporadically, on these and other matters at *hEaD space* (http://legaleducation.wordpress.com).

Introduction

Zenon Bańkowski and Maksymilian Del Mar[1]

General Introduction to the Two Volumes

This present volume is one of two volumes of papers flowing from a project, 'Beyond Text in Legal Education', hosted by the School of Law at the University of Edinburgh. The aim of the two volumes as a whole is to contribute to the reinvigoration of legal education, primarily in law schools but also extending to law firms. We attempt this reinvigoration by introducing the importance and usefulness of pedagogical resources that go beyond text, i.e. resources from the visual and movement arts. Taken as a whole, the two-volume work explores the use of these non-textual resources for legal education and legal scholarship. It is not restricted to any area of law or to any particular form of going beyond text. It includes contributions that explore different ways of visualizing legal knowledge, different ways of designing and interacting with spaces for exploring legal issues, as well as different ways of performing a variety of legal problems. The premise of the work is that the teaching and research of law can be experienced in ways that do not depend exclusively on text, but that have recourse to the full range and diversity of the sensory capacities of teachers, students, professionals and scholars. In that sense, we also recognize that different persons all have different sensory strengths and weakness, that is, that we all experience in different ways and thus also learn via different sensory pathways.

The project that is the subject of this book was part of a UK Arts and Humanities Research Council (AHRC) funding programme called 'Beyond Text in Legal Education'. This funding programme recognized that non-textual material and communication through visual, oral and sensory means were an important part of our culture. We now have the means to reach many quickly and communication becomes rapid and in some cases transitory. The aim was to create a research programme where scholars could study the issues concerning the non-textual dimensions of culture. This would involve, *inter alia*, a study of the material conditions of these non-textual means and also their control and dissemination. Further, it would look at the technology itself and how this impacted upon the culture and tradition. Out of these issues, of particular importance to our project were questions of performativity, of how we transmit multimedia non-textual

1 Our thanks to Martin Taggart for assistance with the finalization of the text of both volumes.

objects, and the impact upon traditional methods of cognition in the transmission and remembering of culture. This implied looking at learning and teaching and the way we might be able to use non-textual methods even in areas that are primarily textual. What would be important here would be the mediation between the text and the non-text aspects, the imagination that would be brought into play and the use that imagination could be put to. How do these new modes that use all the bodily senses play on the imagination and what does that imagination do in helping to create an embodied knowledge?

The role of the imagination in teaching and learning, and the way in which these can be enhanced and enriched by the use of non-textual resources, is a key aspect of the 'Beyond Text in Legal Education' project. Although 'imagination' was understood broadly, one of the most important features of the project was to consider how the ethical or moral imagination could be developed through a combination of text-based and (especially) non-text-based resources properly incorporated into tertiary and professional legal education curricula.

Law is very much a text-based discipline, both in its practice and its education. Legal education, both at the tertiary and continuing professional levels, has been and continues to be dominated by recourse to textual resources. Law students and legal professionals are taught to learn and understand general rules and principles, and apply them to pre-manufactured factual scenarios. This is no different when it comes to the education of legal professional ethics, where, typically, moral theories are presented as consisting of general axioms that allow students and professionals to rationally resolve traditional problem cases (pre-articulated factual scenarios that are designed to produce moral dilemmas). The pursuit of professional integrity is dominated by promoting the ability to use complex systems of ethical postulates to justify the making of a certain decision in relation to a pre-determined set of facts.

There is no doubt that the development and use of text-based resources facilitates the exercise of skills that are important to the ethical development of law students and legal professionals. Learning how to better articulate and justify one's reasoning by reference to complex systems of normative languages is important. However, the exclusive emphasis on textual resources, on languages and their manipulation, carries with it significant dangers. Such an exclusive focus can be restrictive in that it can result in law students and legal professionals never acquiring the skill of coming to see and recognize the ethical complexity of any given situation; it places at risk their ability to overcome the limitation of the categories with which they are working, particularly when the particular situation itself puts into question those categories. Coping with this limit requires the exercise of the (ethical) imagination. Such an exercise enables the person to respond to the complexity and particularity of the situation, and to come up with just and imaginative ways of going forward.

There is a considerable amount of work in this context that has been, and continues to be, conducted by those who emphasize the value of the 'literary imagination' and the use of literature for these purposes. Some of this work has found its way into the post-professional education programmes of major law firms, principally in the USA. While the invocation of the literary imagination in this context is important, it is still too heavily text-based. What the 'Beyond Text in Legal Education' project aimed at was creating a space where the (ethical) imagination can be inculcated and the movement beyond can be experienced in non-textual ways. The project does not wish to suggest that non-textual resources should replace textual ones. It goes beyond text, but does not leave it behind completely. Rather, it seeks to provoke reflection upon the value of non-textual resources in developing imaginative (ethical) perception amongst law students and legal professionals.

In these two volumes, then, it is recognized that legal education and legal practice are both steeped in specific texts and institutions. These texts and institutions define the profession; they orient us; their categories and pathways give us a structure within which we not only participate but also evaluate each other. Yet it is also recognized that the complexity of moral life, and professional life more generally, is not reflected by any one set of texts and institutions. Indeed, it is argued that what is needed, at those moments in which already-existing categories and pathways run out, is the exercise of the (ethical) imagination. However, this (ethical) imagination cannot be understood too cognitively or too rationally; nor can it be said to exist in the manipulation or reorganization of already-existing categories and pathways. This (ethical) imagination is, instead, better understood to be embodied, situated, affective and creative. In constructing this approach to the (ethical) imagination, these two volumes draw on a number of theoretical traditions, including embodied and situated cognition, philosophy of the emotions, theology, aesthetics, and legal and moral theory.

The aim of this volume is to contribute to legal education in a general way, i.e. to the learning and teaching of any area of the law. This volume also includes some chapters that introduce and discuss general resources and issues concerning non-text-based reasoning and non-text-based resources. The remaining chapters in this volume focus on exploring the pedagogical and, to some extent, moral value of non-textual resources in legal education. The companion volume builds on this one and focuses in more detail on the potential contribution of non-text-based resources to moral education in law schools and law firms. The contributors to both volumes include a wide range of theorists and educators, including legal educators in the UK and the USA working in both law schools and law firms, some of whom have used such resources before, and others who did so as a result of the 'Beyond Text in Legal Education' project.

The project started from this thought and this analogy: when people view art objects in galleries, too often they rely on textual explanation, looking for the text in the catalogue to explain it and not letting the object explain itself. Some curators try to get people to engage the art object without text, to use their imagination to let the object speak to them and not be subsumed by the text. Lawyers face an analogous situation when they encounter events that require decisions to be made; too often they look to the text and do not experience the particularity of the situation by letting it speak for itself. Part of the aim, then, practically speaking, was to explore – by working together with an art gallery – this analogy. We wanted to provide a space – literally, a gallery space – where law students and lawyers would be able to experimentally explore legal and ethical skills in unfamiliar ways, precisely by means of non-text-based activities and relying only on non-text-based resources.

Prior to this experiential workshop (about which we will say more below), we held, on 8 November 2008, a one-day workshop, involving a small group of philosophers, theologians and lawyers, who met to discuss the conceptual, ethical and practical implications of this view of law and cognition. These issues were discussed specifically against the backdrop of a provisional programme of activities for the experiential workshop. This initial conference helped us further refine the activities and aims of the experiential workshop.

The experiential workshop itself was the centrepiece of the project. It was held over two days, 7–8 December 2008. The workshop programme and its delivery on the two days was primarily the responsibility of three artists, a visual-based artist (Alicja Rogalska), a movement-based artist (Keren Ben-Dor) and a curator (Zoë Fothergill, who is an artist in her own right). The workshop was held, in large part, in the Talbot Rice Gallery, which is the gallery based at Old College, University of Edinburgh. The participants included legal professionals, legal scholars and legal education (both tertiary and professional) policy makers from the UK and the USA. The artists were all experienced in working with persons who have had no or little exposure to the production and/or appreciation of visual and movement-based art.

The aim of the workshop was in line with the above-described aims of the project, i.e. it aimed to develop non-textually the skills that may enable lawyers to engage the (ethical) imagination, to experience the particularity of the situation and the vulnerability of those in it, and to allow that situation to speak and help them move beyond the law by transforming it, but not destroying it. The experiential workshop, then, delivered on our objective to create a space for legally trained people to explore the production of visually and movement-based art, and also to explore non-textually affective experience and practice in law. It was most certainly a highlight of our project. It was highly risky and experimental. We did things that took us well out of our comfort zones. But the careful planning and skill of the artists made it highly successful both as an event and as a learning experience. The group dynamics that began in this workshop carried over for the whole of the project. We built reflexivity into the workshop so that throughout there was time to reflect together on the exercises and how we felt. The reflexivity included, for instance, randomly placed voice-recorders upon which participants could verbally record their reflections.

The workshop programme has been included as the Appendix to this Introduction. The workshop was also filmed. We hired a film maker, Robert McKillop, who was with us for the entire two days. The film was not a mere record, but was also an artistic outcome in its own right. It also fed into the research itself in that it became part of the research process and interacted with it, and it played an integral role in the succeeding seminars and in our thinking as to how to go forward with the project. In that sense, the film highlighted the 'Beyond Textual' nature of the project and unexpectedly transformed our conception of research method.

After the experiential workshop, we organized two further reflective workshops. The first, held on 6 March 2009, was a small workshop entitled 'Understanding Transformation'. Here, we studied the underlying ethical issues, though more in the context of physical and social processes, bringing together a group of sociologists, philosophers and cognitive scientists with some knowledge of neuroscience to look at the cognitive and sociological processes involved. We looked at the *embodied* nature of what was happening, at the physical and other processes that are involved here, especially legal visualization and what might be called multi-sensory law. We asked: how does the experience of encounter, seeing and vulnerability get played out on the body?

Our second reflective event was a major two-day conference, held on 20–21 June 2009. This conference included some experiential elements, including interactive theatre, but the focus was on the theoretical and practical reflections of participants in the experiential workshop. It is the papers presented at this conference, together with a number of extra specially invited additions, which constitute the chapters published in these two volumes.

Chapters in this Volume

This volume contains nine chapters. The first two, by **Zenon Bańkowski** and **Maksymilian Del Mar** respectively, focus on what happens when we move out and beyond language. In doing so, they set the scene for the remaining chapters in this volume. Both Bańkowski and Del Mar emphasize that they do not want to throw away language, but instead to provide resources when we are in what Bańkowski calls the 'Space to See', that space which is for him ever-present in law but which tends to get overshadowed by language. For Bańkowski, that space is where one develops the moral imagination and encounters the vulnerability of the other. What is vital here for both Bańkowski and Del Mar is how we come to 'see' this vulnerability in the encounter.

For both authors, an arresting image comes from Raimond Gaita's *A Common Humanity* (1996), where Gaita describes and explores the quality of the interaction of a nun with the inmates of a mental hospital. The way the nun relates to the inmates puts, Gaita says, him and others, liberal or not, to shame. For Gaita, the nun treats the inmates differently because she 'sees' something about them which the others miss and it is this which informs the encounter. In confronting this image, Del Mar looks to art and theories of moral perception and shows how the exercises in the experiential workshop were attuned to this process of educating attention and encounter. Bańkowski, on the other hand, confronts the image by looking to analogies with legal reasoning and how movement and patterning help to move the legal narrative imaginatively along.

The next two chapters reflect on these general propositions. In Chapter 3, **Julian Webb** explores further the ideas of attention and encounter and their relationship to text in law. He looks at the relationship of text to 'beyond text' and proposes three broad phenomenological relationships between the self and text that help us better to understand the openness necessary to moving beyond text while not losing it. These are: 'being without text', 'being-with text' and 'being beyond text'. In his commentary on the chapters by Bańkowski and Del Mar, he emphasizes the importance of the 'Beyond Text in Legal Education' project to legal education and the possibility of this helping to achieve justice by transforming not just knowledge but the knower.

In Chapter 4, **Anthony Bradney** locates the arguments about the value or otherwise of the notion of 'Beyond Text' in the context of legal education and especially of law schools in the UK. His claim is that the history of debates about the role of the law school reveals that among the vast majority of legal academics there is now a consensus that the law school is to provide some sort of liberal education. British law schools are now 'intellectually cosmopolitan places' drawing from many disciplines and new ideas and approaches. He does, however, urge caution. First, he argues against Bańkowski's and Del Mar's implicit view that the cultivation of the ethical imagination – and thus in a way a form of moral education – is integral to law and its teaching. Though law and morality are connected and looking at these connections is an important and necessary part of legal education, one does not have to make law students good people. Second, because of the nature of the academy, and given the structural position of law in society, law students and law academics are not going to be a ready audience for this type of beyond-text approach, and the preference in the academy and outside will still be based upon essentially text-based skills.

In Chapter 5, **Paul Maharg** views 'Beyond Text' in the context of the notion of democratic professionalism, a practice that is built around models of active and collaborative democratic change. He argues that Dewey's form of educational praxis is one method by which we can encourage democratic professionalism. He argues, further, that a key element of our approach should be the Deweyan concern with 'associated life' and 'associated thought', namely the cultural and social forms of professional association, and the forms and patterns of social thinking that professionals undertake in practice. Here, learning also includes developing the moral imagination and Maharg seeks to explore the nexus of learning, lived experience and imaginative action. For Maharg, the Internet offers us significant opportunities to engage in new forms of social and educational engagement, and particularly in online games and forms of social software. Two case studies are offered. The first describes a regulatory initiative to embody Deweyan forms of associated life, while the second describes an educational initiative that attempts to embody Dewey's value of associated thinking.

In Chapter 6, **Clare Sandford-Couch** approaches the topic by looking at the different way we move beyond text in the use of visualization in law teaching. She explores the concepts of legal visualization, games, films and television and other non-verbal forms. All of this is for her central to developing wider engagement with legal and moral issues in the education of lawyers. For Sandford-Couch, Mary Warnock sums it up thus:

> It is the representational power of the imagination, its power actually to form images, ideas or likenesses in the mind, which is supposed to contribute to our awareness of the world. (Warnock 1976: 33)

In Chapter 7, **Thomas Wm. Mayo** presents a detailed study of his course 'Law, Literature and Medicine'. Though this course consists in large part of reading various literary materials, it concludes with students creating works of art for their final projects and so it is also in part moving beyond text. This moment beyond is also valuable because for him empathy is an important professional trait and his course aims, through the encounter with art and literature, to model empathy and, through this iterative process, to enhance empathetic abilities.

We come finally to two chapters where aspects of the performative become important. In Chapter 8, **Randy Gordon** shows how law and legal education, because it can benefit from a narrow instrumental way of teaching law, prioritizes rules and familiar forms of legal narrative, which might not in the end be sufficient for legal education. For Gordon, teaching and learning law with contextual-historicist tools provides a way out of this deadlock. He illustrates this by looking at, *inter alia*, cases of self-defence in respect of 'battered women'. But this is more than the still textual way of looking at the material in a historical and literary context. The emphasis on this form of teaching is to provoke the moral imagination that, as Shelley shows, cannot be separated from empathy – something seen in the theoretical context by Neil MacCormick when he crafts Kant on to Smith's sympathetic morality and the 'impartial spectator' (MacCormick 2008). In terms of pedagogy, what is important here is seeing learning and teaching as something that Dewey calls a 'dramatic rehearsal'. This can be extended not only by looking at great drama but also by incorporating play-acting into the learning and teaching process.

Gillian Calder takes this further and discusses how in the context of the University of Victoria's first-year orientation programme one can use the work of Augusto Boal and the Theatre of the Oppressed and Forum Theatre. She shows how in the context of the law school, a relationship between performance and pedagogy, games and exercises, can help in developing the skills of lawyers and teachers of law. This can be used as a means of 'rethinking the relationship between lawyers, legislators and citizens', of helping to develop the empathetic imagination of those who will act for and on behalf of others.

Conclusion

The aim of the two volumes in this 'Beyond Text in Legal Education' series has been not only to stimulate debate in what might be called 'multi-sensory jurisprudence', but also to foster and give examples of pedagogies which involve and enhance the use of the ethical imagination. The development of the ethical imagination, including its empathetic dimension, is something that we think is vital if law is able to structure our life and society in a way that is responsive to vulnerability, not being afraid to go beyond text but at the same time not destroying it.

References

Gaita, R. 2006. *A Common Humanity*. London: Routledge.
MacCormick, N. 2008. *Practical Reason in Law and Morality*. Oxford: Oxford University Press.
Warnock, M. 1976. *Imagination*. London: Faber & Faber.

Appendix

DAY 1

11.00 am Welcome
11.10 am Statement from film maker
11.15 am Ice-breakers led by all three facilitators

1) The name game (15 mins)
2) Visual expectations (15 mins)

11.30 am Warm-up activities with Keren Ben-Dor

1) Familiarity with the space, focus and general awareness
2) From self to other
3) Mutuality, trust and non-verbal listening
4) Directionality. Giving and receiving guidance. Promoting trust
5) Movement witness

12.00 pm Drawing activity with Alicja Rogalska – The space in-between
12.30 pm Movement activity with Keren Ben-Dor – The law of the dance
1.00 pm Sculpture/mixed-media activity with Alicja Rogalska – From textual to visual
2.00 pm Responsive activities with Zoë Fothergill

1) Describe and draw (20 mins)
2) Viewpoints (40 mins)
3) String theories (30 mins)

3.45 pm Installation art activity with Alicja Rogalska – Mute negotiations
4.15 pm Movement activity with Keren Ben-Dor – The great game of power
5.30 pm Informal discussion

DAY 2

10.00 am Movement activity with Keren Ben-Dor leading – Stop and listen
10.30 am Digital photography activity with Alicja Rogalska leading – Respond and capture
11.30 am Movement activity with Keren Ben-Dor leading – Action/reaction and role reversal
12.00 pm Movement activity with Keren Ben-Dor leading – Group response
1.00 pm Visual activity with Zoë Fothergill leading – Visual essays
2.00 pm Visual activity led by all three facilitators – Drawing movement
2.45 pm Visual activity led by all three facilitators – Display time
3.30 pm Reflective activities led by all three facilitators – Creative reflection

1) Drawing activity led by Alicja Rogalska – Visual reflections
2) Combined visual and movement activity led by Zoë Fothergill – Highlights

Performative movement activity led by Keren Ben-Dor – Parting gift

Chapter 1
The Space to See: Law and the Ethical Imagination

Zenon Bańkowski

Introduction

'Beyond Text in Legal Education' was a project designed to see how we could use other resources than text in legal education to stimulate the creativity and ethical imagination which we felt was necessary for the life of law. The centre of the project was a set of experiential workshops, which lasted two days. They were led by artists in the plastic arts and in movement. Lawyers, professional legal educators in the academy and outside, and legal academics took part – the aim being to use experiential and artistic methods to see if they could begin to provide modes to approach the law other than the rich textual resources of the law itself. The point of this chapter is to consider whether we can in this way show the need for, and develop the necessity of, a space for the 'development of moral sensitivity' in law and legal education. We want to look at images and constructions of this space and how it forces us to consider modes of learning other than those of text.

There are two preliminary issues that need to be considered. First, this demands a particular ethical vision of law as an institution. This is not something about acting morally rightly or wrongly; rather, it is about seeing what sort of life, viewed as a whole, is entailed by law as an institution which demands the practice of the moral imagination. Let us take an example to explain. When someone wants to make his career in the army and wonders about the moral implications of doing so, he has to consider two different though in some ways related issues. Initially, there will be issues about what it is morally right to do in the context of army life, questions about the Geneva Convention, the validity of military orders, what counts as a civilian and the like. But there are further broader issues. These concern not the quality of the moral decisions that might have to be made while in the army, but the moral quality of the choice to join the army. This raises questions about a way of life viewed as a whole and not as one composed of good or bad decisions within it. The issue here is how such a life contributes to someone's flourishing and to the good and flourishing of others. This sort of question involves comparisons with other lives and careers: teachers, plumbers, doctors, businessmen and judges. We are asking here about the life rather than the worth or not of the particular actions within it. A judgement about the former might be different from a judgement about the latter. Someone might have acted morally throughout their life but, considered as a whole, did not choose a particularly ethical way of life. For example, some people might think of the military as a regrettable necessity in our world, but not the sort of life that one might ethically aspire to. Thus, a person who has acted honourably in that career might still (justly) be compared unfavourably against those who chose some other life. If we continue with the example, however, we can see that there is much more to it than that, for the ethical value of the military life would depend upon what sort of institution (army) the military life was embedded in. Different kinds of armies might point to different possible answers. Thus, for example, having a career as a soldier in a peace-keeping army, such as a UN army, would be something different from being a soldier in an imperialist or aggressive army.

Our project sees 'living the life of the law' as being embedded in a particular view of the law, one that is based on interactivity and not a top-down management of society. Here we do not think of law as a regrettable necessity, something we have to have because of the defects we have in the state of nature (as in the classical liberal story). Fuller (1969) sees the law as interactive and communicative – it is not as it is portrayed by positivism, which he sees as a unidirectional theory. The lawgiver does not only give; her interaction with the law receiver also changes that law and it becomes a form of life which expresses solidarity through giving and taking. Here there is an emphasis on the mutuality of the interchange, of reaching and responding to the vulnerability and need of the other, and of taking the risk that this entails. On this way of looking at it, law can be viewed as an essential part of the way we connect with others by stepping outside our closed and circumscribed confines and giving ourselves to them. In that sense it is a form of moral community, an enterprise of 'putting ourselves under the governance of rules'. The emphasis on enterprise is important since it has the connotations of a common journey, of something that we all take part in, more than just the technical rational framework for all of us to achieve our individual goods. It becomes part of our common good as well.

Second, as befits a project called 'Beyond Text in Legal Education', we have to look at the constraints of the text and how law appears to be embedded therein. We can view law as a 'Religion of the Book', one of the Abrahamic Faiths which are based on sacred and defining texts that found their belief and practice. The foundational document then serves as a way of defining one's identity and what one has to do. So the word of God becomes solidified in the texts of the sacred scriptures. Of course, this happens to a greater or lesser extent and there are different ways of reading and interpreting the texts, with tradition being an important aspect of it for some. Ultimately, however, it all returns to the text. One cannot be a theologian in these traditions without some reference to the text.

Law is the secular religion.[1] The rationality and order of God are replaced by law and our identity is defined in and through it. We are 'people of the law'

1 Fitzpatrick 1992.

and that defines our identity, whether through a 'constitutional patriotism' as in the USA and proposed for Europe by Habermas,[2] or in the self-identity of the 'common law'.[3] 'In the beginning was the Word' is still the case, but that word is Law. As Carl Schmitt (1985) pointed out, much theorizing in constitutional law is secularized theology, the conceptual problems being of a similar order. Theological questions, as Hegel says, are ways of looking at important philosophical questions. And, in the West, the connection between the two discourses has been close and mutually reinforcing.[4] For Hegel, the Incarnation was the theological way of looking at the central philosophical problem of the relation between the universal and the particular. Similarly, questions around the paradoxes of God's omnipotence can be seen as theological ways of looking at paradoxes of sovereignty in the realms of constitutional theory.

Again, as in the religions of the book, the sacred scriptures of law are also counterposed to a greater or lesser extent by tradition and there are different ways, some stricter than others, of reading the text. But one cannot work as a lawyer without ultimate reference to the text, for it is by the text that ultimately we live. Text and law become synonymous, as this makes it easier to guide our life by the originary experience to which we always have to refer. The *logos* becomes more stable when written down and for those that live by it, that stability is vital for the security of the system and the way of life. And for those who apply it and interpret it, the agents of the text become the text itself; have it inscribed on their bodies. Law, as a text-based discipline, has both strengths and weaknesses. The strength is that it enables decisions to be transparent and constrained by the text. The weakness is that decisions tend to be dominated by text, and situations are shoehorned into the text with stultifying results. The answer is always sought within the text, viewing the situations law encounters through the optic of the text, thus manipulating them rather than transforming them, and not letting the situation speak to the text and the law.

And, of course, as inevitable in all of the 'Religions of the Book', texts run out and gaps appear. What do we do? We might ignore it and become fundamentalists dominating reality with the text. We might expand the gap to such an extent that text becomes irrelevant. Again, we might seek, in these situations, nuanced ways of interpreting the texts. We will however still be in thrall to the texts. We might think that text will run out at its extremities. There, imagination might be required, but that would not be an all-pervasive feature of the system and any imagination required would be strictly confined to these liminal places. Many modern legal theorists, as Del Mar shows, even those who are worried by the stasis of meaning that the law produces when solidifying into this system of clearly organized and timeless categories, do not go beyond language and the text in their efforts to ameliorate this.

2 See Breda 2011.

3 See for example Collins 1995 and Legrand 1996.

4 See Nicholls 1995.

Our project seeks to go further. Let us take an analogy. When people view art objects in galleries, too often they rely on textual explanation, looking for the text in the catalogue to explain it and not letting the object explain itself. Some curators try to get people to engage the art without text, to use their imagination to let the object speak to them and not be subsumed by the text. Lawyers face a similar situation when they encounter events that require decisions to be made; too often they look to the text and do not experience the particularity of the situation by letting it speak for itself. If we want, as we do, to turn away from that, then the implication is that we should not confine the need for imagination to the liminal points that we detailed above, the space that the gap creates. Rather, we should see the need for imagination as all pervasive, as an integral part of law, that there is always within law a need for a space for this imagination to operate. So we should not think of it as a gap only when we approach the limits, but rather as an all-pervasive space that is integral to the law, one that enables the exercise of the imagination and lets the outside in.

In writing about this space and this project, I will use as my organizing principle parables, and specifically the parable of the Good Samaritan. This is so for a variety of reasons: first, for the Hegelian reason outlined above; and, second, because parables in themselves are a sort of parabolic reasoning where paying imaginative attention to the story, to the narrativity, moves one into areas that did not seem possible. The Samaritan story in particular is about the imagination necessary to use the transformative power of attention and encounter to see through patterns and to move to a transformation, and thus regeneration, of present categories of the law. It is about a movement beyond, about the possibility and the potentiality of connection. Attention, encounter, education, and movement and patterns are what this project interrogates.

The Space in Law

The space that this view of law entails has been variously described. Michael Detmold (1989) calls it 'The Particularity Void'. For him, this is the ever-present space that exists between the meaning of the law and its application. Ultimately the law asks what it is reasonable to do and that question is never, for Detmold, exhausted by the reasonableness of the rule. It might be unreasonable to do what is reasonable and reasonable to do what is unreasonable – the answer is never exhausted merely because the law is reasonable. Thus, it is clearly unreasonable to apply the reasonable rule 'Do not get off the bus while the vehicle is in motion' if the vehicle is hurtling down a hill into the sea, for though that rule is reasonable, it still has to be applied in the particular case and this must be separated from the justification of the rule itself.[5] This then is the site where the universalism of the

5 We can put this point more abstractly by following Klaus Günther (1993). For him, following Habermas, one must posit two different discourses. One is the justification

law and the particularity of the object meet and feed off each other. Think of the trial or a decision-making organ as the site of such a space. What this does is to enable 'normative surplus' to be fed into the law because in making the particular decision, the decision-maker is doing so for the particularity of the case. There, 'normative surplus' will be fed into the law, for in making the particular decision, the decision-maker, even though she refers to the general norms of law, is making a decision based on the particularity of the case and the needs of that particular situation. The decision is meant to solve that case and no other. But it will also generate material, 'normative surplus', which will feed back into the general legal norms of the legal system, helping to regenerate and renew it.

Detmold takes this further. He takes us to a concrete example of the particularity void. He takes an example from Tolstoy's *War and Peace* and the confrontation therein between Pierre and Davout. Davout has been given orders to shoot Russian spies, but he does not shoot Pierre. Holding his rifle, he looks at him, hesitates and does not fire. Tolstoy says that at the moment of hesitation, many things passed through Davout's mind:

> Davout lifted his eyes and gazed searchingly at him. For some seconds they looked at one another, and that look saved Pierre. It went beyond the circumstances of war and the court-room, and established human relations between the two men. Both of them in that one instant were dimly aware of an infinite number of things, and they realized that they were both children of humanity, that they were brothers. (1978: 457)

And so, though the moment may be for Detmold mystical, it is also the everyday experience of the law:

> I, the judge, and Davout, at the moment of practicality entered the unanswering void of particularity, the realm of love, about which only mystical, poetic things can be said ... or nothing ... Judges enter this realm every day. (1978: 457)

There are two points to be borne in mind here. First, for Detmold, this space, this meeting of meaning and application, of the universal and the particular is omnipresent in the law. It is about a moment of hesitation and encounter where

---

discourse where norms are justified and where the criteria of universalizability are applied – so norms are justified by the Habermasian universalizing criteria. The other is the application discourse, which decides whether or not a particular justified norm is to be applied. The criteria used here are different from those used in the justification discourse. One might say that a law has a meaning element, whether it is justifiable within the system and a jurisdictional element, whether it ought to be applied in this particular case. It is as though I fire an arrow but I cannot be sure whether what I think of as the target is the target until I hear and examine it, until I let it speak to me. For it can always ask 'Why me?', and that can only be answered at the time of making the decision.

attention is paid, and so it is about that ineffable moment. It is at that moment that Davout sees the particular Pierre – he sees through the enemy and he sees not a brother but someone who should be treated as a brother, and then he imposes that category on him. He pays attention to Pierre. In that moment of attention he comes to realize that he should not shoot him; he should not be instantiated in the rule 'Shoot all enemies'; that will not be attached to him. The particularity void is thus both this ineffable situation and the idea that we have to start from a particular situation. We cannot let the rule make us forget that. Davout does not start from 'All spies should be shot'; he starts from meeting Pierre on a battlefield with all the attendant circumstances, including the rule 'All spies should be shot'. And by paying attention to that, he comes to see Pierre's pain. He sees his need and in doing so regenerates and expands 'All men are brothers and should be treated with compassion' to him.

It is important to stress that this space is not meant to throw away universality. Raimond Gaita (2000) makes this clear when he gives us a striking image of that space 'about which only mystical, poetic things can be said'. He talks of a nun he encountered while working as a student in a mental home. There, as was common in those days, the inmates were treated by the majority of the staff like animals. He and some of the staff tried to treat them, as he hoped, like human beings. But the nun, by the quality of her interaction with the inmates, put them all to shame. A large part of Gaita's book is devoted to seeking to understand the meaning and significance of this encounter and interaction, the quality of what he sees as the nun's love. Kant, he says, would deny that this is something upon which one can base an ethic and, of course, he would be right in that you cannot operationalize an ethical and institutional life by making us all like that nun. Why, however, he goes on, would we want to build societies that care and enable us to live together in peace and justice unless we were touched with something of what that nun had? As such, one can see that at the centre of our Kantian legal universe is that space, the 'realm of love', which nourishes and sustains it.

Seeing and Attention

Gaita recognizes that the nun acts in the way she does because she can see something that he and the others were not able to and that this transforms her interaction with the inmates. Here we can see the influence of Simone Weil. Weil (1951) thinks that all humans have a power or faculty which she calls 'attention' that we should develop. It is a 'method of the exercise of intelligence which consists of looking' (1951: 111). It is both an internal mental state and something that goes outside. It prepares the mind in quietness and readiness but waits for something on the outside, which it will receive with compassion and help. The real key here is that we are to be still, open to that which is outside of us and which will move us in many ways. This can be shown in the way we find God. For Weil, it is not that we actively search for God; rather, it is God who searches for us:

> We do not obtain the most precious gifts by going in search of them but by waiting for them. Men cannot discover them by his own powers, and if he sets out to seek for them he will find in their place counterfeits of which he will be unable to discern their falsity. (1951: 112)

We should not busily seek things out, but rather should rest and wait to be able fully to appreciate it and not busy ourselves in a futile effort to grasp that object:

> The heat of the chase. We must not want to find: as in the case of excessive devotion, we become dependent on the object of our efforts … it is only effort without desire (not attached to any object) which infallibly contains a reward … By pulling at the bunch we make all the grapes fall to the ground. (Weil 1951: 106, quoted by Dietz 1988: 96)

For this you have to cultivate 'attention':

> Attention consists of suspending our thought, leaving it detached, empty, and ready to be penetrated by the object; it means holding our minds within reach of this thought. (1951: 111)

This is both active and passive. We should be open to receive, but this demands active concentration and intelligence. Though it is not a sort of flexing of the muscles that makes you feel that you have been working, to pay attention is the most demanding of things. One needs to be unself-conscious, not grasping but alertly and intelligently waiting. The key is openness and it is in these moments that one is open to illumination. Weil applies this to education, where she argues that students should not struggle immediately to grasp what is being told, for that way they will lose it and not understand; rather, they should 'pay attention' and listen, trusting that the truth will come to them. They should not expect a result or outcome straight away, but should wait for it to grasp them. However, this is not just a sort of active contemplation. Although, as Dietz says, a significant element of it comes from the French connation of *attendre*, to wait for, to expect, to long for, it also has the other connotations of paying attention to and caring for. What is its pay off? For Weil, it is only in this way that we can connect with the reality of the world and our situation. Weil thinks of the world as a text which we cannot read because the symbols of which it consists are solidified and keep us from getting to and receiving its reality. Unless we are still and pay attention, we will be swept along by these solid symbols, the 'force and gravity of the world', unable to pierce through to the reality below.[6]

6 Though this metaphor of 'reading the world' might seem to clash with the idea of 'beyond text', it need not if we view it in the following way. The way the world becomes solidified in symbols is as though it becomes a text and an object of univocal meaning, forcing us within its univocal categories to read it as a book, thus staying within its

For Weil, the spiritual and the political come together for it is, as she says in her essay 'On Education', a way of coming to the love of God and to the love of the neighbour. It is the way we can be moved by and be able to help those in radical need; those whom she calls the 'afflicted'. Attention is a form of discernment: seeing what people are saying when they are hurt, seeing conditions of injustice and, above all, seeing myself as equal in affliction. It is a way of 'reading' others.

This is very far-reaching. With attention the 'unafflicted' help the neighbour, the one who is afflicted. Attention is hard. Self-regarding motives are not enough, even if it is from a wish to help the poor. This patronizes them and sees them as

---

categories. Collins (1990) makes this clearer when discussing digitization and symbols. The meaning resides in the symbol which, within certain tolerances, will always stay the same. When a gold coin, for example, was worth its weight in gold, it mattered whether it was clipped or shaven because its condition affected its value. Now, when it is a symbol for a particular value, its condition is irrelevant. It does not matter if a 50 pence coin gets slightly worn, as it will still retain its face value.

A book and writing can be viewed as digitized speech, which has the effect of making that fluid and uncertain and interactive form (*parole*) clear and univocal by translating it into symbolic form by means of alphabets. And that is why Plato in the *Phaedrus* was against it. Collins (1990: 24) quotes Haugeland: 'But the real importance of digital systems emerges when we turn to a more complicated case. Consider for a moment, the respective fates of Rembrandts' portraits and Shakespeare's sonnets. Even given the finest care, the paintings are slowly deteriorating; by no means are they the same now as when they were new. The poems by contrast may well have been preserved perfectly … we probably have most of them exactly the way Shakespeare wrote them – absolutely without flaw. The difference obviously is that the alphabet is digital … whereas paint colours and textiles are not.'

He also uses a quotation attributed to Galileo used in Abode Systems advertising: 'But above all astonishing inventions, what loftiness was that of the man who conceived of a way to communicate his most recondite thought to whatever other person, though separated from him by the longest interval of space and time! To speak with those as yet unborn, or to be born perhaps a thousand or even ten thousand years hence! And with what ease! All through various groupings of twenty simple letters on paper' (Collins 1990: 24).

But, Collins goes on, things are not quite as simple. The Rembrandt can be viewed in a symbolic digitized way. It might be like money in that we can imagine a perfect Rembrandt forgery that would not be as valuable as an original in worse condition because in the end what is important is, like money, the certification of what it is rather than what it actually is. And the sonnet's meaning changes – it does not contain its meaning just in the symbol: 'What is it that makes us say that there is something uniquely unchanging about the words of the manuscript?' he asks. His answer is that 'it is the deeply in grained and hard learned, almost reflex-like, ability to see written symbols as the same when we do not have a special reason to reflect on their differences' (Collins 1990: 26).

And we regain what Plato thought we were losing by paying attention that becomes the 'special reason' – by being able to pierce through the digitized and solidified text of the world and let the meanings underneath move us. Imagine a long inscription around a church. One might try and walk around to try and grasp its meaning, but if one were open enough, one might pierce through that and see the point as taking one around the church and thus facilitating the contemplation of the sacred with a sacred space.

a type, the poor, and not as people who are in pain. We have to be able to pierce through to that cry of pain and not mask it or hide it through, for example, rights talk. Talking of the rights of the afflicted is rather like saying to girls in a brothel that they have a right to a fair wage – it does not get to their pain. For Weil, affliction is contagious and we will do everything to avoid it. Much of our routines are aimed at avoiding this pain:

> To put oneself in the place of someone whose soul is corroded by affliction, or in near danger of it is to annihilate oneself. It is more difficult than suicide would be for a happy child. Therefore the afflicted are not listened to. They are like someone whose tongue has been cut out and who occasionally forgets the fact. When they move their lips no ear perceives any sound. And they certainly soon sink into impotence in the use of language, because of the certainty of not being heard. (Weil 1990: 285)

We do not want the pain, but it is only when we recognize it that we can do anything. It is to do with a respect for persons, but it is not Kantian. It is not to reduce everything to a rationalistic, objective standpoint. This is not engaging with the person; rather, it is thinking of oneself as superior, to bring them to where your superior knowledge and self already are. There should be no objective distance between oneself and the afflicted.

Weil here makes an important point. She thinks that when the unafflicted truly pay attention to the afflicted, there is no distance between them and they also assume that other person. So Weil says that 'to project one's being into an afflicted person is to assume for a moment his affliction; it is to choose voluntarily something whose very essence consists in being imposed by constraint upon the unwilling' (quoted in Dietz 1988: 130). As Dietz puts it:

> Attention towards others is not an act of impartial disengagement at all, but rather an act through which the unafflicted 'project their being' into the afflicted. Relatedly, she [Weil] insists that attention to the afflicted is not rooted in our recognition of any one attribute, like the rational dignity of man, but instead is consumed by the whole person, the 'neighbour' in his or her completeness. (1988: 129)

For Weil, then, this 'projection' was literal, as her personal life clearly showed. When I project myself into that person, I take on that person's affliction. Attention here then combines the spiritual and the political. The way you help your neighbour who is 'in pain' is by renouncing yourself and embracing their pain.

That is why for Weil the parable of the Good Samaritan was so important, as it emphasizes the creativity of 'attention' to the cry of pain, of 'affliction'.[7]

---

7 For her this was the key to Christianity – Christ taking on the pain of the world and redeeming it.

It takes us on a journey where we are all potential victims, as oppressors and oppressed, and these positions can change at any time. The Samaritan breathes life into he who 'has fallen among thieves', but at the same time takes on the affliction. For Weil, the parable of the Good Samaritan is not merely a matter of grasping what a neighbour is, it is also a constitutive act making the other a neighbour by the act of helping. This is an invitation to go on a risky voyage with the other and thus transform your world – the outcome of which is unpredictable. What that does for Weil is literally to breathe life into someone that was as stone, non-human in their affliction. It is an act of 'creative attention' (Weil 1951: 146–7, cited in Grote, 1990):

> Christ taught us that the supernatural love of our neighbour is the exchange of compassion and gratitude which happens in a flash between two beings, one possessing and the other deprived of human personality. One of the two is only a little piece of flesh, naked, inert, and bleeding beside a ditch; he is nameless; no one knows anything about him. Those who pass by this thing scarcely notice it, and a few minutes afterwards do not even know that they saw it. Only one stops and turns his attention towards it. The attention is creative.

Let us go back to Gaita's nun, for it is she who exemplifies what is going on here. The point is that what makes her attitude one of 'attention' is that she does not feel different or distant from the inmates she interacts with. She embraces them as they are and becomes like them. And this, it seems to me, can be different from the disability approaches of, among others, Nussbaum. They do not embrace the disabled; rather, they want to make them like themselves – they have a cool rationality, albeit full of compassion – their religion is Kant. They are not mutual partners in vulnerability and suffering but are there to help from their superior position. In doing it this way, however, they cannot see. They have empathy and 'feel your pain' but have none of their own.

Watchfulness

We now move on to examine this space in law more closely. What is the process involved here? It is instructive to look to Shytov's (2001) view of legal reasoning. For him, this involves what he calls 'sympathy judgements', which are the main determinant of agapic judgements. This is not about feelings that we might have about the feelings of those upon whom we pass judgement, but our understanding of their feelings and of our own feelings. So 'sympathy judgement' requires from a judge attentiveness both to the feelings and experiences of the litigants, and to his. It is about grasping the situations in all its aspects, including the aspect that you are now in this situation and judging it; to use the Weilian term, 'reading' the situation piercing through to its core. But it is also a situation where there is certain reciprocity, where all must engage. Shytov explains this well by the 'Good Shepherd' imagery in the Bible. The good shepherd is not only the one who cares for his sheep and will lay down his life for them but is also the reason why he is heard and listened to, because the sheep recognize him as such. They listen to him and he to them.

This implies that the litigants' expectations of the judge are important. The judge's taking those into account implies understanding of how they might feel if the judgement goes against them and a sympathetic explanation of that. What is important for Shytov is not just feeling your neighbour's pain but also your experience of understanding it. And this is important because it implies that it is not just related to particulars and people with whom one might empathize and thus decide (correctly) in a particular way – it can also apply to principles and rules. Thus, in *Brown v Board of Education*,[8] he claims that the judges decided in favour of Brown not just because of their empathy for the downtrodden, but because of their sympathy with the concept of harm which was being done to them. It is in this sense that for him, sympathy does not dissolve into free-floating feeling and intuition as it also applies to and is thus constrained by legal rules.

Shytov thinks of sympathy judgements as complex, requiring many skills and above all love for those affected (agapic judgements). But this and knowledge of the law, compassion, etc. are not enough; a special virtue which can be seen as his version of Weil's notion of attention is also called for. He calls this virtue watchfulness:

> Watchfulness means the willingness of the judge to listen to what are the others' moral views on the due application of legal rules in the given circumstances. It is not merely listening but it presumes a readiness to acknowledge the rightness of another's moral perspective. Watchfulness is the result of the humility of the judge who having his own prejudices does understand them, and therefore is open to the different comprehension of the situation. A watchful judge is aware that his own legal reasoning is limited, his justification imperfect, because his knowledge of the facts can never be complete, and his interpretation of legal rules is only his own. (Shytov 2001: 136–7)

This virtue, as elaborated upon by orthodox theologians, originates in the *Philokalia*, a collection of writings of orthodox Greek monasticism. In this view it is a method which keeps one pure because it is internally watchful over oneself and is to be distinguished from a state like stupor, drunkenness, etc. It is of importance in looking at how a judge should examine herself in the struggle for a good conscience and the non-bias and non-prejudice of a decision. It is not just a look into one's inner world but it is also looking outside in order to help reach a just decision. It thus looks at eliminating bias and prejudice, but also for the sources of the correct decision. It could be seen also as a sort of Yoga. This idea was developed monastically into a sort of self-examination through a quasi-Cartesian methodology.

8 347. U.S. 483 (1954).

Shytov develops the notion into something more positive: 'the decision is based on the will to do good to those who are affected by it'. It is a positive element looking outward and being inwardly receptive. One can compare this to 'tuning a radio on the wave sought without necessarily listening to the voices on other waves' (Shytov 2001: 135). It is also active in the sense that it is, as Weil also thought, a work of active intelligence and not something passive. Theophan the Recluse, a Russian Orthodox monk, says:

> Attention to what goes on in the heart and to what comes from it is the chief work of a well ordered Christian life. Through this attention the inward and the outward are brought into due relation with one another. But to this watchfulness discernment must also be added so that we may understand aright what passes within and what is required by outward circumstance. Attention is useless without discernment. (Quoted by Shytov 2001: 136)

As applied to judgements, it implies that, when trying the case, listening to both sides means listening to what they are saying without making one's mind up. This, as Shytov says, requires skill and attention, especially if some of the parties are not particularly articulate or clear as to what is going on. Weil talks about what it means not to listen and not to be engaged with the particular case, for then the law cannot hear the cry – it just hears the rights and entitlements and so the 'vagrant accused of stealing a carrot' stands before the judge who keeps up an 'elegant flow of queries, queries and witticisms while [he] is unable to stammer a word' (Weil 1990: 285).

Attention should be paid not only to what goes on inside the courtroom but also to the internal fears and perspectives of the participants. Shytov exemplifies this in *Remli v France*.[9] The French court did not take seriously, and discounted, a fear of racial bias on the part of Remli. This fear was occasioned by one of the jurors saying in public: 'I am a racist.' The European Court of Human Rights found a violation of Article 6(1) of the European Convention on Human Rights, which guarantees a fair hearing.

Finally, Shytov claims, there is not just a listening to the applicants with equal sympathy for them; the judge also has to look through love to the principles of law and the love which will enable her to apply them correctly. It should be noted that there is a relationship between the judge and the litigants – they expect of her to give a decision and thus she must give reasons. This becomes a way of sharing with them her knowledge of the law and her love for them. This is important because what it shows is that the ethical life of an institution governed by watchfulness will be that interactive and connected view of law which we detailed above – something at variance with the managerial and directive, that is part of people's good and not outside merely helping them to achieve their desires.

9 European Court of Human Rights, 23 April 1996.

Insight

For Bernard Lonergan (1922), what we have here is something he calls 'insight'. This idea forms the basis of his philosophy of science. He defines insight thus:

> In the ideal detective story the reader is given all the clues yet fails to spot the criminal. He may advert to each clue as it arises. He needs no further clues to solve the mystery. Yet he can remain in the dark for the simple reason that reaching the solution is not the mere apprehension of any clue, not the mere memory of all, but a quite distinct activity of organising intelligence that places the full set of clues in a unique explanatory perspective. By insight, then, is meant not any act of attention or advertence or memory, but the supervening act of understanding. It is not any recondite intuition but the familiar event that occurs easily and frequently in the moderately intelligent, rarely and with difficulty only in the very stupid. In itself it is so simple and obvious that it seems to merit the little attention that commonly it receives. At the same time, its function in cognitional activity is so central that to grasp it in its conditions, its working, and its results, is to confer a basic yet startling unity on the whole field of human inquiry and human opinion. (1922: 3–4)

That insight is something that one sees, but is not something that is purely a subjective intuition. It is the ability to see that something makes sense, that it has its own integrity and that often precedes what we think are the principles that guide us in that decision. Thus, *modus ponens* might be seen as the inference rule that licenses certain deductions in logic, but it might also be seen as a description of the insight that one has when one sees that Socrates is mortal from the conjunction of the propositions 'all men are mortal and Socrates is a man'. It is something we can train ourselves in – it is not a just matter of introspection. The process has something in common with what the legal realists called 'hunching', what cognitive psychologists think of as stages of incubation, preparation, etc.

A lot of the activity here consists in a series of questions, an idea which Bruce Anderson (1966) develops. The basic types of insight are 'direct' and 'reflective'. The former is something that gets to see the relations between data and the latter reflects on that and tests it. They are the results of puzzling, of asking questions like 'why?' and 'what?'. Practical insights give you possible courses of action which are then tested by reflective insight. In evaluating practical insights, we look at the relations between our understanding of the event and the implications of the actions. I must have an idea of what sort of situation it is; that precedes my action – for example, I see a situation as a case of delict and not contract, and that makes the solution obvious. There is an understanding phase and a testing phase. We might, says Anderson, think of that as the discovery and justification phases, but we ought not to since the creative act of insight occurs in both and it is to be seen as part of one whole process. We have these insights and cannot know about them, but we can study them and have insight into our acts of insight.

However, says Anderson, this is not to be something spontaneous and unreflective; we must pay careful attention to the various mental activities and describe them. He quotes Lonergan:

> Since sensations can be produced and removed at will, it is a fairly simple matter to advert to them and become familiar with them. On the other hand, not a little forethought and ingenuity are needed when one is to heighten one's consciousness of inquiry, insight formulation, critical reflection, weighing the evidence, deliberating, deciding. One has to know the precise meaning of each of these words. One has to produce in oneself the corresponding operation. One has to keep producing it until one gets beyond the object intended to be the consciously operating subject. One has to do all this within the appropriate context, which is a matter not of inward inspection but of inquiry, enlarged interest, discernment, comparison, identification, naming. (Anderson 1966: 145)

We must, as Anderson says:

> deliberately try to understand the unity and relations among the activities we have identified. We must come to understand, for example, how What-questions are related to sensible and imaginative presentations and to direct insights, how reflective insights related to presentations, direct insight and judgement. (Anderson 1966: 145)

What is important in all of the above comes from the detective story analogy, for it is a sense of how through wonder and the asking of particular questions, one can understand the situation in its own terms. One can understand its internal logic or, as Karl Llewellyn says, one develops a situation sense. In his intellectual biography of Llewellyn, William Twining (1973) gives us the best discussion of this concept. Llewellyn, he says, quotes Levin Goldschmidt in his explanation:

> Every fact-pattern of common life, so far as the legal order can take it in, carries within itself, appropriate, natural rules, its right law. This is a natural law which is real, not imaginary; it is not a creature of mere reason, but rests on a solid foundation of what reason can recognize in the nature of man and of the life conditions of the time and place; it is thus not eternal not changeless nor everywhere the same, but is indwelling in the very circumstances of life. The highest task of lawgiving consists in uncovering and implementing this immanent law. (Twining 1973: 217)

Moving with the Parable

Pattern and Judgement

We might see this 'immanent law, internal logic' as a sort of pattern as in the detective analogy above. What is important here is not seeing legal reasoning as a form of pattern matching in the way that Bernard Jackson (1988) does. According to Jackson, people match patterns against stock stories, and it is the stock story that drives the decision. Thus, we must pay careful attention to the stories we have to match situations. But the stock story, however well constructed, becomes a text. Just as text can be seen as the digitization of parole, so can that stock story be seen as the digitization or freezing of the numerous possibilities in the world (see my discussion of Collins in footnote 6). Rather, what I have in mind here is the way that one might see that paying attention to the story can be an aid to the imagination, in the sense that it drives one to places unknowable in the text. The key is to pay attention, to let the story speak for itself and not be too quick to apply closure by imposing a principle or pattern on it.

Nussbaum (1999) exemplifies this point. She talks of when the novelist Joyce Oates came to her university to give a seminar on her book *Because it is Bitter and Because it is my Heart*. A student denounced one of the characters, Leslie, as a failure and blamed him for refusing to combat the racism in his family. Oates said: 'That's not the way I see it really.' She then, says Nussbaum, went through the story of Leslie's life in detail so that one could see what it was like to be him. Her judgement, which was merciful, was given by telling his story. This is not just paying attention to the particularities but mixing in the concrete with the general principles of moral judgement. For her, you understand what people are and thus what judgement to make by paying attention to their story, by going through the twists and turns of it. It is on this imaginative journey that one gets a sense of a life and a situation and thus what to do. What is key here is the insight one gets from this journey.

Journey and Exploration

Back to parables again. We might, as Jülicher (1899) did, see them as simple stories, complexified by the synoptic Gospels, which essentially were there to give a straightforward moral message. Here they do not disturb what Donald MacKinnon (1974) in his essay on the parables called 'the cake of custom'; there is always an answer that we can read off. Roger White (1989) argues that it would be banal to think that that is all they are; that the dark and complex stories of the parables are just that and something like the parable of the Good Samaritan could be reduced to the principle 'Love knows no limit'. For MacKinnon, they are not there to impose meanings on the world, universalized principles to be applied, but are invitations to embark on a journey which might lead to a radically different view of the world – a journey 'beyond'.

What is important then is the idea of a journey and exploration. This is because, White says, we are invited not just to see illustrations of the Divine – a definition of the Divine and His will which we can then apply – but to take part in an exploration of the Divine which is open-ended, the results of which we cannot prejudge or pre-determine. The parables are there to produce something in the hearts and minds of the listeners, to get them ready for a journey which is itself transformed by their response. Miller says:

> A parable is a way to do things with words. It is a speech act. In the case of the parables of Jesus, however, the performative makes something happen in the hearts and minds of his hearers, but this happening is a knowledge of a state of affairs already existing, the Kingdom of Heaven and the way to get there. (1990: 135)

However, for MacKinnon, the destination is not given – the Kingdom is something to guide and transform the journey. It exists in the transformation of the journey and in that sense is in the 'hearts and minds of his hearers' – the Kingdom is something that transforms our lives (the journey) now and only exists in that transformation, in that opening to the beyond in our day to day lives. We do this, says White, by exploring in detail, by 'paying attention' to the realism of the stories by being taken through their twists and turns. One can never line up the answers easily; there are too many cross-cutting and even apparently blasphemous meanings. Thus, the parables have the capacity to transform their mundane stories of day-to-day activity, transcending them and throwing us out and beyond on an exploration of the Divine. But they can only do so from a base in the ordinary world – where to, however, we cannot tell.

Claire Henderson Davis (2005) develops this theme. We learn a skill like music by practising, repeating until we internalize it in such a way that we can go beyond and express in this language things as yet inexpressible, but which stir us from the outside. Someone skilled in law is much the same sort of person. They can express the inexpressible of the outside they encounter:

> Language moves because we experience the desire to express that which language cannot yet contain. This desire leads us to the limits of our present language, and at the edge, we find what is as yet unspoken within ourselves, within others, within our social world, within the physical world. Working at this edge puts us in touch with what is as yet unknown, where there are no straightforward rules to govern our work because we have exceeded the known territory of the law.
>
> What Jesus teaches is a form of relationship to this outside, a form governed by love instead of judgement. When I judge someone or something, I apply existing categories to the situation before me. But if what is before me cannot

be expressed within existing categories, then judgement is a form of violence enforcing conformity and doing nothing to expand my vision.

The love which Jesus teaches requires that I suspend my adherence to existing categories in order to allow space to the different reality before me. In this form of love, I am seeking to establish a new relationship where one doesn't yet exist. Not a relationship dependent on conformity, but one in which the difference I encounter is allowed to call my own language and vision into question.

Davis illustrates this in a discussion of the parable of the Good Samaritan. What Jesus is doing there is helping, imaginatively, the lawyer to move beyond the limits of his language through love. Jesus does not answer the lawyer's question by straightforwardly saying it is the Samaritan one should love. This would not have given the lawyer the imaginative insight to go beyond, to see the Samaritan as neighbour and to see inclusion as applying to enemies. The parable asks us, says Davis, to identify with the lawyer, the one who is trapped in the old categories, who did not have the imagination to go beyond and let our attention to that story move us beyond.

The Body

We have been talking of patterns and have tried to move away from the cognitive activity of pattern matching to something more dynamic, to the way these patterns might move us, to their performative and embodied nature. The body is important because respect for persons is in some sense bodily. Shusterman says:

In a world where bodies were always mutilated, starved and abused, our familiar concepts of duty, virtue, charity, and respect for others could get no purchase and make no sense. Moreover, bodily abilities set the limits of what we can expect from others and ourselves, thus determining the range of our ethical obligations and aspirations. If paralyzed, we have no duty to leap to the rescue of a drowning child. Virtue cannot require constant labour with no rest or nourishment because these needs are physical necessities. (2006: 5)

It also brings us down to earth. It shows us that we are vulnerable beings; the immortality of our rationality, the universal *logos*, is grounded in a weak and finite body. Recall the nun again. She showed us that Kant is not enough; our bodies make us aware of that and the beauty of our mutual vulnerability:

Kant was marvellously near the mark. But he thought of freedom as the aspiration to a universal order consisting of pre-fabricated harmony. It was not a tragic freedom. The tragic freedom implied by love is this: that we all have an indefinitely extended capacity to imagine the being of others. Tragic because there is no pre-fabricated harmony, and others are to an extent we never cease

> discovering, different from ourselves. Nor is there any social totality within which we can come to differences as placed and reconciled. We have only a segment of the circle. Freedom is exercised in the confrontation by each other of, in the context of an infinitely extensible work of imaginative understanding, of two irreducibly dissimilar individuals. Love is the imaginative recognition of, that is, respect for, this otherness. (Iris Murdoch 1959, quoted by Detmold 1984: 6)

There is a technique common in dance classes and something we did in the project. The participants walk ever faster in the room, all the time trying not to get in each other's way. What they are learning to do, sometimes at a subconscious level, is to negotiate their space with someone else's space, to accommodate their body and its space to the other bodies and their spaces. Here respect for persons becomes embodied and we truly learn a form of liberalism.

Ethics and ideologies, Shusterman goes on, are inscribed on and through bodies. Ethical virtue will depend upon bodily dispositions. How can an act be charitable when it is done stiffly with an angry face? He cites Confucius as emphasizing the importance of proper demeanour in virtue. Being inscribed thus, they are much more powerful and do not need to be made explicit through laws; they are implicit in the body and automatically practised through it:

> Confucius therefore insists that exemplarily virtue is somatically formed through 'the rhythms of ritual propriety and music' and wields its harmonizing power not by laws, threats and punishments but by inspiring emulation and love. (Shusterman 2006: 6)

We can also see this in the models of learning by, among others, Dreyfus and Dreyfus (1986), whose model of skill acquisition shows how rules feature in the early, less advanced stages of learning a skill. They become gradually embedded in the situation so that the rules are no longer a conscious part and are in essence discarded. Rules being invoked imply, on this view, lack of advanced knowledge.

The Dance of Life

How do we marry pattern, movement and the body? Let us start with an analogy. What makes a good footballer is not just the skills that she has but also the ability to locate herself in time and space. What this means is that if you were to stop a game and blindfold her, she would be able to tell you where she was in relation to the rest of the players. And this is not only at one particular time, but also where the positions were before she was stopped and where the positions might be at some time in the future. What she is able to do is to see the game as an ever-changing diachronic matrix and everyone's respective place in it. Thus, part of the training in football (at least in advanced clubs) consists of filming matches from above so that players can get a sense of the game as a pattern which is continually changing shape. But there is more to it than this, for what our player is also able to see in this ever-changing flux of players is connections and embodiments that can change the shape of the play or pattern. As such, the great pass is the ability to be able to see a connection which a lesser player might not have seen. But that pass, through seeing the potentiality of the connection, also unites you in some way with the receiver of the pass and you see yourself and your body as connected with theirs. You and they become in some way part of each other. We can see this in the following exercise. A group sits in a big circle with a ball of string and begins a conversation. Every time someone speaks, they throw the ball to someone else, who then responds and then throws the ball to someone else and so on. At the end you get a visual representation of the connectedness of the arguments and the people with the string crossing between everyone in different ways.[10]

We might then think of morality as a never-ending dance of life and skilled players of it are exactly like our footballer – those who can easily move through the patterns and see connections, and in seeing they can make them happen by passing the ball. All of this, to those less skilled, can be new and disturbing. But this is not a matter of just seeing something that is already there, some pattern that is already established and laid down, for the implication of that would be that what we really need to do is not to go 'Beyond Text' but to get to the bedrock foundation of the true text, and the Religion of the Book really is the Religion of the Book.

I want to emphasize performance to show precisely why this is not the case. Take the Good Samaritan again. This and other parables always start in the context of the Law. Jesus is accused of being outside the law, by consorting with tax gatherers, prostitutes and sinners. His answer to the lawyer's question as to how to gain eternal life is impeccably within the law: 'Love God and thy neighbour as Thyself.' But the story He gives in answer to the follow up question 'Who is my Neighbour?' is not necessarily a wider definition of 'Neighbour'; rather, He is asking for a performance. Make someone your neighbour by treating her like one. When you are enjoined to see the 'one who had fallen among thieves' as your neighbour, seeing implies doing. You see the possibility of the connection and in so doing make it happen. In treating someone as your neighbour, you make her one. The parable is, as Peter Winch (1987) says, both descriptive and performative. Think of the wave function collapse in quantum mechanics. One might think of our lives as a swirling mass of quantum possibilities, which on the interaction and intervention of an observer become just one state.

10 I would like to thank Claire Henderson Davis for introducing me to this exercise.

Conclusion

This fits well into the particular ethical life of the institution of law that I said our project presupposed. The way in which law unites and structures our unity and interconnectedness is by seeing our moral life as a seething mass of possibilities, as a sort of dance in which we are all potentially connected and by its actions, with imagination, making these connections manifest. We can see this more prosaically in the case law. *Donoghue v Stevenson*[11] is the case that founded the law of negligence in the UK. It says that the manufacturer of a product is liable to the ultimate consumer for the negligent manufacture of a product.

What happened was that May Donoghue had some ice cream and ginger beer, in which she found a snail. She felt ill and decided to sue. Within the seething mass of possibilities of the situation, the judges did not focus on the obvious one, the contractual connection between her and the owner of the café where she bought the drink; rather, they saw another possibility and potentiality, that of the manufacturer of the drink. Their intervention, their act of seeing, made that connection real. In terms of our earlier analogies, this decision was the equivalent of the visionary player making the defence-splitting pass.

The judges in that case made reference to the parable of the Good Samaritan:

> The rule that you are to love your neighbour becomes in law: You must not injure your neighbour, and the lawyer's question: Who is my neighbour? receives a restricted reply. You must take reasonable care to avoid acts or omissions which you can reasonably foresee would be likely to injure your neighbour. Who then, in law, is my neighbour? The answer seems to me to be persons who are so closely and directly affected by my act that I ought reasonably to have them in contemplation as being so affected when I am directing my mind to the acts or omissions which are called in question. ([1932] AC 562, 580)

I have used it as a rather wider structuring device for this chapter because the parable talks of attention, encounter and the movement to connectedness, of how the sympathetic recognition of the pain of another moves to connect and help and transform us in our mutual vulnerability. The life of the law must always have a space within for the endless potentiality and possibility of connection which we can use to regenerate and transform its static part. Within that space, we have to use, as our project in its experiential workshop did, methods other than textual ones. In that space at the heart of law, one has to learn to see, encounter and move through the mass of potentialities and possibilities that is the never-ending dance of life. It is that area 'beyond the text' that founds, regenerates and keeps in being the Text itself.

11 [1932] AC 562.

References

Anderson, B. 1996. *'Discovery' in Legal Reasoning*. Dordrecht: Kluwer.
Breda, V. 2011. 'Constitutional patriotism: a reasonable theory of radical democracy?', http://ssrn.com/abstract=1917231 [accessed 14 August 2012].
Collins, H. 1990. *Artificial Experts*. Cambridge, MA; London: MIT Press.
Collins, H. 1995. 'European private law and the cultural identity of states'. *European Review of Private Law*, 3, 353–65.
Davis, C.H. 2005. *Love/Beloved: Dancing the Divine Encounter*, Faith and the Arts, Hugh Price Lectures.
Del Mar, M. 2010. 'Beyond Text in Legal Education: art, ethics and the Carnegie Report'. *Loyola Law Review*, 56, 101–44.
Detmold, M. 1989. 'Law as practical reason'. *Cambridge Law Journal*, 48, 436–71.
Detmold, M. 1984. *The Unity of Law and Morality*. London: Routledge.
Dietz, M. 1988. *Between the Human and the Divine*. New Jersey: Rowan & Littlefield.
Dreyfus, H. and Dreyfus, M. 1986. *Mind over Machine*. New York: Free Press.
Fitzpatrick, P. 1992. *The Mythology of Modern Law*. London: Routledge.
Fuller, L. 1969. *The Morality of Law*. New Haven, CT: Yale University Press.
Gaita, R. 2000. *A Common Humanity*. London: Routledge.
Grote, J. 1990. 'Prestige: Simone Weil's theory of social force'. *Spirituality Today*, 42, 217–32.
Günther, K. 1993. *The Sense of Appropriateness: Application Discourses in Morality and Law.* Translated by J. Farrell. Albany, NY: State University of New York Press.
Jackson, B.J. 1988. *Law, Fact and Narrative Coherence*. Liverpool: Deborah Charles.
Jülicher, A. 1899. *Die Gleichnissreden Jesu*, 2nd edn. Freiburg: J.C. Mohr.
Legrand, P. 1996. 'European legal systems are not converging'. *International Comparative Law Quarterly*, 45, 52–81.
Lonergan, B. 1922. *Collected Works.* Volume 3. Toronto: University of Toronto Press.
MacKinnon, D. 1974. *The Problem of Metaphysics*. Cambridge: Cambridge University Press.
Miller, J. Hillis. 1990. *Tropes, Parables and Performatives: Essays in Twentieth Century Literature.* London: Harvester Wheatsheaf.
Nicholls, D. 1995. *God and Government in an 'Age of Reason'*. London: Routledge.
Nussbaum, M. 1999. 'Equity and mercy', in *Sex and Social Justice*. New York: Oxford University Press, 154–83.
Schmitt, C. 1985. *Political Theology: Four Chapters on the Concept of Sovereignty*. Translated by George D. Schwab. Chicago: University of Chicago Press.
Shusterman, R. 2006. 'Thinking through the body'. *Journal of Aesthetic Education*, 40(1), 1–21.

Shytov, A.N. 2001. *Conscience and Love in Making Judicial Decisions*. Dordrecht: Kluwer.
Tolstoy, L. 1978. *War and Peace*. Translated by R. Edmonds. Harmondsworth: Penguin.
Twining, W. 1973. *Karl Llewellyn and the Realist Movement*. London: Weidenfield & Nicolson.
Weil, S. 1951. *Waiting for God*. New York: Harper.
Weil, S. 1990. 'On human personality', in D. McLellan (ed.), *Utopian Pessimist: The Life and Thought of Simone Weil*. New York: Poseidon Press, 273–88.
White, R. 1989. 'MacKinnon and the Parables', in K. Surin (ed.), *Christ, Ethics and Tragedy*. Cambridge: Cambridge University Press, 49–70.
Winch, P. 1987. 'Who is my neighbour?', in *Trying to Make Sense*. Oxford: Basil Blackwell, 154–66.

Chapter 2

The Education of Attention and Encounter in the Legal Academy

Maksymilian Del Mar[1]

Introduction

Krzysztof Kieślowski's excellent 1985 film *Bez Końca* (*No End*) begins with the death of Antek, a lawyer who had recently taken on the case of Darek. Darek is currently in jail and is alleged to have begun and led a strike. The film takes place during the period when martial law was imposed in Poland and Solidarity was banned. After Antek's death, Darek's case ends up being taken up by Labrador – an ageing lawyer who has not taken on a 'political' case for many years and who has for some time only been involved in criminal defence work. Labrador approaches the case as he believes he must, as a criminal defence lawyer – that is, he does whatever he can to set Darek free. For most of the film, Darek refuses to cooperate with Labrador: for example, although Labrador tells him that there is little proof of his alleged crime and that as long as he remains quiet and cooperative in court, he could walk free, Darek refuses and organizes a hunger strike in the jail instead. Throughout, Darek keeps referring to the different approach taken by Antek to the case; according to Darek, Antek had understood him and would have appropriately represented his dissenting voice. In the end, however, Darek bows to Labrador's pressure, ceases the hunger strike and agrees to cooperate in court. As Labrador predicts, he is given a suspended sentence and is free to go. Labrador's apprentice congratulates Labrador on another victory, but Darek (and his wife) continue to sit in the court (after everyone has left) unable to face each other: clearly, for them, this is a humiliating defeat.

The contrast between Antek and Labrador is instructive. The very first opening lines of the film are by Antek, who has just died and who says, looking directly at the camera: 'I have died.' A similarly powerful line is delivered by Labrador, who, addressing some of the concerns of his apprentice over Labrador's treatment of the case, says: 'We are only defenders.' Although Labrador is aware that Antek

1 An earlier version of this chapter was delivered at the 'Beyond Text in Legal Education' final conference on 20–21 June 2009 at the School of Law, University of Edinburgh. I am very grateful for questions and comments made by the participants at that conference, especially Anthony Bradney and Julian Webb. Special thanks to Zenon Bańkowski for many discussions on the issues raised here.

had given Darek something that Darek was seeking – recognition of his humanity and his courage – he nevertheless recedes into what he sees as his role as a legal professional: to defend Darek. Kieślowski suggests that he achieves the opposite, defending only the system that provides Labrador with the role in the first place. And, by opening with the lines 'I have died', Kieślowski also suggests that the humanity and courage exemplified by Antek has died in Polish society (or at least is dying). Nevertheless, Kieślowski did not choose to portray only the actions of Labrador. By including the figure of Antek and by showing us the resistance offered by Darek, he also gave Polish viewers a sense of what he thought was missing: a way of resistance that was not withdrawal. The film, then, can be read as a very powerful reminder that although we can survive without the courage and humanity exemplified by Antek and Darek, that may not be a life not worth living, or at least not a life we can live with our heads held high.

Poland in the 1980s was, of course, a very specific time, with its own unique difficulties (no less so for lawyers than for other citizens), but the contrasting portraits of the two lawyers – Antek and Labrador – are generalizable and of relevance to contemporary times. One need only consider, for example, the role of lawyers and legal institutions in the legitimation of the sanctions regime in Iraq in the 1990s, which had resulted in the deaths of 200 Iraqi children a day. As Scott Veitch has pointed out, the death and suffering of the Iraqi population would not have been possible without the coordination of the world's most important institutions, including the United Nations (see Veitch 2007: 12–19).

This chapter is not the occasion for an enquiry into the capacity for legal systems as a whole to facilitate moral catastrophes, but it is about the moral quality of the life of the law lived by individuals who learn it and work within it on an everyday basis: lawyers, legal academics and law students. One of the basic difficulties for such a life is the role-differentiated behaviour required by the system. The pressure imposed by such roles, and the potential for moral blindness resulting from uncritical involvement in them, is exemplified in Kieślowski's film by the figure of Labrador. Veitch also pays a good deal of attention to the capacity for role-differentiated behaviour to enable us, often without us realizing it, to disavow responsibility: to distance ourselves from the consequences of our actions and to fail to even consider, let alone feel anxious about, the ends supported or created by the system of which our role is a part (Veitch 2007: *passim*). For present purposes, however, a particularly astute discussion of the dangers of role-differentiated behaviour in the context of legal practice is offered by Richard Wasserstrom (1975–76).

Writing in the mid-1970s, Wasserstrom argues that the world created by the lawyer's role is 'at best … a simplified moral world; often it is an amoral one; and more than occasionally, perhaps, an overtly immoral one' (1975–76: 2). He provides a striking example of the number of lawyers involved in the Watergate affair and offers the following hypothesis: 'that the fact that they were lawyers made it easier rather than harder for them both to look at the things the way they did and to do the things that were done' (1975–1976: 3).

For, he continues, it is the principal feature of role-differentiated behaviour that it 'makes it both appropriate and desirable for the person in a particular role to put to one side considerations of various sorts – and especially various moral considerations – that would otherwise be relevant if not decisive' (1975–76: 3). In her relentless pursuit of the client's ends, said Wasserstrom, the lawyer was always at risk of becoming 'an amoral technician whose peculiar skills and knowledge in respect to the law are available to those with whom the relationship of client is established' (Wasserstrom 1975–76: 6). Wasserstrom acknowledges that there are strong arguments in favour of the role to be played by lawyers: individuals who may not otherwise have access to legal representation – such as those ostracized and condemned by the majority and the media – are protected by a system that gives them the right to be represented in court. But the anxiety he articulates is positioned at a more personal (and less systemic) level: he asks, in essence, what is the effect, on the moral sensitivity of specific individuals, of a way of life that requires one to inhabit a 'simplified moral universe'? He says: 'Role-differentiated behaviour is enticing and reassuring precisely because it does constrain and delimit an otherwise intractable and confusing moral world' (Wasserstrom 1975–76: 9), and given his characterization of legal work, he expresses serious concerns about the effect of such constraints and delimitations on the moral development of those immersed in the legal life.

Wasserstrom's identification of the potentially dangerous effects of role-differentiated behaviour is one of the greatest challenges for moral education in the legal academy. It is a challenge that seeks to be met in this chapter by reference to what is here called 'the education of attention'. Given that role-differentiated behaviour simplifies the moral universe and influences those who come to learn and master that role to notice only certain things rather than others, there is an important role to be played by reorienting and relocating – or, better still, unlearning – attention. Although the education of attention can be furthered in many different ways, including by way of text-based resources, this chapter focuses on resources that go beyond text.

The education of attention is, however, only one part of the vision for moral education in the legal academy articulated here. The other fundamental component is 'the education of encounter'. The need for this approach is identified, once again, by Wasserstrom. Legal work is characterized, according to Wasserstrom, not only by role-differentiated behaviour but also by the kind of encounter with others, particularly clients, that lawyers engage in on an everyday basis. This relationship is, he says, an intensely unequal one, i.e. it is one in which the client is dependent on the lawyer's expert knowledge. As a result, and somewhat paradoxically, 'the lawyer can both be overly concerned with the interests of the client, and at the same time fail to view the client as a whole person, entitled to be treated in certain ways', i.e. 'with the respect and dignity that he or she deserves' (Wasserstrom 1975–76: 16). This kind of encounter, says Wasserstrom, is characteristic of professionalism generally (whether it be lawyers, doctors or other experts). Accordingly, the education of encounter is an education based on providing circumstances and situations, and modes of engagement, where those immersed in legal life can encounter other individuals in different ways and, in particular, in ways that do not enable (or that frustrate) the tendency to take up a position of dominance and control over dependent others.

Some readers may feel that in all of the above, the legal life has been hard done by: that the characterizations (by Wasserstrom) or the examples (in Kieślowski's film) do not do justice to the complexities, including moral complexities, of legal life. This is undeniably so. There will always be enormous variety in how individuals will respond to the requirements imposed upon them: for example, there will always be those who will be more akin to the character of Antek, and those more like Labrador. It is not altogether clear that Antek is a moral saint[2] or that Labrador is the opposite. This chapter does not wish to sit above the difficulties experienced by those involved in the legal life and pass easy judgement on the rights and wrongs of professional conduct. Rather, the departure point for this chapter is the hypothesis that there are certain aspects of the legal life – role-differentiation and professionalism – that indicate that there is a need for a kind of education that gives individuals the opportunity and the resources to develop an ability to distance themselves from what they have learnt, both in the sense of what they have learnt to pay attention to and in the sense of how they have learnt to relate to others. The claim, then, is that without the education of attention and encounter, the legal life can all too quickly become a hotbed for moral blindness.

In the background here is a particular vision of what it means to lead a legal life, i.e. to learn the law, live in legal institutions and work as a lawyer. The departure point, to reiterate, is that in the course of the legal life, individuals come to acquire what we might call 'patterns of embodied and embedded salience'; in other words, over a certain period of time, and as a result of learning and working in specific environments, individuals come to be sensitive to certain kinds of things (for instance, to certain kinds of narrative patterns which are associated with certain legal rules and principles) and to certain ways of being and doing, and thus also to certain ways of relating to others. In this respect, this departure point is informed by recent work in the cognitive sciences and the philosophy of mind that argues that human cognition operates beyond the skull or the brain. The 'embodied' aspect of this view focuses on the ways in which our thinking is integrated with, or indeed subsists in, our embodied abilities and skills.[3] The 'embedded' aspect,

---

2 I should point out now that nothing in this chapter suggests that we either should strive, or can strive, for moral sainthood. A powerful critique of such an ideal is provided by Wolf (1982).

3 The contemporary literature here is extensive. In fact, it is now common to incorporate the embodied and embedded features of cognition together, sometimes together with other dimensions, such as the enactive dimension, i.e. the sense in which thinking is integrated with action. For a brief account of perception that refers to these 'E' dimensions of perception, see Gallagher 2008.

in turn, looks at the ways in which the environments we act in store some of the information we draw on when exercising those abilities and skills.[4]

Although articulating this picture is beyond the scope of this chapter,[5] it is important to note that nothing in the picture is meant to denigrate the role of language (or symbolic instruments more generally). This is particularly important to mention given the focus of this chapter – and, indeed, of the 'Beyond Text in Legal Education' project as a whole – on pedagogical resources that go beyond text. Nothing, then, in this chapter's departure point of individuals as acquiring patterns of embodied and embedded salience, or in its focus on providing resources that go beyond text, should be read as ignorance of the importance of language.

Let me elaborate on this briefly, for it is important to keep it mind in what follows. A fully-fledged picture of legal life constructed around the idea of patterns of embodied and embedded salience, and also a fully-fledged account of legal education (including moral education in the legal academy), would need to find a middle path between overestimating and underestimating the role of language.

That legal scholars and legal educators are particularly prone to overestimating the role of language is hardly news. The history of legal epistemology – of theoretical pictures that describe how it is that individuals come to learn and know the law – is filled to the brim with talk of the alleged inherent properties of linguistically articulated rules and of how these guide legally trained individuals to reason their way to legal solutions. On this picture, individuals come to acquire legal knowledge in the form of knowledge of the rules, going on to reason in accordance with them whenever they take those rules to apply to the situation at hand (indeed, in some versions, it is the rules themselves that tell us when they apply). This epistemological picture has heavily informed legal education and it has been one of the aims of the 'Beyond Text in Legal Education' project to move away from it – hence, indeed, the departure point of this chapter, i.e. the idea that individuals learn in the context of and come to acquire patterns of embodied and embedded salience. The departure point is necessary, then, in order not to overestimate the role of language.

Equally misplaced, however, would be the underestimation of language – a risk to which those who speak of know-how, abilities and skills, and generally

4 For a recent account of 'externalism', which also combines features of embodiment, see Clark 2008. Clark's term is 'supersizing the mind', i.e. the way in which the environment contains information that augments our cognition.

5 Relevant resources for a picture specifically of the legal life so construed (as subject to the development of embodied and embedded salience) would include (to mention just a few): Winter 2001 (on cognitive legal studies); Meyer 1998 (on the 'handiwork' of legal knowledge); Robertson 2007 (on the 'always already constrained legal actor'); Legrand 1999 (on legal *mentalité*); Bell 2006 (on legal cultures); Johnson 2002 (on embodied knowledge); Samuel 2003 (on non-propositional forms of legal knowledge); Jackson 1998 (on narrative patterns); White 1973 (on the legal imagination) and 2001–2002 (on legal knowledge as an activity); and Lerner 2004 (on emotionally charged patterns of neural connections).

non-propositional forms of knowledge, are especially prone. Language can be underestimated in at least two ways: first, its role in how we learn and in how we store knowledge, for part of our learning (certainly in law schools) consists in learning swathes of propositions and systems of propositions; and, second, in its capacity to help us 'break the spell' (as Andy Clark has put it in a number of papers)[6] of cognitive salience. In other words, language is involved in both shaping salience – in us learning to see certain things rather than others – as well as in helping us to disassemble salience, and thus to unlearn how we see things. A fully-fledged account of legal life (including legal epistemology) and legal education would include discussion of these roles of language. Given space restrictions, and also the focus of this chapter and the project as a whole, this task is not undertaken in this chapter – but, to repeat, this is by no means to suggest that such a task ought not to be undertaken.

Having articulated the departure point, it is now important to elaborate on the education of attention and encounter. I turn first to attention and second to encounter. Note, finally by way of a preliminary observation, that the object of the discussion below is not to offer resources for the development, within legal academies, of moral sensitivity: instead, it is to offer resources (in this chapter, resources that go beyond text) in order to assist legal academies to help individuals avoid some of the dangers involved in becoming sensitive to a certain limited range of features of the world and ways of relating to others (where these dangers are precisely the result of learning to think and act like a lawyer). It is important to see from the outset that the work of education and encounter is ongoing and never complete: its aim is not to teach individuals to attend to specific things or to relate to others in specific ways, and then rest on its laurels, claiming that one has produced morally sensitive lawyers. On the contrary, the aim is to encourage and help individuals acquire a taste for, and develop the ability to, unlearn: to distance themselves, such that they are not trapped within the confines of the patterns of embodied and embedded salience that they come to acquire in the course of the legal life.

The Education of Attention

The concept of attention has had comparatively little exposure in moral philosophy. In what follows below, I consider how it has been used, and how its importance has been articulated, by a number of different philosophers. All these uses identified are important aspects of the role that the concept of attention can play in our understanding of the moral life. Following such an account, this part

6 For instance, Clark 1996 and 2000; and Clark and Wilson 2008. A revised version of Clark 1996 is included as a chapter in Volume I of this Beyond Text in Legal Education series.

turns to the development of beyond-text resources for an education of attention in the legal academy.

Attention in Murdoch and Weil

One of the most important, and also most influential, articulations of the concept of attention in contemporary moral philosophy comes from the work of Iris Murdoch. Murdoch herself attributes the notion of attention to Simone Weil (Murdoch 1970: 33), though, as we shall see, this is not without controversy. Although she herself does not present it in this way, it is clear that Murdoch is working with two concepts of attention: first, in negative form, as a way of criticizing the focus within moral philosophy on cases of isolated choice, rather than on a person's history of seeing; and, second, in a more positive guise, this also being the use Murdoch attributes to Weil, as a 'just and loving gaze directed upon an individual reality', which Murdoch believes 'to be the characteristic and proper mark of the active moral agent' (Murdoch 1970: 33).

The function of the first use, then, is to wean moral philosophers off the reliance on isolated moments of choice. Connected with this reliance is a picture of an autonomous agent, who freely decides whether, in a particular isolated incident, she should follow this or that moral prescription. Against this view, Murdoch argues that 'I can only choose within the world I can see' (Murdoch 1970: 36). Indeed, more strongly, she points out that one is 'often compelled automatically by what one can see' (1970: 36). Of course, the fact that we are so compelled, and that we can only choose within what it occurs to us to choose (based on what we see can be chosen), does not come from nowhere: there is a story to tell, peculiar to each person, about the 'prior work of attention' (1970: 36). Furthermore, there being a story to tell about such prior work does not mean that the work is not ongoing; on the contrary, the work of attention goes on 'continuously', and often 'imperceptibly', building up 'structures of value round about us' (1970: 36). If we neglect this prior and ongoing work of attention, and focus only on isolated moments of choosing, we will neglect to see 'that at crucial moments of choice most of the business of choosing is already over' (1970: 36). Murdoch is careful to note that by no means does this imply 'that we are not free, certainly not. But it implies', she says, 'that the exercise of our freedom is a small piecemeal business which goes on all the time and not a grandiose leaping about unimpeded at important moments' (1970: 36).

It is important to see how radical – in light of contemporary trends (especially those inspired by Kant) – Murdoch's view is (of course, in some ways, Murdoch's view is classical and recalls Aristotelian ideas). Contemporary moral philosophy's focus on choice, and thus also its bank of examples of isolated acts of choosing (we all know these from exposure to cases of 'moral dilemma'), gives us, says Murdoch, a distorted picture of what it is to be a moral agent or, better, what it is to lead a moral life. On Murdoch's view, 'the moral life ... is something that goes on continually, not something that is switched off in between the occurrence of explicit moral choices. What happens in between such choices is indeed what is crucial' (Murdoch 1970: 36). And what happens prior to, in between and after those choices is precisely the work of attention.

The autonomous agent, who 'chooses his reasons in terms of, and after surveying, the ordinary facts which lie open to everyone', and who is offered by some philosophers as a description and by others as a norm (Murdoch 1970: 34), is a myth. Such a mythical picture of the agent, 'thin as a needle' (1970: 52), is said by some moral philosophers to be guaranteed by moral language. Murdoch is certainly not opposed to the value and importance of moral language; she says, for example, that 'words are the most subtle symbols which we possess and our human fabric depends on them', that is, as long as we remember 'the living and radical nature of language' (1970: 33). However, she stresses that we learn to use such words (such as 'vulgarity', or 'courage') 'in the context of particular acts of attention' (1970: 30). In other words, our knowledge of these moral concepts is dependent on the prior and ongoing work of seeing. Our knowledge deepens, and also becomes more complicated, with time, as we learn to pay attention; as we do so, the words themselves become associated with certain contexts of seeing. 'We learn', says Murdoch, 'through attending to contexts'; 'vocabulary develops through close attention to objects' (1970: 31). Moral knowledge is inextricably tied to what we might call our attentional biography – our own idiosyncratic (and always ongoing) history of associating certain concepts, including words, with certain contexts and certain objects. For Murdoch, then, focusing exclusively on an isolated moment of choice leads theorists to miss these extra, vital dimensions of the moral life.

Such is the negative use of the concept of attention: it serves, to recall, to wean us off certain ways of thinking about the moral life. What about the second, and also the more positive, use? Here, the focus is on the quality of our attention. 'Goodness', says Murdoch, 'is connected with … a *refined* and *honest* perception of what is really the case, a *patient* and *just* discernment and exploration of what confronts one' (Murdoch 1970: 37, emphasis added). Achieving such quality, however, is not only a matter of effort in the moment: it is not a mere matter of 'opening one's eyes but of a certainly perfectly familiar kind of moral discipline' (1970: 37). Exercising one's vision as a form of moral discipline 'goes on all the time' and equally so 'at apparently empty and everyday moments' (1970: 42). The quality of our attention is being formed all the time, such that small incremental changes at any one moment will often have 'important cumulative results' (1970: 42).

Murdoch's suggestions for the development of the quality of one's attention are a mix of both positive models and warnings. On the positive side, she argues that the development of that 'refined and honest perception of what is really the case' can be furthered by the appreciation of 'great art'. However, she tempers this with the warning that 'great art' is few and far between, for 'almost all art is a form of fantasy-consolation and few artists achieve the vision of the real' (Murdoch 1970: 63). 'The talent of the artist', she says, 'can be readily, and is naturally, employed to produce a picture whose purpose is the consolation and aggrandisement of the author and the project of his personal obsessions and wishes' (1970: 63). 'Great art', by contrast, is able to 'silence and expel self, to contemplate and delineate nature with a clear eye' (1970: 63). It is 'impersonal' because 'it shows us the world, our world and not another one, with a clarity which startles and delights us simply because we are not used to looking at the real world at all' (1970: 63). 'Great art', she continues:

> teaches us how real things can be looked at and loved without being seized and used, without being appropriated into the greedy organism of the self. This exercise of detachment is difficult and valuable whether the thing contemplated is a human being or the root of a tree or the vibration of a colour or a sound. Unsentimental contemplation of nature exhibits the same quality of detachment: selfish concerns vanish, nothing exists except the things which are seen. Beauty is that which attracts this particular sort of unselfish attention. (Murdoch 1970: 64)

The positive model of 'great art', then, is combined with a warning: 'the chief enemy of excellence in morality (and also in art) is personal fantasy: the tissue of self-aggrandising and consoling wishes and dreams which prevents one from seeing what is there outside one' (Murdoch 1970: 57). If we are able to 'overcome prejudice, to avoid temptation, to control and curb imagination, to direct reflection' (1970: 39), then we would have a chance to transcend the fantasy self, and look out, into the world, doing so, furthermore, in a just and loving gaze, i.e. one that does instrumentalize that which it sees, but simply looks, contemplates, loves. Indeed, Murdoch reiterates many times that it is the 'capacity to love, that is to see, that the liberation of the soul from fantasy consists' (1970: 65). In a particularly moving passage, reminiscent of a literary rather than philosophical register, Murdoch says:

> I am looking out of my window in an anxious and resentful state of mind, oblivious of my surroundings, brooding perhaps on some damage done to my prestige. Then suddenly I observe a hovering kestrel. In a moment everything is altered. The brooding self with its hurt vanity has disappeared. There is nothing now but the kestrel. And when I return to thinking of the other matter it seems less important. (Murdoch 1970: 82)

It is difficult to look – just look – and also difficult to learn to look. This so because 'we are anxiety-ridden animals. Our minds are continually active, fabricating an anxious, usually self-preoccupied, often falsifying veil which partially conceals the world' (Murdoch 1970: 82). To learn to look is to learn to love, and to learn to love is to face others and the world as 'they really are'; it is to be able to face 'real death and real chance and real transience' (1970: 100) without distancing ourselves from it by the 'consolations of self-pity, resentment, fantasy and despair' (1970: 89). Here we reach the pinnacle of Murdoch's second use of the concept of attention: to attend to is to love, to see things as they really are, to not project one's own fantasies such that one sees what one desires to see, and such that one instrumentalizes what one sees.

Recall that this second use of the concept was also what Murdoch attributed to Weil. On the surface, there are indeed some similarities – for example, in her paper 'Human Personality', Weil states that 'the spirit of justice and truth is nothing else but a certain kind of attention, which is pure love' (Weil 2005: 92). Elsewhere, Weil also asserts that 'attention is the only source of perfectly beautiful art', though she does add (thereby going beyond Murdoch's celebration of 'great art') that it is also the only source of 'truly original and brilliant scientific discovery, of philosophy which really aspires to wisdom and of true, practical love of one's neighbour' (2005: 273). However, Weil also uses the concept of attention in a different way:

> Attention consists of suspending our thought, leaving it detached, empty and ready to be penetrated by the object. It means holding in our minds, within reach of this thought, but on a lower level and not in contact with it, the diverse knowledge we have acquired which we are forced to make use of. Our thought should be in relation to all particular and already formulated thoughts as a man on a mountain who, as he looks forward, sees also below him, without actually looking at them, a great many forests and plains. Above all, our thought should be empty, waiting, not seeking anything, but ready to receive in its naked truth the object which is to penetrate it. (Weil 2005: 8)

There is some echo of this in Murdoch's call to look and not cover the object with one's anxieties and fantasies (as with the episode of the kestrel). But Weil's notion, at least in the above passage, is not limited to the overcoming of the selfish ego: rather, there is a more basic entreaty to wait, to suspend the work of one's mind, to withhold the rapidity of one's thought and, just as – if not more – importantly, to be willing to be transformed by what may come. In Murdoch, the object is something to be admired. Certainly, the kestrel will not be noticed unless the person can brush aside her consolations, but it remains outside; it does not 'penetrate' one's mind, one's thought. Arguably, then, Weil's notion requires one to take a greater risk: not only to look, and look again, but also to open oneself up to be transformed, overcome by the experience.[7]

Furthermore, Weil's use of the concept of attention also does not lay claim, as Murdoch's does, to the ability to see things 'as they really are'. True, Weil does speak of the 'naked truth' of the object, but we need not read this to suggest the

7 There is also a form of objectification in the recurring example Murdoch uses in *The Sovereignty of Good* (see Murdoch 1970: 16–18). The example refers to M, the mother in law of D. D is either no longer alive or has emigrated. There is certainly a change that occurs in M's mind, but it is a change from a comfortable distance, in the absence of D. There is no interaction, no dialogue, and thus no opportunity for D to directly affect M, or for M to show that she is open to being transformed by D.

same simple divide between the projection of personal fantasies on the one hand and things as they really are (warts and all) on the other. Weil's use, then, can be read without any metaphysical bite, as a purely epistemological point, encouraging us to look at things in the corner of our eye, beyond our natural tendency to grasp them or master them. Her notion of attention is a little more awkward, askew, off-key, and all the more powerful for that. Assuming this reading of Weil's notion is accepted, we can treat this as a third use of the concept of attention (we could call it 'transformative attention').

Moral Perception: Obstacles and Gestalt Shifts

I would like to look now at two further theorists, both of whom speak of vision as moral discipline, or 'moral perception'[8] as it has more recently been referred to: Lawrence Blum and Peggy DesAutels. The change in locution here from attention to perception does not render the work any less relevant for present purposes.

Blum explicitly refers to and wishes to build on Murdoch's account. He refers, for instance, to Murdoch's first use of the concept of attention, as indicating how important is much of the work of seeing that goes on before any moment of choice (or, in his language, judgement): 'in a given situation', he says, 'moral perception comes on the scene prior to moral judgement' (Blum 1991: 702). But Blum also incorporates aspects of Murdoch's second use of the concept of attention. Thus, he speaks of perception as recognition that something is so (Blum 1991: 703, fn 3). The best illustration of what he means by recognition is from a more recent paper where, relating his visit to Auschwitz, he speaks of the importance of recognizing – and communicating the recognition of – others as human beings. Thus, he says, 'as human beings, we care not only about what people do for and to us, but how they feel about us; … their concern or its absence can be particularly heightened in certain situations' (by 'concern' here he means the recognition of the common humanity of stigmatized and persecuted groups – see Blum 2004: 143). This form of attention clearly closely resembles Murdoch's just and loving gaze.

Importantly for present purposes, though, Blum also goes further than Murdoch. He does so when he draws on psychological literature concerning the kinds of obstacles we may have to attending to certain features of situations – features that have clear moral valence. A useful illustration of Blum's approach is the following example: a white male is standing by the roadside awaiting a cab. Earlier along the same road, there is a black woman with a child. As a cab comes into view, both the white male and the black woman begin to hail the cab. However, the cab drives past the black woman and picks up the white male. What Blum is interested in is the capacity of the white male to notice the cab driver's 'presumed racism'. Blum uses this example in two ways: both negatively and positively. Negatively, he uses it to point out the problem with

8 The literature on moral perception is much too large to consider here in any detail. For a recent helpful overview, see Starkey 2006.

'principle-based traditions', which, he says, even when they are supplemented by the acknowledgement that agents need to know how to apply principles to particular situations,[9] do not guarantee that the white male 'perceives the racism in the driver's behaviour in the first place' (Blum 1991: 711). No matter, then, how thick our conception of moral judgement, it is always moral perception that individuates a situation 'as a moral situation in the first place ... thus providing a setting in which moral judgement carries out its task' (1991: 712). In light of Murdoch, this is nothing new: it resembles Murdoch's first use of the concept of attention.

However, the more positive use is novel. Here, Blum refers to what he calls 'attention laziness' (Blum 1991: 704). According to him, a person may, without realizing it, have developed certain habits of non-attentiveness. Part of this may be situational, in that there is no relevant prior personal history that makes the person non-attentive. But part of it may indeed be biographical: individuals may have 'obstacles ... to being sensitive to particular sorts of moral features', such 'as injustice, racism, physical pain, discomfort' (1991: 715). Blum further argues that there may be 'some morally distinct features of situations which some individuals may be better at perceiving than others' (1991: 716), for example, some may be better at noticing dishonesty, others better at recognising violations of someone's rights. This can be illustrated by returning to the above example of the taxi: imagine that nearby to the black woman with her child is an elderly, poor-looking man (of whatever skin colour), and that the white man is affluent-looking; Blum's point is that someone could see the taxi driver driving past the elderly, poor-looking man as a moral wrong and yet miss the moral wrong done to the black woman and her child. In other words, someone could be particularly sensitive to how elderly, poor people are treated (to age/socio-economic discrimination), but less sensitive (or not sensitive at all) to racism.

Blum concludes that the education of moral perception ought to proceed by way of a mix of activities designed to train the 'imagination, attention, empathy, critical reason, habit, exposure to new moral categories': all of these, says Blum, 'can contribute to the formation of moral sensitivities' (Blum 1991: 715).[10] Blum's notion, then, of attentional obstacles – the idea that we may be disposed, without realizing it, to not notice certain forms of injustice – can be counted as a fourth use of the concept of attention.

The last theorist I wish to consider briefly here is Peggy DesAutels. In a paper dedicated to exploring Gestalt shifts in moral perception (1996),[11] DesAutels does not rest on describing the value and importance of, as well as the kinds of skills

9 As emphasized, for example, by Herman (1993).

10 In his later work, Blum appears to have focused his attention on obstacles to the recognition of racism: see Blum 2002. Examining this in more detail falls beyond the scope of this chapter. For Blum's book-length treatment of moral perception, see Blum 1994. For a direct discussion of Murdoch by Blum, see Blum 1986.

11 See also DesAutels 1998 and 2012.

involved in, perceiving moral features of situations, but she also considers some of the ways in which our perception can (and indeed ought to) shift and how we can develop the ability to be open to performing such shifts. Her focus, then, on the possibility of such shifts, and on the ability to perform them, within any one situation may be counted as a fifth use of the concept of attention – one that we may call 'situational attention'.

Like Murdoch, DesAutels acknowledges the ways in which our daily lives, and involvement in certain tasks, may guide perception so as to make our attention differential: focused as we may be on one task after another, our attention turns to the features of the situation that fit our pragmatic involvement. It follows that one of the most effective ways of switching Gestalts, and thus of heightening one's situational attention, is to shift tasks, for example, shifting from the task of determining what is fair to the task of determining what is most caring.[12] Paying attention, then, to the kinds of tasks demanded by the roles we play, and switching tasks – such as by switching roles – can help us to loosen the hold that those tasks have over that which we notice and recognize as relevant and/or valuable.

Shifting tasks is an important method for Gestalt shifts, but is not the only one. We can also switch analogies, metaphors and concepts. Drawing on the work of Paul Churchland (1989), DesAutels says that we can call on the services of 'conceptual redeployment', a process which involves transferring a concept usually found in one conceptual framework to another one, used for the first time in that domain. What is interesting here about DesAutels' approach is that it warrants taking seriously, and indeed celebrating rather than bemoaning, a plurality of moral theories. Each theory, rather than being seen to be a rival, is understood to be one component of a more robust toolbox, all designed to help individuals heighten their situational attention: a utilitarian theory, for instance, might help us pick out features that we might otherwise (for example, because we were informed by a virtue theory) not notice. Of course, none of this is to suggest conservativism about the theories we have, as if we need no longer reflect critically on the theories we have constructed, or attempt to build new theories. But it does build in modesty: it asks us to see each theory as inevitably limited, as inevitably helping us to bring to light only some of the potentially relevant moral features of situations; indeed, it might also help us to come to terms with the likelihood (I would prefer to say the certainty) that there is no sense in which we will ever be able to speak of having the complete moral toolbox, which would enable us to exhaust our detection of all potentially morally relevant features of situations.[13]

---

12 Carol Gilligan's work on 'the ethics of care' (as distinct from 'the ethics of justice') is an important reference for DesAutels (see Gilligan 1982).

13 Another way to put this is that we do not need to be anti-theorists in order to embrace theoretical pluralism. A recent endorsement of pluralism amongst moral theories can be found in Hamalainen (2009), who also discusses the anti-theory strand in moral philosophy. Hamalainen quotes Tim Dare, with approval, who says that 'theories and principles are used as one part of a process of approaching moral problems. They are tools

Attention and Beyond-Text Resources

We have now considered four theorists – Murdoch, Weil, Blum and DesAutels – and have come up with five different uses of the concept of attention: first, a negative use that points to the impoverishment of our understanding of moral life if we focus solely on isolated moments of choice and do not ignore the prior and ongoing work of attention; second, a positive use that focuses partly on the way in which we learn the meaning of moral words in certain contexts of attention and partly emphasizes the need for a just and loving gaze; third, and again a positive use, which encourages us to suspend our thought and to look at things from the corner of our eye, where we may be most likely to avoid seeing it exclusively as part of some task-oriented scheme; fourth, a use where the focus is on attentional obstacles or, in other words, barriers that we may have unwittingly picked up to seeing certain kinds of moral infractions; and, fifth, a use that points to the need for exercising situational awareness, including by using moral theories and other conceptual resources to help us make Gestalt shifts.

In fact, all five uses have their place, and all can be – and indeed should be – used to counter the very powerful effects of the acquisition of patterns of embodied and embedded salience. On this view, we need acknowledgement of the importance of attention and we need to build pedagogical resources around the idea of attention (guided, at least initially, by these five uses), precisely because, in the absence of such an education of attention, we may only be strengthening the potentially disastrous effects of patterns of embodied and embedded salience. After all, if it is true that so much depends – as all the four theorists above emphasize – on vision as moral discipline, then we have to do all we can to give individuals in our pedagogical care the opportunities and the resources to develop that discipline (realizing, of course, that the work is ongoing and can never, in principle, be completed).

It was mentioned earlier that a fully-fledged account of such an education would need to incorporate both text-based and beyond-text resources. Given the focus of this book, however, it is apt to fasten on to the latter here. Part of the background work that needs to be done in this context is an examination of how the above uses of the concept of attention might help us incorporate, but also move beyond, the many excellent efforts that have been made in the uses of art for the purposes of moral education. As I have discussed this, in part, elsewhere, I shall not repeat the task here.[14] Instead, I shall focus on listing a number of the resources developed as part of the 'Beyond Text in Legal Education' project at the School of Law at the University of Edinburgh.

---

in moral reasoning rather than self-contained machines for the generation of moral answers' (Hamalainen 2009: 12).

14 See my 'Beyond Text in Legal Education: art, ethics and the Carnegie Report' (Del Mar 2010).

The examples below draw on some of the activities designed in collaboration with three artists: Alicja Rogalska (visual artist), Keren Ben Dor (dance educationalist) and Zoë Fothergill (artist and curator at the Talbot Rice Gallery). I say 'collaboration' because the project involved several meetings and much correspondence between the artists and both Zenon Bańkowski (the lead investigator) and myself, all of which aimed at finding a middle path between appreciation and involvement in the creation of imaginative works and the distinctive challenges of legal education. In other words, our aim throughout was to construct activities that would speak to, and would thus be found relevant, by law students and lawyers, while nevertheless being somewhat 'deconstructive or even destructive' (as Aiden O'Neill QC, one of the participants, put it) of their habits and professional requirements. Once finalized, the activities were collated into a two-day programme, in which law students, law teachers and professional lawyers, from both the USA and the UK (including both Zenon and I), all participated.[15] The activities were introduced and supervised by the three artists (who each took primary responsibility for a certain number of activities).

A list of these activities can be found elsewhere in this volume.[16] Here, I limit myself to six examples. Some of these, as shall become obvious, focused on participants confronting their own limitations – not artistic limitations (though inevitably many of us confronted these as well), but limitations resulting precisely from certain professional habits or certain ways of noticing that result from the acquisition of patterns of embodied and embedded salience in the legal life. These included, then, limitations of noticing as well as limitations of certain forms of expression and communication. Here are the examples:

1. Participants chose a word from a collection based on legal vocabulary, but which were also everyday words (e.g. 'causation', 'attempt', 'discovery'). Participants were then given a large black sheet of paper, as well as soil, nails of all kinds, bits of plastic, scissors, gloves and the like. They were asked to come up with a sculpture, or any other kind of work, that responded to the word chosen. Participants were also asked not to create word shapes to represent their responses (the work had to be non-textual). This exercise proved very effective in showing how much we relied on text-based communication, but also in exploring non-textual associations with certain words commonly not noticed by legal professionals (precisely because they are so familiar).
2. In the Talbot Rice Gallery, which is located across the courtyard from the School of Law at Edinburgh, participants were asked to look, as a group, at video installations and use string and blu-tack to respond, in diagrammatic

15 A film of this practice-led workshop (held in Edinburgh in December 2008) was made by Robert McKillop and is available at the following website: www.law.ed.ac.uk/beyondtext/film.aspx [accessed 14 August 2012].

16 See the Appendix to the Introduction to this volume.

fashion, to those installations. One of the most difficult things here (or so I personally found) was to resist the temptation to represent, or attempt to faithfully depict some feature of, what the installation could be understood to be depicting. The installation one of the groups responded to was an electronic game version of (with matchstick to navigate around) Osama bin Laden's hideout. This group (of which I was a member) found it difficult to resist the temptation to represent, and ended up mapping with the string, the layout of the buildings depicted in the game.[17] This activity confronted participants not only with images to respond to, but also with forms of expression that were inherently non-textual. The very fact that participants could not resist providing a simple representation of what was depicted highlighted the difficulties in communicating non-textually.

3. Three boxes of all kinds of materials (toys, odds and ends) were made available to two groups, who were given the task of making an installation from those materials in a confined space. The trick was that there was to be no talking to each other; participants could only rely on non-verbal communication (e.g. pointing to objects, matching objects, acting out potential links between objects). One of the interesting things to observe here was how individuals who were normally dominant in verbal communication receded into the background. Another interesting feature of this exercise was the difference in how quickly the two groups came to converge on a theme: one of the groups did so very quickly, thereafter choosing materials that represented the theme, while the other group kept exploring what the theme would be right to the end.
4. Participants were matched in pairs and asked to pick up separate instructions (one for the drawer and one for the describer). Each pair then sat with their backs to each other, and each was asked to read the instructions, but not to let the other person know about them. In general, the activity required the describer to describe an artwork (in the Talbot Rice Gallery), which the drawer had to draw (without seeing it). The instructions, however, were designed to rupture expectations. They included, for example, an instruction to the drawer to draw the opposite of what the describer was describing or to draw the way the voice of the describer sounded rather than what the describer was describing. An example of an instruction to the describer was to describe an imaginary artwork, or to describe with one's eyes closed. The activity was effective in many different ways, including having to translate linguistic instructions into images and, perhaps most powerfully for legal professionals, placing in doubt and indeed frustrating one's tendency to control outcomes.

17 The installation referred to here, and elsewhere in the descriptions referring to installations in the Talbot Rice Gallery, was by Ben Langlands and Nikki Bell. See www.trg.ed.ac.uk for more information.

5. Participants were asked to approach three chosen artworks in the gallery. Each participant was given three envelopes with instructions or materials and asked to open one when he or she was about to approach each artwork. The instructions included standing very close to the artwork (almost touching it), using a magnifying glass to look at it or facing away from the artwork. In all cases, this activity was designed to make one realize how limited (and how standardized) one's usual way of experiencing artworks is. It also brought to light the standardized ways in which one often confronts that which one is asked to assess or respond to, and thus to allow participants to experience the powerful effect of changing perspectives.
6. Participants were given a digital camera and three envelopes with three different kinds of prompts. They were given 45 minutes to make one photograph each in response to each prompt (so 15 minutes per prompt). They were then asked to go outside into the streets of Edinburgh to take photos. This activity proved very popular. The prompts included coloured pieces of paper, as well as things like tablets, string, SIM cards, etc. Participants reported being both encouraged and 'permitted' to look much more carefully at their surroundings than they were used to doing. Many produced photos that were only orthogonally (and thus, one might say, creatively) related to the prompts. (A version of this activity allows for the prompts to be legal terms.)

In all these cases the link with certain professional habits or other forms of salience, acquired as a result of involvement in the legal life, are not spelled out (and were not on the day). This was done by design, so that the links might not be obvious (thereby avoiding participants over-intellectualizing what they were doing or what the activities were trying to achieve). Indeed, this may be what contributed to their effects, which were felt by most participants (certainly, different participants responded more to some rather than other activities).[18] Participants articulated this by saying that they found the activities liberating: 'liberating' here can be read partly as permission to do what one normally would not do, but also partly as precisely not requiring any meta-level cognition and thus control by deliberation of what one was doing. In some cases, special effort was made to link the activities to legal practice (e.g. in the first activity, use was made of legal terms), and it is certainly the case that more legally relevant features can be worked into the various activities (for example, the second activity could be amended to involve communication of the principle(s) of a case). But even without adding such features, the above activities highlighted, just by having individuals involved in forms of seeing, doing and being that they would not

18 Participants' reflections were recorded in a number of different ways, including by making available to each participant a notebook, a voice recorder, as well as having a communal feedback board where anonymous comments could be posted.

otherwise get involved in, the limitations of the acquired patterns of embodied and embedded salience of the legal life.

Put differently, we can say that in all these activities, what is being targeted is the decoupling of the usual paths relied on by the agent to engage with the environment. Whether it be by sight or by any other sense, individuals tend to be oriented – as a result of a long and continuing learning process in repeated environments, especially when playing roles with repetitive tasks – to notice certain things, and approach and respond to things in certain ways. Individuals also come to acquire certain ways of expressing and communicating, which are effective in those environments, but which also have their limitations. To reiterate, then, the mode of instruction for the education of attention is not so much learning as it is unlearning: unravelling, disentangling and extricating the agent from that which is most familiar to him or her. Although this can also be attempted by text-based activities, it is very effectively pursued by resources and activities that go beyond text.

The Education of Encounter

Whereas the focus of the education of attention is on a person's relationship to the world – to what they see or do not see in the environments they interact with as a result of immersion in certain kinds of practical contexts – the focus of the education of encounter is on a person's relationship with other individuals. Nevertheless, despite the change of focus, there are some overlaps between attention and encounter. For a start, Murdoch's notion (her second use) of attention as a just and loving gaze can be said to form part of the quality of interpersonal relations. Blum's emphasis on the importance of recognition of the humanity of others also has obvious implications. Indeed, it will pay here to begin with yet another theorist, Sven Arvidson, who has spoken of attention, but in a way that offers us a neat bridge from the education of attention to that of encounter. As we shall see, Arvidson also draws helpfully on Martin Buber's work, which can further help us understand the moral dimensions of person-to-person relations.

From Attentional Character to I–You Relations

Arvidson works with the concept of 'attentional character', which he defines as a 'way of thinking about what is relevant in a human life, what is meaningful and how it becomes so' or, more succinctly, with the idea that 'we are what we attend to' (Arvidson 2008: 540). Most of the time, he says, attention – including the shifting of it – is 'automatic, bottom-up, exogenous, involuntary' (2008: 540). If it were otherwise, such that 'we had to start anew in visual search each time, imposing order and organisation on experiential flux, we would not be measuring reaction times in milliseconds' (2008: 546). For Arvidson, and in a way that echoes this chapter's departure point, 'the sphere of attention is a dynamic, embodied attending in the world, and attentional character is the relatively stable style of this attending' (2008: 552). By 'style', Arvidson means 'a particular manner of opening onto the world, an idiosyncratic, describable way of letting things appear as salient in attending', and by 'stability of character', he means 'a learned, organisational ordering of the attentional system, an initially limited capacity for attending in a given environment, such that some content is more likely to segregate into gestalts, as theme and context, than others' (2008: 552).

Given this chapter's departure point, and also some of the discussion of attention above, these ideas will seem familiar. But what is particularly useful for present purposes is that in an earlier paper (Arvidson 2003), Arvidson had taken this account of attention and combined it with an exploration of Martin Buber's work (1970), thereby leading us to see the relevance of the quality of attention for interpersonal relations. And it is this particular focus, of ways in which we relate to each other – including how we look at, but also act towards or interact with, others – that is the focus of encounter.

Buber, a Jewish theologian and philosopher, famously argued, though in a style that many have found impenetrable, for the fundamental importance, for moral life, of the I–You encounter. Arvidson offers a neat summary and helpful interpretation of Buber's concept of the I–You encounter. According to Arvidson, 'an encounter is I–You to the extent that the importance of means and practicality diminishes' (Arvidson 2003: 74). Arvidson quotes Buber: 'No purpose intervenes between I and You, no greed, no anticipation … Every means is an obstacle. Only where means have disintegrated encounters occur' (Buber, quoted in Arvidson 2003: 74). The I–You encounter 'is a tense and intense moment of conscious experience … The inner sense of my embodied consciousness is the context for You as the focus of attention … in encountering You, You confront me in an original way, such that You are presented as immediately and directly relevant and significant in my ongoing conscious life' (Arvidson 2003: 82).

Helpfully, Arvidson also discusses a number of obstacles to such an encounter or, differently, circumstances under which the possibility for such an encounter dissipates. Thus, for example, he quotes Buber: 'I can abstract from him the colour of his hair or the colour of his speech or the colour of his graciousness; I have to do this again and again; but immediately he is no longer You' (Buber 1970: 59, quoted in Arvidson 2003: 86). Arvidson goes on to explain that the moment I place You in a context, or thematise You – indeed, even when I reflect upon You – I 'destroy the mode of direct and immediate relation between You and I'; I transform the I–You relation to an I–It relation (Arvidson 2003: 87). For example, 'I can envision You now as a member of a family or as part of what is exciting in the room', but if I do that, then to that extent I no longer encounter You (2003: 87). Similarly, if I 'place him there (in any Somewhere and Sometime)', then, again, 'immediately he becomes a He or a She, an It, and no longer remains my You' (Buber 1970: 59, quoted in Arvidson 2003: 87).

Buber's account, as reconstructed by Arvidson, of the I–You encounter is clearly very demanding, but it is made even more difficult by Arvidson's reminder that Buber insisted that there was no prescription – no method – that can lead us from an I–It relation to an I–You encounter. Arvidson himself says that 'some attentional preparation' may make 'encountering you more likely' (Arvidson 2003: 88). Buber, on the other hand, says that we can only 'prepare with grace' and that 'grace concerns us insofar as we proceed toward it and await its presence: it is not our object' (Buber 1970: 124, quoted in Arvidson 2003: 88–9). The I–You encounter is defined negatively, as the absence of the features that would make it an I-It encounter and, furthermore, it is not one – at least according to Buber – that we can prepare for in any way but to approach any potential encounter with grace.

The Quality of Interpersonal Relations

Buber's call to grace, and also for waiting, may rightly remind us of Weil's sense of attention as suspension, and in that sense it offers us yet another intersection between attention and encounter. But it can also remind us of another theorist, who has also reflected deeply about the quality of interpersonal relations: Raimond Gaita.

There is a famous passage in Gaita's *A Common Humanity* (2000), where Gaita describes how, when he was 17 years old, he worked as a ward assistant in a psychiatric hospital. Gaita recalls that 'the patients were judged to be incurable' (this was in the 1960s) 'and they appeared to have irretrievably lost everything which gives meaning to our lives' (Gaita 2000: 17). Although there was, he says, 'a small number of psychiatrists' who worked 'devotedly to improve their condition' and 'spoke, against all appearances, of the inalienable dignity of even those patients', the majority not only treated the patients 'brutishly', but they also thought the above-mentioned minority of psychiatrists were 'naïve, even fools' (2000: 18). One day, however, an event occurred, which remains forever etched into Gaita's memory:

> One day a nun came to the ward. In her middle years, only her vivacity made an impression on me until she talked to the patients. Then everything in her demeanour towards them – the way she spoke to them, her facial expressions, the inflexions of her body – contrasted with and showed up the behaviour of those noble psychiatrists. She showed that they were, despite their best efforts, condescending, as I too had been. She thereby revealed even such patients were, as the psychiatrists and I had sincerely and genuinely professed, the equals of those who wanted to help them; but she also revealed that in our hearts we did not believe this. (Gaita 2000: 18–19)

Gaita's reaction here, and the very fact that he noticed, let alone interpreted, the nun's behaviour in the way he did, is important. Feeling ashamed himself, and ashamed too for the minority of psychiatrists he admired, Gaita provides us with an example of the exercise of grace. Without Gaita, it is unlikely that the nun's behaviour would have been noticed (by other onlookers), let alone thought important enough to describe to others. As he showed in his incredibly moving autobiography *Romulus, My Father* (1988), Gaita's sensitivity to the quality of encounter extended not only to members of his family, but also to other human beings excluded by the community (he and his father befriend an outcast, whom they allow to live on their property) and, significantly, to animals.

Gaita's work and Arvidson's reading of Buber both allow us to focus on the importance of the quality of how we encounter others. In a paper examining moral judgement in Conrad's *Lord Jim*, Daniel Brudney articulates this quality in the following way:

> The moral life is the life between people, and the structure of that 'between' is important. To treat others as rational beings or as sentient beings or even as beings who (like every snowflake) are unique is not enough, nor is having any particular set of feelings or motives. All these are compatible with looking over or through or beyond the other person. Of course, to acknowledge the other's reality can be less important than one's actions with respect to him or her. Nevertheless, as part of a picture of human relationships, such acknowledgement is important. (Brudney 1998: 274)

The phrase Brudney uses, i.e. 'the acknowledgement of another's reality', is significant. For one it may remind us, once again, of Murdoch's sense of the importance of not projecting one's own reality but of seeing things as 'they really are'. However, it may also remind us of another theorist who placed the quality of relations between individuals at the very epicentre of philosophy: Emmanuel Levinas.

Like Buber, Levinas' style is extraordinary difficult; fittingly, and perhaps necessarily, it makes one proceed slowly, reading sentences over and over again. Levinas famously asserted that 'ethics is first philosophy'. Responding to the dominance of metaphysics in the history of philosophy, and versed in Judaic theology, Levinas sought to replace the primacy of what he called 'ecology' (i.e. a person's ontological relation to himself) and 'cosmology' (i.e. 'the totality of things that we call the world') with a person's relation to the other (Levinas, in Levinas and Kearney 1986: 21). Even for those, like Heidegger, who used the notion of the interhuman relationship to dislodge what he called 'the metaphysics of presence', the fundamental notion was said to be a 'being-in-the-world', a kind of intelligibility – the forms in which the world always and already discloses itself to us. For Levinas, on the contrary, the interhuman relationship is 'considered from another perspective – the ethical or biblical perspective that transcends the Greek language of intelligibility – as a theme of justice and concern for the other as other, as a theme of love and desire, which carries us beyond the infinite being of the world as presence' (Levinas, in Levinas and Kearney 1986: 20). Our relationship to the other cannot be a matter of intelligibility. Intelligibility suggests a form of a-temporality: something present to be possessed. Rather, Levinas says:

> The relationship with the other is *time*: it is an untotalisable diachrony in which one moment pursues another without ever being able to retrieve it, to catch up with, or coincide with it. The non-simultaneous and non-present are my primary rapport with the other in time. Time means that the other is forever beyond me, irreducible to the synchrony of the same. (Levinas, in Levinas and Kearney 1986: 21, emphasis in original)

So Brudney's phrase, 'the acknowledgement of another's reality', is correct, but only if we understand that reality to remain always on the horizon: out of our reach, out of our grasp; not something we can understand, let alone control, dominate and manipulate, but something we can, and should, approach with grace, awaiting its never-complete emergence. Further, the other, in all his or her particularity, places a demand on us: an infinite demand, which we can never completely satisfy.

Dialogically Ethical Phenomenology

Some strands of more recent work in phenomenology have returned to the primacy of the relation with the other that Levinas placed at the foundation of philosophy. For example, Beata Stawarska's book *Between You and I: Dialogical Phenomenology* (2009) speaks of the notion of 'primordial duality', which is 'irreducible to the usual metaphysical categories such as the singularity of the one and an impartial multiplicity of the many' (Stawarska 2009: xi). This emphasis on dialogue, and the kind of turn-taking that characterizes the 'between us' when we relate to one another, has also begun to influence contemporary accounts of social cognition. For example, in their recent call for 'strong interactivity', and thus for the centrality of second-person relations (again, like Stawarska, warning against reducing second-person relations to first- or third-person viewpoints), Hanna De Jaegher, Ezequiel Di Paulo and Shaun Gallagher (2010) speak of the sense in which (for example, in conversations or in dance) individuals who relate to one another must each be autonomous, i.e. able not only to be influenced, but also to influence the other. Without such mutual autonomy, we would not have a person–person relation, but a person–object relation, where the object remains passive and susceptible to the unilateral exercise of autonomy of one participant in the relation (see also De Jaegher and Di Paulo 2007).

This emphasis on the distinctiveness, but also the quality, of second-person relations has been recognized to be important not only as part of a theory of social cognition, but also ethically. Thus, in their paper on 'Emotions and ethics: an inter-(en)active approach' (2009), Giovanna Colombetti and Steve Torrance build on De Jaegher and Di Paulo's enactive (and second-personal) approach to social cognition (2007) by speaking of its affective and ethical dimension. Their contrast between two forms of encounter, taken from a handbook for carers, which was based on a series of studies made in various care homes in the UK (see Perrin and May 2000), is particularly instructive for present purposes. The interactions both feature Audrey, a person with advanced dementia, where the first relation is between Audrey and a regular member of the care staff, and the second (significantly for present purposes) by a volunteer with little prior exposure to caring practice:

> It was mealtime in the home, and Audrey was wheeled into the lounge. Audrey … can say only a few phrases (like 'Go to bed', 'I love you' and a few swear words) … Audrey also has very bright blue, large, expressive, beautiful eyes.
>
> The [first] care assistant … placed the bowl of splodge on her lap, and started to put spoonfuls into Audrey's mouth – all the while looking out of the window. Audrey's eyes tracked left, right, left, right – looking for a face to hook herself into. But there wasn't one, just more faceless spoonfuls of food arriving out of nowhere into her mouth. When she was finished, the care worker stood up, stood over Audrey and wiped her mouth – still with no eye contact, and Audrey's eyes scanning her face.
>
> Later that afternoon, when a new shift was on duty, a punk walked into the day room. She had bright blond dyed hair … lots of earrings … Doc Martens … She pulled the low stool up next to Audrey, and sat astride it so that her face was right up close to Audrey's face. Audrey beamed as her eyes hooked in with the punk's eyes. Both women were twinkling at each other. Without any words, the punk slowly and gently fed Audrey sips of tea, eyes still locked together and smiling, beaming, deeply communicating. The punk stroked Audrey's face every so often, and Audrey nuzzled in for more.
>
> The punk was new, she didn't have any training and she didn't know that she was keeping Audrey in the world for a little longer. (Perrin and May 2000: 51, quoted in Colombetti and Torrance 2009: 521)

As Colombetti and Torrance say, 'there is clearly a marked difference in the style of interaction between the participants in the two cases'; their way of articulating it is that the first encounter is essentially a third-person interaction, where Audrey is treated as a 'her' rather than a 'you' or a 'thou', while the second interaction is a 'second-person interaction' (Colombetti and Torrance 2009: 521). When they come to articulate the ethical and affective dimension of the two interactions, they say that the first has 'a closed, blocked character … the carer is not affectively attuned to Audrey, and Audrey's responsivity is frustrated accordingly … the individual autonomy of both participants is diminished' and, importantly, they add: 'a reasonable interpretation of the first care worker's style of encounter is that she seems bored by her task, hemmed in by a role' (Colombetti and Torrance 2009: 522). By contrast, in the second interaction, the relation is 'less conflictual, more open, and more mutually facilitating … there is a strong sense of affective attunement on the part of both participants … individual autonomy is being mutually reinforced' (2009: 522).[19]

Colombetti and Torrance's example and discussion raises an issue most pertinent to the present chapter: the potentially dangerous effect of role-differentiation and immersion in professionalism. After all, it is the professional care worker who fails to relate to the other person in a mutually affectively attuned manner. The affective dimension, it seems, is missing precisely because of the routine nature of the work: the worker simply goes about fulfilling the requirements of her role, mechanically acting out her duty. It is the newcomer, who finds herself in an unfamiliar environment and in an unfamiliar relation, who manages to not only attune herself affectively, but also to spark an emotional response in the other. Of course, none of this is to suggest that role-differentiation and professionalism must have the effect it had on the care worker in this example (though it is telling that the nun in Gaita's example is also not one of the ward's psychiatrists), but it does point to the possible danger that can flow from mindless, or thoughtless, emotion-bereft immersion in one's professional role.

By no means is the above a complete survey of the ways in which theorists, from many different disciplines, have noticed the importance of the quality of encounter. I have not spoken, for instance, of Mikhail Bakhtin's (1984) emphasis on dialogue in Dostoyevsky's work (to take one example from literary theory)[20] or John Shotter's (1997) Wittgenstein-inspired account of the importance of 'dialogical realities' for our understanding of social behaviour (to take an example from social theory). Indeed, Wittgenstein's work can be drawn on very helpfully in understanding the quality of face-to-face interaction: 'My attitude towards' an other, said Wittgenstein, 'is an attitude towards a soul', and he adds, 'I am not of the opinion that he has a soul' (Wittgenstein 1953: II, iv). Others, like Gilligan (1982), for example, have also spoken of the importance of seeing 'others thickly, as constituted by their particular human face, their particular psychological and social self' (quoted in Flanagan and Jackson 1987: 623) – a reminder, once again, of the importance of responsiveness to the particularity, including physical particularity, of another.

19 I should add that the absence of conflict, as Colombetti and Torrance describe it, in the second relation is not a necessary part, as I see it, of the quality of an encounter: we can be in conflict and (for instance) argue, but still relate to each other in a way that is mutually reinforcing of each other's autonomy. Of course, there are limits – one would not wish to endorse violence – but it is important to see that no defence of second-person relations, or the quality of encounter, needs to require all such relations to be completely without conflict and disagreement.

20 See Friedman 2001 for a comparison of Buber and Bakhtin on dialogue.

Encounter and Beyond-Text Resources

We have now, it is hoped, a sufficient grasp of what it means to speak of encounter, as well as some sense of the kinds of ways in which we can prepare ourselves (though never in a way that can guarantee we are prepared) for such encounters. We have also seen that part of the obstacle to the flourishing of such encounters may be our immersion in role-differentiated behaviour and other pressures flowing from our interaction with others in professional environments. We have also seen above how some of the activities relevant to the education of attention are clearly also relevant to the education of encounter. Nevertheless, there are also activities that can be more specifically designed for the education of encounter. In offering five examples below – all taken from the same Edinburgh workshop as part of the 'Beyond Text in Legal Education' project – it is important to underscore that their aim is not to offer any particular model of relating to others, or any one ideal of what it may mean for an encounter to be an ethical one. No such vision of an ideal encounter is presupposed. Rather, the point is to give individuals the opportunity to encounter one another in ways that – given their immersion in the legal life – are unfamiliar and thus necessarily to some extent uncomfortable. This dimension of the unfamiliar and some discomfort is part of the strategy behind these activities: indeed, to match the powerful effects of learning (of the acquisition of patterns of embodied and embedded salience), and thus to enable unlearning, these activities must match the familiarity and comfort of learning with the unfamiliarity and discomfort of unlearning.

Here are the examples:

1. Participants were matched in pairs and asked to draw the body of their partner, who stood on the other side of a transparent sheet and who, in turn, drew them at exactly the same time. In my case, I struggled to keep up with my partner's body – for he too was moving while he drew me – and I noticed that he was experiencing the same difficulties. The outline that my felt pen produced was very erratic, the lines were wobbly, some of the features (such as the nose, the eyes and the mouth) were overlapping and the proportions were all out of whack. What I, and other participants, found powerful was not our technical failure, but rather the sense of how unfamiliar and (certainly initially) uncomfortable was this intense mutual attention to each other's physicality, not mediated by any words or any other social rituals.
2. Participants were matched in pairs and asked to stand next to each other with a large piece of white paper before them. One participant held a piece of charcoal in their hand and was to allow the other person to take their hand and let them draw with it on the piece of paper. Once again, this involved trusting each other in very physical terms, requiring one participant to be particularly vulnerable.

3. Participants were asked to group together in threes. Two individuals stood opposite each other and one of them was asked to lead, while the other had to mirror the moments. At any moment, the person mirroring could take over the lead and the other person had to follow. The third person observed, but could also tap one of the other individuals on the shoulder, which had the effect of freezing the situation and enabled the swapping of the observer for one of the individuals engaged in the mirroring exercise. One of the fascinating things about this exercise was to see how differently people moved, which one only noticed when one had to pay such close attention. For example, some would make grand movements with their whole body, while others made very subtle movements with their fingers. Indeed, some of us had great difficulty in mirroring the movements made by others. Once again, this activity enabled participants to experience each other as very distinct human beings that could nevertheless share an encounter with no pre-determined end, and thus in a way that was not mediated by any role or task requirements.
4. The group as a whole was asked to move in a large space. At first, participants were asked to move about as they wished. Then different kinds of instructions were used: for example, participants were asked to become gradually more aware of where everyone else in the group was; or, more confrontationally, one half of the group was given the task of doing everything they could do to make contact (for example, shake hands) with others, while the other half, in turn, had the task of doing everything they could to avoid contact. The instructions had the effect of problematizing the usual social rituals individuals rely on when interacting with each other, especially in professional environments.
5. The group was divided into three smaller groups and was asked to compose a dance. Each group had different instructions. One group had no rules at all. The other two had either very complex rules or simply a picture. Interestingly, the group with no instructions composed a dance that gradually involved all the members of the other groups (they began in a circle, and repeated a simple pattern, and every so often gestured towards an outside observer to join in). This activity was challenging on many levels, including having to choreograph a dance together in a short amount of time, while keeping in mind the differing physical abilities of participants.

To reiterate, none of the above activities aimed at prescribing any one way of relating to each other. Their aim, instead, was to offer individuals the opportunity to relate to each other in ways they are likely to find unfamiliar and uncomfortable. One large aspect of this unfamiliarity and discomfort, which was particularly powerful for those immersed in the legal life, was the emphasis in all the activities on physicality, which sometimes involved experiencing one's own limitations (though also abilities), sometimes one's own vulnerability (and sometimes that of others) and sometimes simply experiencing the other as a moving, constantly changing, autonomous and radically other body.

Conclusion

One of the potential criticisms of the activities listed above in both the education of attention and encounter is that the individuals who undertake them – especially seasoned professionals – will happily perform them in an environment such as the open space of a workshop (where, say, they are playing the role of an enthusiastic project participant), but will not see the relevance of what they have learnt for other contexts (especially their work context). In other words, no matter how hard teachers try, there is always a risk that individuals already adjusted to role-differentiated behaviour will not be transformed by such experiences.[21] This is an important criticism. It is not met satisfactorily by suggesting that one cannot force transformation on anyone, though that is obviously true: the activities listed above are not meant to be coercive; they can only work when individuals allow themselves to engage. Rather, what the criticism raises is the significance of institutional environments: the efforts of individual law students and legal professionals, as well as individual teachers, are very important, but they are not enough. Introducing the education of attention and encounter into both tertiary and professional legal education requires institutional changes at all levels within the institution.

At first glance, these institutional changes may seem to be too demanding, especially in the current climate of financial difficulties for universities, where the focus turns back on what is most essential and most professionally useful to teach. However, the requirements are not as prohibitive as they first appear and, indeed, the need for them arises precisely because of the current climate's heightened instrumentalism and professionalism.

All legal academies have access, or can easily obtain access, to open spaces, such as those found in a gym or even a local art gallery. The real cost comes not in terms of spaces, but in terms of the knowledge and experience of instructors. The know-how and sensitivity of the instructor in such activities changes everything: it is they who can create a sense of trust and openness, and an atmosphere of willingness to experiment and to enter into zones that are unfamiliar and uncomfortable. The 'Beyond Text in Legal Education' project at Edinburgh was blessed with three extraordinary artists who had extensive experience of working with individuals without any prior artistic background. Indeed, inviting an artist-in-residence to coach other members of staff – beginning with a workshop just for the staff (so they themselves can experience it first) – is an excellent starting point for academies who wish to explore going beyond text. The costs of such an artist, especially for short periods of time, is not as prohibitive as one might

21 I am grateful to Daniel Augenstein for this point.

think, and there are of course many funding schemes available (the artists often know these schemes very well, for many are forced to live from one such grant to another). Certainly, the teachers who participated in the Edinburgh workshop all spoke of how refreshing and liberating it was to be involved in such experiences themselves, but also of how grateful they were for the opportunity to learn from the artists' methods and strategies for devising such activities and managing them in practice.[22]

The greatest difficulty in any such project is relating these activities back to law, to showing the students why involvement in such activities is beneficial and should be part of *legal* education. In the context of the present chapter, this task is doubly difficult, for the aim of the activities is deconstructing, or unlearning, the learning habits one acquires in the course of a traditional legal education. In that sense, the justification is paradoxical: it is useful precisely because it helps you distance yourself from what you are learning. To defend such a pedagogy – namely, one that argues that learning and unlearning ought to go hand in hand – is clearly beyond the scope of this chapter, but neither it does not seem altogether unreasonable, even if it is somewhat counterintuitive at first blush (especially from the perspective of a streamlined, professionally geared educational philosophy).

Some years ago, Roger Cotterrell (2000) spoke of the vital role that jurisprudence can play in the legal academy, enabling students to stand back from, and look critically at, the habits (I would say, patterns of embodied and embedded salience) that they have acquired, and are acquiring, in the context of their immersion in the legal life. Jurisprudence certainly can play an effective role in this process of unlearning. However, it tends to be a text-based discipline, and even attempts to move beyond canonical jurisprudential texts, such as using literature, still rely heavily on text. It has been the aim of the 'Beyond Text in Legal Education' project to suggest that it is time to go beyond text in the legal academy. It has been the aim of this chapter to offer – via an analysis of the concepts of attention and encounter – a way of thinking about how such beyond-text resources can have vital moral significance in the legal academy.[23]

---

22 In a follow-up, reflective, workshop, organized in June 2009, the artists got all the participants to form groups and devise and then manage their own activities. Many participants found this very difficult though rewarding. Other chapters in this volume and the first volume discuss the various beyond-text resources and activities that teachers have developed or all developing.

23 In this chapter I have ignored the efforts made by many law clinics to go beyond text, including clinical approaches to teaching professional ethics (see e.g. Lerner 2004 and Lerner and Talati 2006). The activities offered here are not in competition with those efforts, for many of those focus precisely on the teaching of professional requirements; the focus here has been on the importance, within the legal academy, of deprofessionalizing students' understanding of the moral life (for more discussion on this, see Del Mar 2010).

References

Arvidson, S. 2003. 'Moral attention in encountering You: Gurwitsch and Buber'. *Husserl Studies*, 19, 71–91.

Arvidson, S. 2008. 'Attentional capture and attentional character'. *Phenomenology and Cognitive Science*, 7, 539–62.

Aydede, M. and Robbins, P. (eds). 2008. *The Cambridge Handbook of Situated Cognition.* Cambridge: Cambridge University Press.

Bakhtin, M. 1984. *Problems of Dostoyevsky's Poetics*, translated by C. Emerson. Minneapolis: University of Minnesota Press.

Bell, J. 2006. *Judiciaries within Europe: A Comparative Review.* Cambridge: Cambridge University Press.

Blum, L. 1986. 'Iris Murdoch and the domain of the moral'. *Philosophical Studies*, 50(3), 343–67.

Blum, L. 1991. 'Moral perception and particularity'. *Ethics*, 101, 701–25.

Blum, L. 1994. *Moral Perception and Particularity.* Cambridge: Cambridge University Press.

Blum, L. 2002. *I'm Not a Racist, But ...: The Moral Quandary of Race.* New York: Cornell University Press.

Blum, L. 2004. 'The Poles, the Jews, and the Holocaust: reflections on an AME trip to Auschwitz'. *Journal of Moral Education*, 33(2), 131–48.

Brudney, D. 1998. 'Lord Jim and moral judgement: literature and moral philosophy'. *Journal of Aesthetics and Art Criticism*, 56(3), 265–81.

Buber, M. 1970. *I and Thou*, translated W. Kaufmann. New York: Simon & Schuster.

Campbell, R. and Hunter, B. (eds). 2000. *Moral Epistemology Naturalized: Canadian Journal of Philosophy Supp. Volume 26.* Alberta: University of Calgary Press.

Churchland, P. 1989. *A Neurocomputational Perspective: The Nature of Mind and the Structure of Science.* Cambridge, MA: MIT Press.

Clark, A. 1996. 'Connectionism, moral cognition, and collaborative problem solving', in L. May, M. Friedman and A. Clark (eds), *Mind and Morals*. Cambridge, MA: MIT Press, 109–28.

Clark, A. 1997. *Being There: Putting Brain, Body and World Together Again.* Cambridge, MA: MIT Press.

Clark, A. 2000. 'Word and action: reconciling rules and know-how in moral cognition', in R. Campbell and B. Hunter (eds), *Moral Epistemology Naturalized: Canadian Journal of Philosophy Supp. Volume 26*. Alberta: University of Calgary Press, 267–90.

Clark, A. 2006. 'Language, embodiment and the cognitive niche'. *Trends in Cognitive Science*, 10(8), 370–74.

Clark, A. 2008. *Supersizing the Mind: Embodiment, Action and Cognitive Extension.* Oxford: Oxford University Press.

Clark, A. and Wilson, R. 2008. 'How to situate cognition: letting nature take its course', in M. Aydede and P. Robbins (eds), *The Cambridge Handbook of Situated Cognition*. Cambridge: Cambridge University Press, 55–77.

Cohen, R.A. 1986. *Face to Face with Levinas*. New York: State University of New York Press.

Colombetti, G. and Torrance, S. 2009. 'Emotion and ethics: an inter-(en)active approach'. *Phenomenology and the Cognitive Sciences*, 8(4), 505–26.

Cotterrell, R. 2000. 'Pandora's Box: jurisprudence in legal education'. *International Journal of the Legal Profession*, 7(3), 179–87.

De Jaegher, H. and Di Paolo, E. 2007. 'Participatory sense-making: an enactive approach to social cognition'. *Phenomenology and the Cognitive Sciences*, 6, 485–507.

De Jaegher, H., Di Paolo, E. and Gallagher, S. 2010. 'Can social interaction constitute social cognition?' *Trends in Cognitive Sciences*, 14(10), 441–7.

Del Mar, M. 2010. 'Beyond Text in Legal Education: art, ethics and the Carnegie Report'. *Loyola Law Review*, 56, 101–44.

DesAutels, P. 1996. 'Gestalt shifts in moral perception', in L. May, M. Friedman and A. Clark (eds), *Mind and Morals*. Cambridge, MA: MIT Press, 129–44.

DesAutels, P. 1998. 'Psychologies of moral perceivers'. *Midwest Studies in Philosophy*, 22, 266–79.

DesAutels, P. 2012. 'Moral perception and responsiveness'. *Journal of Social Philosophy*, 43(3), 334–46.

Flanagan, O. and Jackson, K. 1987. 'Justice, care, and gender: the Kohlberg-Gilligan debate revisited'. *Ethics*, 97, 622–37.

Friedman, M. 2001. 'Martin Buber and Mikhail Bakhtin: the dialogue of voices and the word that is spoken'. *Religion & Literature*, 33(3), 25–36.

Gaita, R. 1988. *Romulus, My Father.* Melbourne: Text Publishing.

Gaita, R. 2000. *A Common Humanity: Thinking about Love and Truth and Justice.* London: Routledge.

Gallagher, S. 2008. 'Intersubjectivity in perception'. *Continental Philosophy Review*, 41, 163–78.

Gilligan, C. 1982. *In a Different Voice: Psychological Theory and Women's Development.* Cambridge, MA: Harvard University Press.

Hamalainen, N. 2009. 'Is moral theory harmful in practice? – relocating anti-theory in contemporary ethics'. *Ethical Theory and Moral Practice*, 12(5), 539–53.

Herman, B. 1993. *The Practice of Moral Judgement.* Cambridge, MA: Harvard University Press.

Jackson, B. 1988. *Law, Fact and Narrative Coherence.* Merseyside: Deborah Charles Publications.

Johnson, M. 2002. 'Law incarnate'. *Brooklyn Law Review*, 67(4), 949–62.

Legrand, P. 1999. *Fragments on Law-as-Culture.* Deventer: WEJ Tjeenk Willink.

Lerner, A. 2004. 'Using our brains: what cognitive science teaches about teaching our students to be ethical, professional lawyers'. *Quinnipiac Law Review*, 23, 643–707.

Lerner, A. and Talati, E. 2006. 'Teaching law and educating lawyers: closing the gap through multidisciplinary experiential learning'. *International Journal of Clinical Legal Education*, 9, 96–133.

Levinas, E. and Kearney, R. 1986. 'Dialogue with Emmanuel Levinas', in R.A. Cohen (ed.), *Face to Face with Levinas*. New York: State University of New York Press, 13–33.

May, L., Friedman, M. and Clark, A. (eds). 1996. *Mind and Morals.* Cambridge, MA: MIT Press.

Meyer, L. 1998. 'Is Practical Reason Mindless?' *Georgetown Law Journal*, 86, 647–75.

Murdoch, I. 1970. *The Sovereignty of Good.* London: Routledge.

Perrin, T. and May, T. 2000. *Wellbeing in Dementia: An Occupational Approach for Therapists and Carers.* London: Churchill Livingstone.

Robertson, M. 2007. 'Does the unconstrained legal actor exist?' *Ratio Juris*, 20(2), 258–79.

Samuel, G. 2003. *Epistemology and Method in Law.* Aldershot: Ashgate.

Shotter, J. 1997. 'Dialogical realities: the ordinary, the everyday, and other strange new worlds'. *Journal for the Theory of Social Behaviour*, 27(2–3), 345–57.

Starkey, C. 2006. 'On the category of moral perception'. *Social Theory and Practice*, 32(1), 75–96.

Stawarska, B. 2009. *Between You and I: Dialogical Phenomenology.* Athens: Ohio University Press.

Veitch, S. 2007. *Law and Irresponsibility: On the Legitimation of Suffering.* London: Routledge.

Wasserstrom, R. 1975–1976. 'Lawyers as professionals: some moral issues'. *Human Rights*, 5, 1–24.

Weil, S. 2005. *An Anthology*, edited by S. Miles. London: Penguin.

White, J.B. 1973. *The Legal Imagination: Studies in the Nature of Legal Thought and Expression.* New York: Little Brown & Co.

White, J.B. 2001–2002. 'Legal knowledge'. *Harvard Law Review*, 115, 1396–431.

Winter, S. 2001. *A Clearing in the Forest: Law, Life and Mind.* Chicago: Chicago University Press.

Wittgenstein, L. 1953. *Philosophical Investigations*, translated by G.E.M. Anscombe. Oxford: Blackwell.

Wolf, S. 1982. 'Moral saints'. *Journal of Philosophy*, 79(8), 419–39.

Chapter 3

On Encountering Life and Learning With/out the Text: Reflections on Bańkowski and Del Mar[1]

Julian Webb

Introduction

Zenon Bańkowski's and Maks Del Mar's contributions are extremely welcome in a field that, with some notable exceptions, often lacks this depth of philosophical engagement. The ethical challenges of attention and encounter that they identify deserve to be taken seriously in our scholarship of learning and teaching, and in this chapter I intend not so much to comment on what they say as to use a number of their ideas as a point of departure for my own.

The gravitational pull of written text and the importance of thinking and acting 'beyond text' have also been brilliantly highlighted for us in their chapters. Written text without doubt dominates the law and legal education – even here. It is hard to miss the obvious irony that in a project dedicated to what is 'Beyond Text', we began – and have ended – with text and commentary on text. The temptation for academics in particular to return to and capture experience in the written word is clearly hard to resist!

At the same time, beyond text is never *without* text. We cannot seriously do law without text. But this project, it seems to me, offers some timely challenges. It raises serious questions: how do we, as legal academics, conceive of our relationship with text? What expectations do we have of our students' relationship to the text? What are the consequences of privileging the textual, and overlooking or subordinating that which is not text – to quite literally reduce the legal

1 My thanks to Maks Del Mar and Zenon Bańkowski for inviting me to participate in this project and for their generous comments on the original presentation from which this chapter has evolved. I would also like to acknowledge the work and influence of my friends and colleagues Andreas Philippopoulos-Mihalopoulos and Oren Ben-Dor, whose continuing journeys through phenomenology have done much to inspire my own, and to Liza and John, whose apartment in Frigiliana provided a wonderfully relaxed setting in which to complete this chapter.

environment (and everything else) to *con-text*?[2] And, perhaps most importantly, how does moving beyond text change our relationship to text itself? In exploring some of these questions I will adopt a consciously phenomenological-hermeneutic viewpoint, drawing largely on the work of Hans-Georg Gadamer, which I think is both sympathetic to the ambitions of 'Beyond Text' and may offer a way of further opening up the unspoken of this particular 'beyond'.

Why Phenomenology?

The attraction of phenomenology is quite simply that it offers a distinctive way of looking at the world and provides some important insights for pedagogy. I think it is no coincidence that, in mapping the territory of attention and encounter, Bańkowski and Del Mar both draw extensively on a number of theorists who themselves reflect the phenomenological tradition of European philosophy, and I want to build on that here.

Phenomenology seeks to uncover the meaning of things in themselves, as manifested in the lifeworld of human beings – that is, as the things that are there, in the manner that they appear to consciousness. Phenomenology emphasizes description of the world rather than the search for causal explanation, but not description in the classical objectivist sense. A phenomenological account recognizes that knowledge does not exist prior to experience, and brings a more holistic approach than do more traditional 'rationalist' theories to the relationship between objective reality and consciousness, recognizing, for example, the mediating effects of the body and the horizons set by culture and our established ways of being.

Closely associated with phenomenology is one of the root questions of hermeneutics: how is it that meaning emerges in the world? For both Heidegger and Gadamer, in particular, the questions of hermeneutics and the radical scepticism of phenomenology come together. Hermeneutics for them is an ontological rather than merely a methodological concept. Understanding is not just a question of epistemology, of knowing that, and knowing how we know; rather, it is the fundamental way of human being-in-the-world. The origin of meaning lies not in some primordial or pre-phenomenological realm, but right here and now, in the actions and practices of everyday life. From a phenomenological point of view, we make meaning out of the dialectic of *lived experience*, the 'what happens to us,

2 As will become apparent, this chapter assumes that 'text' exists not just as a representation of some reality beyond itself, but as a being-in-the-world with a physical presence and cultural history of its own – see Said (1983: 33). This assumption also informs the distinction between the limited notion of 'con-text' adverted to here and a richer understanding of 'context'. If con-text is subordinate to (written) text, then context is something which is both outside and other than (and hence beyond) text but also absolutely integral to it, in that it forms part of its *textuality* (which is discussed further below).

over and above our wanting and doing' (Gadamer 2004: xxvi). Experience matters because it provides the access both to self-understanding, 'the way one finds oneself' (Heidegger 1962: 172), and a greater understanding of, and connection with, the external world.

The relationship between experience and understanding is central to the phenomenological-hermeneutic view. Gadamer, like Dewey, distinguishes normative from generic experience (see Higgins 2010). In its ordinary, generic sense, experience is simply what happens; it need not have any particular significance. Normatively, however, experience is always significant. Normative experience is difficult, disruptive and unsettling: it implies a new insight, something that stands out and 'pulls us up short' (Gadamer 2004: 270; see also Kerdeman 2003). These normative experiences matter because they 'create the genres which generic experiences fill out' (Higgins 2010: 324). Those raw experiences that are powerful enough to pull us up short tend to be immediate, subjective, embodied and often initially experienced as beyond or outside of language. Language, however, is critical in converting such experience into understanding. In Gadamer's (1971: 31, 2004: xxxi–xxxii, 470) rather Delphic phrase, 'being that can be understood is language'. As Doran (2000: 269) observes, this re-asserts the Heideggerian view that being is a sense-making activity that is only realized – and realizable – in language. 'Linguistic being', as Davey (2006) distinguishes it, is thus both our access to knowledge of the self and the world, and more than that, since it also constitutes the *ontological source* of understanding. In short, there is always an articulation and a listening implicit in any situation; the spoken is always already embedded in our being, whatever we may subsequently say or not say.

To have an experience, then, requires not just an attitude of reflection, as educationalists often characterize it, but that we approach life in a state of openness and attentiveness, both to what may be encountered and to the nature of the encounter itself. It is in this normative sense of experience as the pathway to a deeper kind of understanding that we come closest to many of the ideas explored by Bańkowski and Del Mar in their chapters.

The Encounter in Bańkowski, Del Mar and Gadamer

In introducing us to legal education beyond text, Bańkowski and Del Mar focus on two related features or forms of learning: an education of attention and an education of encounter. Each follows Simone Weil in describing attention as, in Bańkowski's words, 'both an internal mental state and something that goes outside'. It is an active passivity; a purposeful, intelligent, stillness; a detachment from but also openness to that which is outside of us and has the power to move us. Attachment in this sense is both an epistemological and moral conception. Epistemologically it calls on us to look closely at the world, and particularly to attend to those things that we would not normally notice. As Del Mar observes, quoting Murdoch, 'we learn through attending to contexts' (Murdoch 1970: 31). This insight is also fundamental to understanding the moral work of attention. It is a reminder that, as Iris Murdoch (1970) also asserts, in moments of moral choice, our choices are commonly limited by our past – our personal history of seeing, or 'attentional biography' (Del Mar 2012: 40). But the work of attention also offers a way out of the moral constraints of history. Attention implies an attitude of solicitude or care. It calls us to attend (*attendre*) to the needs of the other, not simply out of a Kantian respect for that person, but as an active and deeply personal experience of the other in all her naked subjectivity.

The idea of the encounter thus reminds us of two things: the essential truism that lived experience is always situated in the world – that there is no possibility of abstract 'living' – and also that not every engagement with another has the qualities of a true encounter. There are different ways of engaging with the world, mapped out, *inter alia*, by our commitment in the moment to engage the other openly, and with empathy and understanding.

What Bańkowski and Del Mar have called the encounter is, without doubt, central to the process of Gadamerian understanding. For Gadamer, the encounter itself creates an ontological opening – a dialectical and deeply affective being-with another that seeks to understand the truth of that other.[3] At the same time, and through the power of attention, it becomes a challenging process of identity construction and self-cultivation. The encounter is where we experience both engagement with another and the shadow of what Gadamer calls 'tradition': those things that have historically become significant in shaping our personal and cultural narratives. Although tradition limits the scope of what appears possible in engagement, it also serves as a condition for engagement in the first place. Tradition determines 'in advance both what seems … worth enquiring about and what … appears as an object of investigation' (Gadamer 2004: 300). It sets both the ground for inquiry and its horizon. Tradition thus prepares us not only for the familiar, but for the unfamiliar as well; it enables us to recognize that which is alien or other, precisely because it is 'not-us'. It is this experience of difference that may provide the element of shock, of being 'pulled up short' that is our access to understanding, which necessarily challenges and stretches our perceptions and expectations (Davey 2006: 33). The encounter matters because it is thus the space in which we can question tradition, the place from which new 'horizons' (quite literally the limit beyond which it is not possible to see – Gadamer 2004: 305) may appear.

The importance of tradition in shaping our worldview also points us to the centrality of open-mindedness to the hermeneutic method. Tradition constitutes a constraint on what is thought and what is possible for human beings. Whether as

3 In this context, Gadamer uses truth not to connote a/the criterion for interpretation, but drawing on the Heideggerian sense of *a-letheia*, the openness of *Dasein* to the whole world of meaning, to indicate openness to the other – see Svenaeus (2003: 414). We return to the importance of openness to Gadamer's hermeneutics below.

participants in a conversation or readers of a text, we bring numerous assumptions and prejudices to the subject matter. These constantly undermine our liberty to think or act otherwise. Whilst we might, through a process of reflection and critical self-evaluation, peel these back like the layers of an onion, the rationalist assumption that we really can reach a view from nowhere is an Enlightenment fiction belied by experience. Perspectives are particular. Though each perspective, each interpretation, has the capacity to bring a different aspect of the intended object into view, meaning cannot be finalized. There will always be, as Eugene Kaelin (1999: 172) observed in commenting on Wallace Stevens' poem *Thirteen Ways of Looking at a Blackbird*, a fourteenth view of the blackbird. All we can do, then, is modify our particular set of beliefs and prejudices through dialogue with another, and that requires open-mindedness.

Openness in the encounter itself requires that we engage the other in 'genuine dialogue' (Gadamer 2007: 68–70). In a genuine dialogue we are committed to coming to an understanding – not necessarily to agreement, but to a point where 'one understands and is understood'. 'Good' understanding is only possible in the encounter through the merging of horizons (*horizonverschmelzung*), a fusion of the limited worldviews of self and other, or text and interpreter.

Gadamer's insights thus both reinforce the importance of attention and encounter to human understanding, but also differ from Bańkowski and Del Mar in at least two material respects. First, by suggesting that openness can never be other than openness from a position, Gadamer emphasizes that 'pure' perspectivelessness (even if it were possible) would in fact rob the encounter of meaning. Without what Gadamer calls the 'biases of our openness to the world', the encounter would say nothing to us (Gadamer 2004: 9) – and it could not challenge us. Second, it suggests that attention must extend as much inward as it reaches outward, to recognize our situatedness in our own views and preconceptions. Attending to our own values, beliefs and preconceptions means caring enough about them to be willing to change them. It is this quality of attention that provides the opening to open-mindedness in the encounter with another (whether person or text).

The openness we are exploring here is, I suggest, no less radical than Bańkowski and Del Mar's. By engaging with the other, we risk an element of ourselves. In this process one cannot maintain a superior position in relation to one's own understanding, but must come to recognize that it too should be 'put to the test'. Gadamer's openness to the other thus becomes, ultimately, an openness to the mystery of the self. A 'true' experience of difference cannot but leave us open to the possibility of other narratives of ourselves. By being open to these other possibilities in the encounter, often in the very moment of covering up (since the self-perceptions we defend the hardest are typically our greatest self-deceptions and failures – see Kerdeman 2003: 296), we become more present to our prejudices and the limits we set on our understanding. In that moment our openness not just to ourselves but also to the world increases: we experience in the encounter 'the revolutionary consciousness that unhinges … tradition through emancipatory reflection' (Gadamer 1971: 31) and 'a shared interpretation of the world which makes moral and social solidarity possible' (Gadamer 2007: 96).

This emphasis on the morality of the encounter draws in yet another dimension of philosophical hermeneutics that is relevant to Bańkowski's and Del Mar's concerns: the way in which ethical reasoning is both hermeneutically difficult and yet made possible by hermeneutic method.

For Gadamer, the difficulty can be understood thus. In approaching a particular moral or ethical problem, moral reflection as we generally think of it demands that I draw on my general understanding of what is right or good. In so doing, however, I am faced with a circularity that is at the heart of ethical evaluation. In short, the problem is that I cannot fully know what the ethics of a given situation demand until I am in that situation and, at the same time, it is only *post hoc*, by engaging in such situated ethical reasoning, that I can really begin to grasp what ethics more generally 'means'. So, without a general sense of what makes a particular dilemma 'ethical', I might not have the capacity to see it as an ethical problem, but at the same time my general understanding, by virtue of its very generality, will also be of limited value. Indeed, it may even get in the way of dealing with the situation effectively.

Gadamer's 'solution' (such as it is) to this problem is to return to the Aristotelian notion of *phronesis* or 'practical wisdom'.[4] *Phronesis* is both an intellectual virtue and a practical capacity. It is central to Aristotle's view of ethical decision-making, since it shapes our capacity for moral judgment and the ability to do the right thing in a specific situation. Ethical choices are not made purely on the basis of moral precepts; they also require the exercise of practical wisdom, which is, in large part, the product of experience. It is, as Martha Nussbaum expresses it, the outcome of 'a loving conversation between rules and concrete responses, general conceptions and unique cases' (Nussbaum 1990: 95, cited in Higgins 2010: 320). In Gadamerian terms, it also begins with an openness to ethical experiences, and specifically the willingness to question, refine and develop one's general ethical principles in the light of that concrete experience. Let us now begin to apply these insights to what we might call the 'legal encounter'.

The Legal Encounter

The idea of encounter as explored so far is intuitively attractive to a phenomenological account of law and 'lawyering'. From this point of view, being a lawyer may be seen as a reflective exploration of what it is like, moment by moment, to live in the encounter with law, and with the other in law. In short, the legal encounter could be said to constitute in and of itself the space within which knowledge *and* professional identity are constructed in practice.

4 On Gadamer's indebtedness to Aristotle, see e.g. Figal 1995; Svenaeus 2003; and Higgins 2010.

In academic legal education, however, we tend to focus primarily on one part of that experience: the encounter with the law as written text. This is not surprising in one sense, given the primacy of written text in defining and understanding law. Du Plessis (2001: 795) thus observes that 'whatever we can say and know about the law comes to us as text(s). There is no law "out there." The law is thoroughly textual and textualized'. However, there are of course other possible encounters in law that are not shaped quite so exclusively by written text.

From the lawyer's perspective, the primary encounter is often the face-to-face meeting between the client and herself. If we look at the lawyer–client relationship as encounter, it usually begins with an experience and a conversation. A client (to be) is one who has experienced events that stand out as significant, perhaps disturbing or disruptive of the ordered pattern of their life. By the time they present themselves to the lawyer, they will have decided that these events are – or at least may be – unfolding within a particular interpretative framework: that is, that they constitute a potential *legal* problem (see e.g. Felstiner, Abel and Sarat 1980). In most matters, other than those that are sufficiently routinized to require little direct communication between lawyer and client, they will then set up an initial meeting to establish a mutual understanding of the circumstances, their legal significance, and to determine what can be done next to forward some purpose of the client's (see e.g. Sherr 1986 on the significance of the 'first meeting'). One purpose of the initial consultation, then, will be to resolve uncertainty about the nature of the problem and to fix it within or outside of legal discourse – to create, at least provisionally, a new problem frame. Though there will be significant commonalities, in this process lawyer and client will be working essentially with different texts.[5] This difference and distance in understanding has both positive and negative consequences. The difference in the horizons of lawyer and client are part of the reason why clients visit lawyers, so they can get a new (legal) understanding of their problem. In the process, the lawyer will take the client's narrative and translate it into the recognized problem categories provided by law, recreating and redrawing the highlights and boundaries of that narrative in the process, perhaps giving voice, or enabling the client to give voice, and put into language some of their concerns for the first time. On the other hand, the encounter may also become an event in which the client's concerns, particularly their emotional or social needs, are lost in the search for the certainty of a legal solution (see e.g. Sarat and Felstiner 1988; Alfieri 1991). In other words, there is also inherent within the encounter the risk that only limited understanding is achieved.

Moreover, the legal encounter is not just constructed out of this initial narrative. It is a living, changing, created thing. It becomes refined, perhaps even refashioned, as the legal process unwinds by the interplay not just of the continuing lawyer–client dialogue, but of a whole range of what I will call *formal* and

5 See similarly Leder (1990: 17–18) on the nature of the clinical encounter in medicine.

authoritative texts. These formal texts will include written legal sources – cases, statutes, regulations, legal principles, forms and precedents, judicial directions and evidence that, at whatever distance, will shape the telling of the client's story. To these will be added the gloss of a range of authoritative texts that help manage the legal process itself as well as continuing lawyer–client interaction – letters and other communications between lawyer and client; communications between the lawyer and third parties; conferences with and advice from counsel and so on, all of them ultimately captured in the technology of 'the file' (see Tuitt 2005). This process in itself resembles the classical hermeneutic circle – a process in which meaning is given by a particular interpretative framework and is then modified by the text itself. Just as the lawyer and client work with a range of texts, so too the texts work with them.

Then there are also those elements that have relatively little or nothing to do with law or the legal nature of the problem as such. This is particularly apparent in the way that the emerging relationship has a set of affective components. It will often begin as a meeting between strangers, and even if familiarity between lawyer and client grows, the relationship will still tend to be circumscribed by some sense of 'professional' formality or distance – an often unspoken sense that there are particular social 'rules of the game' that govern this encounter. There is commonly an asymmetry of knowledge, and hence a potential difference in power and authority between the participants (though not always in favour of the lawyer). There may also be strong emotions at play, particularly in private client work. The client may be angry or actively distressed by their circumstances. They may be worried about whether they can trust the lawyer, whether she will do a good job for them, concerned about the costs and consequences of any action, and possibly uncomfortable that the meeting itself may require disclosure of quite personal details of their life. For the lawyer too, there may be a whole array of cognitive and affective attitudes at play. The nature of the problem or the way in which the client presents may generate a range of feelings, from distaste, through ennui to moments of sympathy for or genuine empathy with the client. The nature of the problem may sometimes generate confusion or doubt, a tentativeness about the best advice to give, and behind it all will be the usual noise created by the stresses and strains of personal and professional life.

Both lawyer and client also bring their own histories to the meeting – the assumptions and contingencies of their identity, ethnicity, class and culture. They will both come with their own preconceptions of professionalism – what a lawyer should look and sound like, the kind of language they should use and so on. The lawyer's words and actions will be influenced by her own sense of role morality, the cultures and practices of her firm, and her training and educational experiences more generally. These reflect what, following Knorr-Cetina (1997), we might call the 'epistemic culture' of law. An epistemic culture is built up of 'knowledge objects', that is, those:

> Centering and integrating devices for regimes of expertise that transcend an expert's lifetime and create the collective conventions and the moral order communitarians are concerned about. Object worlds also make up the embedding environments in which expert work is carried out, thus constituting something of an emotional home for expert selves. (Knorr-Cetina 1997: 9)

The tools of legal analysis, the norms and values of professionalism, and the often unconsidered ways of doing and being that have become a feature of the legal identity all form part of this epistemic culture, and all play a part in shaping the legal encounter. The ways in which the client and lawyer each present their selves in the meeting, through their appearance and non-verbal communication (the embodied features of language), will be critical in developing understanding between the parties in its fullest cognitive and affective sense. For the client, there may be the story of previous encounters with lawyers, or other professionals, and the lawyer will have her own history of clients too. These elements all combine in constructing a richly layered, dialogical story out of the interaction between lawyer and client, whether they will it or not.

Moreover, from the layperson's point of view, this may be one of only a number of possible encounters with and stories about law. For some, the law may be personalized in encounters with the police, immigration officials or others who exercise coercive state power. Or the primary encounter may have been with a civil court or tribunal as an unrepresented party, or as a witness or juror in a criminal case and so on. Each of these encounters may represent very different but nonetheless 'true' perspectives on the law and lawyers. One could develop a description of each of these that is equally as rich as a description of the lawyer–client encounter, though they tend to get even less 'air time' in legal education and training.

And that really is the point. If we reflect on this complex pattern of encounters, we may be struck by how much is going on and how far the representations of law and lawyering in legal education tend to fall short of capturing the 'thickness' of that reality. This failure adequately to capture the truth of the encounter is both a failure of imagination and of ethics. In saying this, I am conscious that, once again, I am largely in agreement with Bańkowski and Del Mar. Like them, I would treat openness to the other as having a strong moral quality; it is a starting point for ethical understanding and growth. In this context, real ethical experiences should be distinguished from situations of 'ethical comportment' (Dreyfus and Dreyfus 1990) or mere rule-following. Real ethics, I assert, requires an authentic response to each direct, unique situation that presents itself (Heidegger 1962: 346; Webb 2002). Ethical understanding in such situations begins phenomenologically as an experience, a 'felt demand' emanating from beyond the self (see e.g. Mandelbaum 1955: 54; Levinas 1969), but which is also grounded in the reflexive judgment that a contemplated action (or omission) is inappropriate or 'unfitting' (Mandelbaum 1955: 55).

I am not suggesting by all this that the idea of the encounter needs to become a dominant motif in legal education, but I do agree that taking the encounter much more seriously would prepare our students better for the interpersonal and ethical experience of 'doing law', and I suggest it might even encourage them to be open to the possibility of lawyering (in whatever guise) as a meaningful, perhaps even transformative, expression of the self. What I want to consider next is how might we use attention and encounter to those ends – even in relation to written text.

Applying a Phenomenology of Attention and Encounter in Legal Education

This analysis has started from a recognition that originary communication is not the written text, but conversation,[6] whilst also acknowledging that, from a hermeneutic point of view, there are dangers in overstating differences that are based simply on the distinction between written and unwritten forms of communication. Modern approaches to 'textuality', which treat it as an active practice, acknowledge this. Texts in this sense are best understood as complex entities, constructed out of signs (not exclusively written) that convey meaning (Gracia 1995: 7–14). Though the text is the thing that is 'read', the text itself cannot tell us how it will be read and understood. Meaning does not simply reside in the text, waiting to be discovered, it is actively constructed out of its textuality.[7] 'Beyond Text' in this sense is relevant to our understanding of law as a set of written and non-written forms and practices; indeed, it might thus be understood quite simply as a plea for a far greater awareness of textuality in legal education and training.

In this spirit, I want to suggest that the experience of textuality in legal education can be viewed through three broad phenomenological relationships between the self and the text (including the person-as-text). These are described in the following pages as 'being without the text', 'being-with the text' and 'being beyond text'. I suggest that these represent different sites, perhaps even 'levels' of attention and encounter. I also argue that this formulation may help us identify coherent forms of educational *praxis* – that is, of theoretically informed practice

6 Gadamer (2007: 96) thus asserts that all non-verbal or 'extra-verbal' forms of understanding refer back to an understanding 'that unfolds in speaking and in speaking with another person'. Paul Ricouer also argues that writing 'intercepts' the relation to the world and the relation between subjectivities that exist in the situation of speech (1981: 147). The emphasis on textual interpretation so apparent in the first two parts of Gadamer's *Truth and Method* is best seen, in the light of Part III and his later work, as illustrative of more general hermeneutic processes.

7 Thus, Gadamer (2001: 529) also observes, in talking about education, that 'to lecture is not to speak, as these are two different things. When one speaks, one speaks to somebody, when one lectures, then this paper lies between the speaker and the audience'.

– that will enrich our students' understanding and engagement with law as a rich textual, interpersonal and ethical phenomenon.

Being without the Text

'Without' here is used in the sense of being outside. It thus connotes an absence of being-with; a separateness, perhaps even a state of alienation, between the self and the text. The state of being without the text of law is, I suggest, a common experience, especially for the neophyte lawyer. Legal texts constitute a new genre for most of our students and occur as hard work. The style of writing (and sometimes speaking too) is often dry, pedantic and devoid of emotion. The content is invariably technical, sometimes highly so. There is an unaccustomed level of detail and an expectation that one is attentive to often hair-splitting differences of fact and principle. Legal texts must therefore be navigated and pored-over rather than read. The focus in legal education on the outputs of appellate courts also means that much of the human context has been sifted out of the primary sources long before we get to them. They are no longer able to speak to us affectively.[8] No wonder that Scott Turow (1978: 30–31) has memorably described his experience of reading a legal case for the first time as being like 'stirring concrete with your eyelashes'.

Educationally, the problem here is not just the difficulty of legal texts *per se*. Learning needs to be challenging, and we might think that being without the text is simply a necessary threshold that has to be crossed before deeper understanding can be achieved. To be sure, developing familiarity with legal texts and becoming more 'expert' as a reader will make a difference – it may even make for a more successful law student (see e.g. Dewitz 1996), but that is not my primary concern here. Being without the text describes a level of understanding that is inadequate in a deeper, more humanistic, sense, one which (though I cannot prove this empirically) I suspect many of our students struggle to surmount. Being without the text implies an impoverished relationship to legal narrative and to the real object of legal narrative – the human being who is both an object and (ethical) subject of law.

This tendency is not just a feature of legal education, but a characteristic of our culture's increasing emphasis on technical knowledge over *phronesis*.

8 There are exceptions, of course, but they stand out for that reason. The impact and distinctiveness of Lord Denning as a teller of human stories has been widely commented upon. See, for example, his judgment in *Hinz v Berry* [1970] 2 QB 40 with its famous opening line: 'It was bluebell time in Kent …' Compare also, for example, the relative power of the unemotional and logical analysis of Blackman J in the US Supreme Court in *Furman v Georgia*, 408 US 238 (1972), 405 with the more personalized and rhetorical critique of capital punishment in Camus' *Reflections on the Guillotine* (see White 1973: 131–2, 137–9).

The modern abandonment of wisdom is clearly highlighted by Dickens in the opening classroom scene of *Hard Times* (1854: 5–7):

> 'Girl number twenty', said Mr. Gradgrind, squarely pointing with his square fore-finger…, 'Give me your definition of a horse.' (Sissy Jupe thrown into the greatest alarm by this demand.)
>
> 'Girl number twenty unable to define a horse!' said Mr. Gradgrind, for the general behoof of all the little pitchers. 'Girl number twenty possessed of no facts, in reference to one of the commonest of animals! Some boy's definition of a horse. "Bitzer"', said Thomas Gradgrind. 'Your definition of a horse.'
>
> 'Quadruped. Graminivorous. Forty teeth, namely twenty-four grinders, four eye-teeth, and twelve incisors. Sheds coat in the spring; in marshy countries, sheds hoofs too. Hoofs hard, but requiring to be shod with iron. Age known by marks in mouth.' Thus (and much more) Bitzer.
>
> 'Now girl number twenty', said Mr. Gradgrind. 'You know what a horse is.'

In Mr Gradgrind's world, Bitzer 'knows' everything about horses when he actually has no comprehension of the animal beyond these memorized facts. Sissy Jupe, by contrast, knows far more than Bitzer about the being of horses; her father belongs to the 'horse-riding', and she lives and works with the animals every day. The privileging of knowledge-as-facts in the schoolroom, as advocated by the Gradgrinds of this world, both reifies the 'thingness' of things over their being and silences the deeper, perhaps more intuitive, order of knowing (wisdom) possessed by Sissy Jupe and her kind.

It is certainly tempting to see this emphasis on *techne* at the expense of *phronesis* as part of what is at the source of many of the ethical limits of modern legal education (compare Economides and Rogers 2009), including lawyers' oft-noted lack of empathy (see e.g. Vanilla Research 2010), and the tendency, particularly of less-experienced lawyers, to treat the client as a walking exam question. Phenomenology, by comparison, seeks to recover wisdom for education, and it does so by emphasizing the importance of relationships that are both with and, in a sense that I shall define below, beyond the text.

Being-with the Text

What does it mean to be-with a written text or a conversation? Another way of asking the same question might be, as an interviewee in the *Sociologists Talking* project at Warwick put it: 'how do you learn to live in a text?' (Reinvention Centre 2009).

In Gadamer's hermeneutics, a text is understood because of our participation in the subject matter communicated by the text. To be-with the text implies a joint project between text and interpreter that is both intellectual and fully embodied. The embodied nature of the encounter is obvious where that encounter is face-to-face, as in many lawyer-client interactions, but it equally applies in the context of a written text – where it may approximate the ideal of the Barthesian encounter between the absent body of the writer and the present, indeed attentive, body of the reader.

The aim of any normative reading experience should be to achieve an authentic understanding – this is at the core of being-with. In the legal context, authenticity does not equate to the pursuit of authorial intent, let alone authorial being in some pure, unmediated form. As I have sought to demonstrate above, it is our own anticipatory understanding, our own sense of tradition that provides both the context and the challenge for being-with. The challenge is, as Gadamer himself observed, that we fall prey to the preconceptions of our 'own rough drafts' (1979: 149). To really be-with a written text, or another person, we must be constantly aware of and question the origin and adequacy of our preconceptions, and genuinely open to the otherness of the text. Our relationship with the text is thus dialogical, in the classical, Socratic sense. It is marked by a willingness to engage in a playful dialectic with serious intent: 'to let the subject under discussion lead the way' (Gadamer 2007: 234). In this way interpretation becomes a joint project capable of (newly) generating an authentic understanding of the text or situation.

The implications of this approach for legal education and scholarship are significant. For the present purposes, I will focus on three key observations. First, what Gadamer's methodology points to is the importance of developing an *attitude* rather than any fixed techniques. At the heart of this attitude are two things: an appropriately critical awareness of one's own place in a received tradition (see also Sherman 1988: 396) and the recognition that understanding really is a project, not just a set of right answers. Authentic understanding requires that we be-with what is being said and not said; in other words, that we attend to communication – we both care *about* and *for* (perhaps we might even say be for – Webb 2002) what is said and the person saying it.

Second, we also need to attend more closely to the idea of legal tradition – though, again, not in an uncritical sense. Viewed positively, legal tradition can also become a useful way of encapsulating and emphasizing the connections between knowledge (both as personal knowledge and that embedded more generally in legal norms and culture) and identity – the links between epistemology and ontology, as it were, on a local scale. But it is also highly significant for the limits it imposes on Bańkowski's 'space to see'. The complexity of the legal tradition, and the limited amount of agency any actor has to step outside the parameters of the tradition, has to be acknowledged and understood (Sherman 1988). At the very least, we cannot conceptualize other ways of law and lawyering without recognizing what is already there and, so far as possible, clearing the ground so that something else can grow in the space we have created.

Finally, despite this emphasis on tradition, Gadamer gives us the freedom to acknowledge that, while there may be limits on what we can see, there is no absolutely privileged place from which to see. There is no primacy of authorial intent, let alone 'originalism' in a Gadamerian hermeneutics. Thus, for example, legal interpretation itself becomes a 'reflective enterprise' which requires the interpreter to reach out beyond legislative intent to see the instant case against the backdrop of the law in general (Patterson 1989: 83).

Together, these three observations, I think, focus the attention of legal education on a range of skills, attitudes and knowledge that students are too often left to develop incidentally (if at all) as a byproduct of their substantive learning.

At the heart of being-with is the capacity for open-mindedness. In sum, therefore, legal education should be much more about developing open-mindedness; aiming to broaden rather than narrow the mind by enabling us to question our conceptual horizons. If legal education is to be open to open-mindedness, what will this in turn require? First, contrary to the tendency of hyper-specialization, a key function of legal education must be to develop understanding both of the law in its broad social, historical and cultural contexts, and of the general principles that have helped shape and direct law's purposes. Second, legal education needs to become more relational and dialogic in approach: experiencing others' perspectives is a key to understanding and changing our own. Third, open-mindedness also creates an opening for creativity. An open-minded person is less likely to be dogmatic about how things 'are' and more likely to be skilled at viewing the world from different perspectives, and thus, perhaps, more effective at using a range of viewpoints productively to generate solutions to problems. Gadamerian hermeneutics therefore adds value in pinpointing the limitations that tradition can impose on our ways of seeing, on the impossibility of perspectivelessness, and consequently on the importance of what we might call 'perspectivalism', and the need to develop the epistemological tools that will help us develop and evaluate a multiplicity of perspectives on law.

Being Beyond Text

If the key capacity we need to develop is the ability to be-with the text, what is the added value of being beyond text? This question states simply the challenge to Bańkowski and Del Mar – precisely because a Gadamerian perspective might seem to put in doubt the very possibility of the 'beyond' of their title.

On balance, this concern is probably unfounded. The underlying binary text/non-text distinction itself remains useful insofar as too little attention has been paid in the past to the non-textual in legal education. Even if nothing more, it demands that we pay attention to other forms of or contexts for learning. It also usefully reminds us that writing can be safer, more distant, more 'cooked' than speech (and perhaps by extension we might say the same about other non-textual forms of representation).

At the same time, however, there is a danger that 'Beyond Text', like 'skills' or 'jurisprudence', can be reduced to *techne*, and thereby made safe and accommodated in some more-or-less marginal niche in the curriculum.

This, of course, is not Bańkowski's or Del Mar's intention. If we are to uncover students' 'patterns of embodied and embedded salience' (Del Mar 2012: 36), a rich understanding of how legal tradition is constructed out of both textual and non-textual forms and processes is required, and this begs not just the introduction of more non-textual exercises and experiential ways of teaching, but perhaps a more radical rethink of the curriculum itself.

And that I think brings us back to Bańkowski's emphasis on the need to create 'a space for the development of moral sensitivity'. One way in which we can meaningfully move the academic encounter beyond text (even in a Gadamerian sense) is to uncover what is always already unspoken in the legal encounter and, as Bańkowski and Del Mar intimate, that is commonly the moral or ethical understanding that sits behind, but is critical to, the situation. Much of our traditional curriculum and pedagogy does not simply fail to uncover the ethical subject of law, it actively hides it behind a thick veil of rules and abstractions, an approach which often serves to depoliticize the political and demoralize the ethical. Like Pether (2005: 2423), I make a plea for reading law *improperly*: to interpret back into the law all its messy textuality and intertextuality, for, as Pether (2005: 2421) also succinctly observes, 'with the interpretivity that is law's substance and best method comes the possibility of ethics in Levinas's sense'.

If we are to open the door to ethics, then we need to address law's human context, its intersubjectivity, as a key element of its textuality. Del Mar's descriptions of the various exercises participants undertook reminded me of one of the most difficult and powerful things I have ever done in a classroom. This was to participate in an activity that is used in a variety of personal development work. In this process you stand face to face with a partner, a couple of feet apart, and without speaking or touching, your task is simply to 'be' with that person over a period of three or four minutes. It feels like a lifetime. It starts off feeling extremely odd and unnatural; most of us I think are not used to that degree of proximity to another human being, or at least not outside of our more intimate and family relationships. To seriously engage in that process, I had to keep giving up a whole range of learned behaviours, thoughts and responses. In the process, that actual experience gradually transformed into something extremely moving and powerful, as each of us became aware of the other in a way that is hard to put into language – a deep sense of being-with, and perhaps even being-for another human being. I think it approaches the sense of originary encounter that Bańkowski and Del Mar have sought to capture. Levinas (1969), of course, as Del Mar notes, put this encounter at the heart of his ethics; the originary encounter with the face of the other; a face to face which is also a face to faith; a call to respond to the other that speaks directly to our deepest-held beliefs, and demands that we open ourselves to the possibility of another human being (compare Webb 2002 and Nicolson 2004).

In addressing the ethical demand of 'Beyond Text', I want also to focus on the problem of autonomy, which we have not so far expressly considered in this chapter. This is, of course, a big topic, so what I will argue here is perforce brief, and steps over a number of complex conceptual issues, though I think it is nonetheless of value. The reason for my doing so is, however, straightforward: the problem of autonomy is important in understanding how *phronesis* could become a key concept for legal ethics, and hence for legal ethics' education, particularly in the context of current discussions about the move away from ethical rules to more outcome-focused regulation of the English legal profession (see Boon 2011).

Autonomy obviously plays an important part in liberal political and ethical theory. To put it simply, a liberal education is commonly characterized as one that promotes personal autonomy, and both client and lawyer autonomy are central values for legal ethics. What we have said so far does not create a problem for autonomy. Even our (re)conceptualization of open-mindedness as a dialogical concept can be squared with liberal education's commitment to the development of critical autonomy. But autonomy, at least as traditionally understood by liberal theory, serves as a(n even) more problematic foundation for ethical theory than it does for education (see e.g. MacIntyre 1981; Schmitt 1995; Nicolson and Webb 1999). Central to this criticism is the extent to which modern legal ethics has tended to draw on a relatively thin conception of autonomy and one that particularly emphasizes individual choice over other values. Responsibility in this model also tends to be construed relatively narrowly as responsibility for oneself in the context of other, quite limited, dyadic relationships, usually captured by specific duties and obligations to foreseeable others.

Let us now take a step back to *phronesis.* We might say that a wise lawyer is simply one who knows what is the right or good thing to do for this client at this particular time. A model of legal ethics that privileges client autonomy would support this view: the right thing to do is what the client chooses, provided that that choice is one permitted by law. A potential strength and weakness of our focus on the encounter is that it may actually put the client's wants and needs more centre stage than at present. This may be a morally 'good thing' in situations of under-representation, but may seem more morally problematic if it leads to problems of what Dare (2004) calls 'hyper zeal'.

Reference to general principles and rules, however, runs counter to the idea of *phronesis* as Gadamer articulates it. Legal ethics cannot be properly understood simply as a rule-based endeavour: it also has *phronetic* characteristics. So, how do we assess the *phronetic* thing to do? One obviously Gadamerian answer is by reference to embedded experience, but also, perhaps less obviously, it requires us to consider the phenomenological structure and goals of the law, since law in itself is a phenomenological being-in-the-world. Law in this sense is purposeful. It can be seen as part of a set of systems geared to enabling human beings to lead the good life (health, politics and economics similarly contribute to other aspects of *eudaimonia*).[9] In addressing the needs of the client, the lawyer therefore needs to understand that client as a concrete being-in-the world, but not just in the client's own terms. The client is one of many participants in a wider moral conversation

9 In straightforward terms, we might say that, if the goal of medicine is health, the goal of law is (or should be) justice (compare Svenaeus 2003).

about what that good life involves, and their perspective may similarly be but one of many. This recognition is not an opening for lawyer paternalism, but it does allow that it may be a legitimate part of the lawyer's role to make the client aware of the limits of their own horizon, and of the consequences for others who may be impacted by the client's decisions, whether proximally or not.

If we are serious, then, about the transformative potential of legal ethics education, then we need to think carefully about *how* we move beyond talking broadly about 'moral sensitivity' and 'attention', and the importance of acknowledging another's reality. Much of what passes for attention in education today is a relatively passive state. We need, first, to ensure that attention is, as Bańkowski observes, a deeply active process. That is a necessary first step, but I am not sure it sufficiently gets us down in the dirt of experience. As I argued some years ago (Webb 2002), at the centre of any project to construct what I have called an 'authentic legal education' is the task of 'constructing a self that can take responsibility' (Dennett 1993: 430). The opportunity of moving beyond the comfort zone of the inauthentic self and exposing one's self to the active demands of law's other(s) seems to me to go to the heart of that project.

This will require from our students an element of unlearning and therefore, above all, a willingness to engage in a process of rewriting the self. As Gadamer shows us, this is unlikely to be an easy or short-lived task, but it seems an ethically necessary commitment. To blindly turn one's back on the possibility of greater self-knowledge would seem to be a significant act of bad faith, particularly at the hands of those who are committing themselves to a professional calling (if that phrase is to mean anything at all). It will also require us, the teachers, to create normative experiences that will enable growth. These will need to deliver, like the best clinical programmes, some fairly prolonged engagement in activities that bring a real mix of interpersonal and ethical challenge. The call to step beyond text certainly reminds us that we have probably made learning too safe, too sanitized. We need to re-introduce some element of 'danger', of learning at the edge, into the process if we are to ensure that our students are indeed pulled up short by more of their learning experiences.

There are also questions about how we help capture and assess such experience. These issues are sufficiently complex to merit separate discussion beyond what is feasible here. Nevertheless, I will express some reservations in this context about the use of even quite personalized learning tools such as reflective journals and portfolios. These may be pretty good at capturing and distilling 'reflection on action', to use Schön's (1987) term, as a kind of *post hoc* reflection and rationalization of experience, but I worry that, without more, they may in the process contribute to the objectification of that same experience. It requires both moral courage and probably a quite different learning culture from the current norm to reflect deeply on experience and in a way that will lead to moral growth.

Conclusion

Zenon Bańkowski has modestly described 'Beyond Text' as a project 'designed to see how we could use other resources than text in legal education'. What these chapters disclose however is much more than that. Despite its limitations, what we get a sense of is the distance that engaging in the kinds of activities created in 'Beyond Text' enables one to travel, and, moreover, that the journey itself promises an energy and excitement that is often lacking in more traditional educational processes. 'Beyond Text' as a project illustrates what those of us who engage in student-centred experiential education already 'know' from our practice: that experience has the capacity to transform not just the knowledge but the knower, and that opportunity is there for each of us as teachers and scholars, as well as for our students. It is an opportunity which no one should be[10] spared.

What I have sought to show here in my commentary is that the promise of 'Beyond Text' is central, not marginal to the concerns of legal education and, specifically, that its insights also extend back into the (written) textual realm. My personal hope is that the outcomes of this project will also provide access to ways of recovering for legal education the possibility of doing justice that is always already waiting in the wings at the moment of applying law.

References

Alfieri, A.V. 1991. 'Reconstructive poverty law practice: learning lessons of client narrative'. *Yale Law Journal*, 100, 2107–47.

Bańkowski, Z. 2012. 'The space to see: law and the ethical imagination', Chapter 1, this volume.

Boon, A. 2011. 'Professionalism under the Legal Services Act 2007'. *International Journal of the Legal Profession*, 17, 195–232.

Dare, T. 2004. 'Mere zeal, hyper-zeal and the ethical obligations of lawyers'. *Legal Ethics*, 7, 24–38.

Davey, N. 2006. *Unquiet Understanding: Gadamer's Philosophical Hermeneutics.* Albany, NY: SUNY Press.

Del Mar, M. 2012. 'The education of attention and encounter in the legal academy', Chapter 2, this volume.

Dennett, D.C. 1993. *Consciousness Explained.* London: Penguin.

Dickens, C. 1854. *Hard Times.* London: Bradbury & Evans.

Dreyfus, H. and Dreyfus, S. 1990. 'What is morality? A phenomenological account of the development of ethical expertise', in D. Rasmussen (ed.), *Universalism vs Communitarianism: Contemporary Debates in Ethics*. Cambridge, MA: MIT Press, 237–65.

---

10 Or could be – compare Gadamer (2004: 350): 'Experience as a whole is not something that anyone can be spared.'

Dewitz, P. 1996. 'Reading law: three suggestions for legal education'. *University of Toledo Law Review*, 27, 657–73.

Doran, M. 2000. *Introduction to Phenomenology*. London: Routledge.

Du Plessis, L. 2001. 'Lawspeak as text and textspeak as law: reflections on how jurists work with texts – and texts with them'. *South African Law Journal*, 118, 794–811.

Economides, K. and Rogers, J. 2009. *Preparatory Ethics Training for Future Solicitors*. London: The Law Society. Available at: http://www.lawsociety.org.uk/influencinglaw/policyinresponse/view=article.law?DOCUMENTID=419357 [accessed 16 August 2012].

Felstiner, W.L., Abel, R.L. and Sarat, A. 1980. 'The emergence and transformation of disputes: naming, blaming, claiming …'. *Law and Society Review*, 15, 631–54.

Figal, G. 1995. '*Phronesis* as understanding: situating philosophical hermeneutics', in L.K. Schmidt (ed.), *The Spectre of Relativism: Truth, Dialogue and* Phronesis *in Philosophical Hermeneutics*. Evanston, IL: Northwestern University Press, 236–47.

Gadamer, H.-G. 1971. *Philosophical Hermeneutics*, translated by D.E. Linge. Berkeley, CA: University of California Press.

Gadamer, H.-G. 1979. 'The problem of historical consciousness', in P. Rabinow and W.M. Sullivan (eds), *Interpretive Social Science: A Reader*. Berkeley, CA: University of California Press, 103–60.

Gadamer, H.-G. 2001. 'Education is self-education'. *Journal of Philosophy of Education*, 35, 529–38.

Gadamer, H.-G. 2004. *Truth and Method*, 2nd revised edn. Translated by J. Weinsheimer and D.G. Marshall. London: Continuum.

Gadamer, H.-G. 2007. *The Gadamer Reader: A Bouquet of the Later Writings*, edited by R.E. Palmer. Evanston, IL: Northwestern University Press.

Gracia, J.J.E. 1995. *A Theory of Textuality: The Logic and Epistemology*. Albany, NY: SUNY Press.

Heidegger, M. 1962. *Being and Time*. New York: Harper & Row.

Higgins, C. 2010. 'A question of experience: Dewey and Gadamer on practical wisdom'. *Journal of the Philosophy of Education*, 44, 302–33.

Kaelin, E.F. 1999. *Texts on Texts and Textuality: A Phenomenology of Literary Art*. Amsterdam: Editions Rodopi.

Kerdeman, D. 2003. 'Pulled up short: challenging self-understanding as a focus of teaching and Learning'. *Journal of the Philosophy of Education*, 37, 293–308.

Knorr-Cetina, K. 1997. 'Sociality with objects: social relations in postsocial knowledge societies'. *Theory, Culture and Society*, 14, 1–30.

Leder, D. 1990. 'Clinical interpretation: the hermeneutics of medicine'. *Theoretical Medicine*, 11, 9–24.

Levinas, E. 1969. *Totality and Infinity*. Pittsburgh, PA: Duquesne University Press.

MacIntyre, A. 1981. *After Virtue: A Study in Moral Theory*. London: Duckworth.

Mandelbaum, M. 1955. *The Phenomenology of Moral Experience*. Glencoe, IL: The New Press.

Murdoch, I. 1970. *The Sovereignty of Good.* London: Routledge.
Nicolson, D. 2004. 'The theoretical turn in professional legal ethics'. *Legal Ethics*, 7, 17–23.
Nicolson, D. and Webb, J. 1999. *Professional Legal Ethics: Critical Interrogations.* Oxford: Oxford University Press.
Nussbaum, M.C. 1990. *Love's Knowledge: Essays on Philosophy and Literature.* New York: Oxford University Press.
Patterson, D.M. 1989. 'Authorial intent and hermeneutics'. *Canadian Journal of Law and Jurisprudence*, 2, 79–83.
Pether, P. 2005. 'Is there anything outside the class? Law, literature, and pedagogy'. *Cardozo Law Review*, 26, 2415.
Reinvention Centre. 2009. 'Sociologists talking'. Available at: http://www2.warwick.ac.uk/fac/soc/sociology/rsw/undergrad/cetl/filmspublications/sociologiststalking/ [accessed 16 August 2012].
Ricouer, P. 1981. *Hermeneutics and the Human Sciences*, translated by J.B. Thompson. Cambridge: Cambridge University Press.
Said, E.W. 1983. *The World, the Text and the Critic.* Cambridge, MA: Harvard University Press.
Sarat, A. and Felstiner, W.L. 1988. 'Law and social relations: vocabularies of motive in lawyer-client interaction'. *Law & Society Review*, 22, 737–69.
Schmitt, R. 1995. *Beyond Separateness.* Boulder, CO: Westview Press.
Schön, D.A. 1987. *Educating the Reflective Practitioner.* San Francisco, CA: Jossey-Bass.
Sherman, B. 1988. 'Hermeneutics in law'. *Modern Law Review*, 51, 386–402.
Sherr, A. 1986. 'Lawyer and client: the first meeting'. *Modern Law Review*, 49, 323–57.
Svenaeus, F. 2003. 'Hermeneutics of medicine in the wake of Gadamer: the issue of *phronesis*'. *Theoretical Medicine*, 24, 407–31.
Tuitt, P. 2005. 'Legal practice and modes of dying: Bruno Latour, technology and the critical legal instance'. *Law and Critique*, 16, 113–29.
Turow, S. 1978. *One L: An Inside Account of Life in the First Year at Harvard Law School.* London: Penguin.
Vanilla Research. 2010. 'The quality of legal services: report prepared by Vanilla Research for the Legal Services Consumer Panel September 2010'. Available at: http://legalservicesconsumerpanel.org.uk/publications/research_and_reports/index.html [accessed 16 August 2012].
Webb, J. 2002. 'Being a lawyer/being a human being'. *Legal Ethics*, 5, 130–51.
White, J.B. 1973. *The Legal Imagination.* Boston, MA: Little Brown.

Chapter 4
A University is Not the World: And Nor is its Law School

Anthony Bradney

Introduction

In this chapter I will put the arguments for moving beyond text in university law schools that are explored elsewhere in this volume into the context of the changing nature of UK law schools.[1] I will consider only the provision of academic legal education. Law schools that are involved in this constitute the vast majority of British university law schools. However, there are a small number of law schools in the UK that also teach professional courses, usually in departments that are separate from those parts of the school concerned with academic education. For reasons that will become apparent later in the chapter, these professional departments fall outside of my scheme of analysis.

Any argument for changing the practice of legal education always needs to be examined in the context of what that practice is at present and what it has been in the past. Present and past practice plainly should not determine the nature of what can be done in the future. To suggest otherwise would be to plead for stasis in legal education – something that would not be desirable and something that has never been part of the history of legal education in the UK. Even in its most lethargic periods, the nature of legal education in British university law schools has always been the subject of continual debate and change.

Twining has written that '[a]cademic law in England, as embodied in the full-time scholar-teacher of law, had, by and large, a secure and somnolent infancy' (Twining 1974: 149).[2] Whilst this is doubtless correct, it does not mean that there

---

1 This chapter will focus on UK university law schools. Comparative analyses of university law schools from different traditions are possible. However, since these traditions vary in so many respects, such work has to be done cautiously and carefully if the variations in the traditions are not to be distorted or ignored (Bradney 2007). Given the length of this chapter, I will not attempt to do this here. There are differences between the university law schools in the various legal jurisdictions in the UK, but I would argue that these differences are not relevant to the points that I make here.

2 Others have been more acerbic in their descriptions of British university law schools in the first part of the twentieth century. Duxbury, for example, writes of 'a fairly moribund, amateurish profession' (Duxbury 2001: 71).

was no deliberation about the nature and practice of legal education during this time. General academic law journals in the UK have always included articles on legal education in their contents. Thus, for example, in 1924 the first article in the first issue of the *Journal of the Society of Public Teachers of Law* took as its subject the changing nature of legal education (Hazeltine 1924). Cownie and Cox observe that:

> the capacity to write on educational issues in the new *Journal* did much to enliven the Society [of Public Teachers of Law], and by the mid-1930s there were important debates reflected in articles and the published records of Annual General Meetings. (Cownie and Cocks 2009: 80)

Debate about legal education at this time was not confined to the *Journal of the Society of Public Teachers of Law*. The main law journal of the time, the *Law Quarterly Review*, also published articles on legal education. Its first issue contained an article on legal education (Clark 1885). In the twentieth century, the first article on legal education in the same journal was published in 1902 (Brown 1902) and others followed thereafter. New general journals in law that were established in the first half of the twentieth century in the UK were, amongst other things, new places for the publication of articles on legal education. Thus, for example, the first volume of the *Cambridge Law Journal* contained a note by Holland on the revision of the Law Tripos at Cambridge (Holland 1922). The first article about legal education in the *Modern Law Review*, first published in 1937, was not until its ninth volume in 1946 (Simpson 1946). However, both the unsigned 'Editorial Notes' and Lord Macmillan's 'Prefatory Note' in the first issue of the first volume had contained reflections on legal education (Editorial Notes 1937; Macmillan 1937). In Scotland, the first volume of the *Juridical Review* carried an article on legal education in Italy (Kirkpatrick 1889), although the first contribution on legal education in the UK, entitled somewhat ironically, given the journal's provenance, 'Legal Education in England', was not published until 1898 (Raleigh 1898). In Northern Ireland, the first volume of the *Northern Ireland Legal Quarterly* contained an article on legal education in Northern Ireland (Reid 1936), as did the second volume (Unsigned 1938). Both journals have continued to publish articles on legal education through the decades.[3]

Change and discussion of change is clearly part of the history of legal education in university law schools throughout the UK that continues in the present day. Precisely because of this, each proposed reform has to be measured against present and previous practice in order to assess not just the coherence and validity of the particular reform in its own terms but also the impact that it will have on other

3 The first volume of the *Cambrian Law Review*, which was begun as a law journal for Wales (Llewelfryn Davies 1970: 11), was not published until 1970. Its first volume contained an article on legal education (Holland and McNair 1970) and other articles on legal education have appeared in subsequent volumes.

aspects of legal education within the law school. British university law schools are not a blank canvas on which any picture can now be painted; they have their specific history which has resulted in their particular culture. That culture can be and should be changed as conditions elsewhere in the wider university change. Moreover, reforms can be either incremental or revolutionary in their nature. Both types of change are useful and even necessary. Nonetheless, one of the things that law schools need to know when assessing the utility of a suggested change is what type of reform is being suggested and what reordering of law school culture is being proposed.

The History of UK University Law Schools

The Doctrinal Paradigm

Contemporary UK law schools are plainly not the places that they once were, the latter quarter of the twentieth century having seen a dramatic change in their nature.[4] Before this period, British law schools had been under the sway of a strict doctrinal paradigm.[5] They saw both their teaching and research almost solely in terms of an analysis of legal rules and principles that was to be accomplished on the basis of an internal reading of those texts and only those texts that had legal authority, that is, appropriately reported judgements and statutes; this is something that Twining has termed the 'Expository Orthodoxy' (Twining 1974: 161–3; 1979: 558).[6] The dominance of this paradigm is not inconsistent with variations in what doctrinalism meant to different authors. The doctrinalism of Pollock, as analysed by Duxbury, with its search for legal principle (Duxbury 2004: Chapter 5), is, for example, markedly different from Goodhart's stress on the importance of rules

4 A detailed history of British university legal education has yet to be written. For accounts which are either of a limited period or which are relatively brief, see Sugarman 1986; Twining 1994: Chapter 2; and Cownie 2000. For histories of individual institutions, see, for example, Lawson 1968; Mulholland nd; and Twining 1987. For a history of the largest British professional association for legal academics, see Cownie and Cocks 2009. In addition to these sources, there are also several studies of individual legal academics such as Cocks' study of Maine (Cocks 1988) and Duxbury's study of Pollock (Duxbury 2004), whilst Neville Brown published a memoir of his life as a legal academic between 1953 and 1990 (Neville Brown 2004).

5 I use the term 'paradigm' in the sense that Kuhn uses it in relation to what he terms 'normal science' (Kuhn 1970: Chapter 2). Kuhn's work has, of course, generated a wealth of literature. For an assessment of Kuhn, see Barnes 1982. For Kuhn's own reassessment of his position, see Conant and Haugeland 2000.

6 Other writers have used different terminology, Murphy, for example, writes of the dominance of 'School law' (Murphy 1990), whilst Murphy and Roberts write of 'the central core of commentary upon the products of legislative and adjudicative activity' (Murphy and Roberts 1987: 677), but their conclusions are much the same as Twining's.

and *rationes* (Goodhart 1931: Chapters I and III). However, what divided legal academics who held to the doctrinal paradigm was much less important than what united them. For much of the twentieth century, most British legal scholars believed that law lay in cases and statutes and that questions about what that law was were the only things that were of concern for those in the law school (see, for example, Stallybrass 1948: 164).[7]

There have always been some subdisciplines of law that have had a wider remit, asking questions about things other than the content of legal rules and principles. For example, doctrinalism has never held sway in either legal history or jurisprudence, although, in the case of jurisprudence, it is both arguable that the tradition of analytical jurisprudence legitimated doctrinalism (Sugarman 2005: 275–6) and that its teaching in the twentieth century did, at times, have a doctrinal element to it (Stallybrass 1948: 164; Hart 1953: 358–9; Abel-Smith and Stevens 1967: 372). Equally, there have always been some individuals and some law schools that did not wholly accept the doctrinal approach. Thus, for example, part of the reason for the start of the *Modern Law Review* was a perception by its founders that there was a need for a wider form of legal scholarship than that which dominated other academic journals of the time (Editorial Notes 1937: 1–2; Glasser 1987).[8] Nevertheless, the pervasive nature of the doctrinal approach in British law schools until the last quarter of the twentieth century, permeating almost all aspects of its culture, should not be underestimated.

Law Schools and the University

Whilst doctrinalism prevailed, because of their method of working, academics in law schools, at least in their professional lives, had no intellectual need for any connection with other academics within the university (Bridge 1975: 493). The only materials that legal academics needed were legal materials and the only acceptable method for interrogating those materials was a method known only to legal academics and professional lawyers outside the university. What other academics did was not relevant to what happened in the law school. Whilst all academic disciplines had, and have, a tendency to develop their own tribal

7 The picture in the nineteenth century was somewhat more complex. Whilst the legal academics were, in modern terminology, doctrinal in their approach to law, Collini, Winch and Burrow argue that legal scholars such as Bryce, Dicey, Maine and Pollock were 'authors of several of the most widely cited works of political science' at the time (Collini, Winch and Burrow 1983: 359). Equally, Duxbury suggests that Pollock's monograph on Spinoza, an aside from his legal scholarship, was 'arguably his most impressive intellectual accomplishment' (Duxbury 2004: 92).

8 Although the *Modern Law Review* was associated with the London School of Economics (LSE) from its foundation, not everybody at the LSE actively supported it at the time that it was started. Hughes Parry, the then head of the School of Law, does not appear to have been involved with it (Gwynedd Parry 2010: 54–5).

practices (Becher 1989; Becher and Trowler 2001), law was unusual in the degree to which it separated itself off from the rest of the university.[9]

Not everybody in the law school during this period saw law's isolation as being desirable. Thus, for example, Wade wrote of the need to make contact with academics in other disciplines (Wade 1947: 288). Some academics within the law school did make some connections with those outside it, as is illustrated by Goodhart's (1955) foreword to Gluckman's *The Judicial Process among the Barotse of Northern Rhodesia (Zambia)*. Glasser (1987: 695; see also Gwynedd Parry 2010: 43) writes that in the late 1930s academics in the LSE's School of Law had made contacts with academics in other disciplines. However, notwithstanding exceptions to the general rule, the discipline of law was largely self-sufficient in its teaching and scholarship (Bradney 2003a: 1–9).[10]

Change in the Law Schools

What led to a radical change in the nature of British university law schools in the latter part of the twentieth century is a matter for conjecture. The major innovation in British universities during this period was the introduction of a variety of audit regimes (Bradney 2003a: Chapter 7). Many commentators have seen the introduction of the Research Assessment Exercise in particular as being of unique significance in changing university culture, Halsey, for example, describing it as 'a dramatic moment in the decline of donnish dominion' (Halsey 1992: 189). Some later assessments of the impact of the RAE have, however, been more nuanced. Henkel, for example, acknowledges the importance of the changes that the RAE brought to British universities but also observes that:

> the RAE at one level exemplified a successful response by a co-opted academic elite to a combination of external and internal pressures for a more accountable and rationalised resource allocation process. It had a structure within which

---

9 This is not to argue that law was unique. Medicine, for example, has been taught in English universities since the late medieval era (Getz 1995: 85–8). Nevertheless, despite this long history, medicine, even in the present day, is only semi-connected with the university. Sinclair's ethnographic account of medical education observes that 'the physical surroundings of the medical school can in fact act as … a total institution in Goffman's own terms' (Sinclair 1997: 108) and notes elsewhere that '[f]rom an institutional point of view, while the medical school is part of a wider college … [but] the school maintains a distinct identity' (Sinclair 1997: 105). For a similar account of medical education in Scotland, see Atkinson 1997.

10 Other academics at the time saw those who worked in law schools as being 'not really academic – one critical respondent described them as "arcane, distant and alien: an appendage to the university world"' (Becher 1989: 40), an observation that mirrors Thorstein's much earlier statement, made in the context of universities in the USA, that 'in point of substantial merit the law school belongs in the modern university no more than a school of fencing or dancing' (Veblen 1919: 212).

> academic values and academic culture were sustained. The academic profession could be seen to have taken a new opportunity to regulate itself in the new political and economic environment. (Henkel 2000: 115)

In law schools the advent of the Research Assessment Exercise in 1985 doubtless played a part in producing reforms by focusing academic attention on the quality and quantity of publishing that was being undertaken within law schools.[11] More than this, many legal academics have seen the RAE as a process that not merely encouraged more research but shifted the focus of academic writing in law schools from material intended for practitioners or students to more scholarly work published as monographs or in academic journals (Vick et al. 1998: 556). However, the role of the RAE in reforming law school culture can be overemphasized. Critical comments from within law schools about the law school's attitude towards research predate the RAE by some years. Thus, for example, 10 years before the introduction of the RAE, Bridge, in an inaugural lecture later published as an article, argued that '[i]f academic lawyers are honest they will admit that there is still too little legal research being done' (Bridge 1975: 494). A few years later in his Presidential Address to the Society of Public Teachers of Law (now the Society of Legal Scholars), Street stated that '[my] overall view of English law teachers' periodical writing is that the standard is indefensibly low. The choice of topics is often unimaginative' (Street 1979: 247). In the following year, Street's successor as President, Twining, observed in his Presidential Address that there was no 'highly developed tradition of committed and sustained scholarship which is central to the culture of academic law' (Twining 1980: 5). The implementation of research audit is plainly part of the process of change within UK law schools, but it is difficult to argue that it was the cause of this change. The RAE was implemented after legal academics' attitudes towards the place of research in British university law schools had already begun to alter. The factors driving this shift in culture lay elsewhere.

Rapid growth in the number of law schools in the UK and, arguably, the consequences this had for the kind of people who became legal academics are important factors that had an impact on the culture of law schools. The 1960s saw the beginning of a significant rise in the number of university law schools and, consequently, a large rise in the number of full-time legal academics. In 1966 the first survey of legal education conducted by the then Society of Public Teachers of Law reported that there were 23 law schools that provided full law degrees in the UK (Wilson 1966: 10). In England and Wales, these law schools had a total of 448 academic staff of whom 113 were part-time. In Scotland, there were 110 academic staff of whom 82 were part-time (Wilson 1966: 26). What is important in these statistics is not just the fact that there were a relatively small number of legal academics. Before the 1960s and into it, a significant number of

11 The manner in which the exercise was introduced is described in Kogan and Hanney 2000: 96–8.

legal academics had been part-time practitioners (Sugarman 1991: 54). Indeed, the survey figures do not fully reveal the extent of part-time practice amongst legal academics. Street has written that in the period immediately after the Second World War, '[most] departmental heads, though on full-time appointments, were also local practitioners, and so were many of the other full-time staff' (Street 1979: 244).[12] Whilst Street's observation is merely anecdotal, being based on no survey evidence, it is an observation about an era that he lived through, having been first appointed in the Faculty of Law at the University of Manchester in 1946 (Street 1979: 243). The place that professional practice had had in the university law school in the first three-quarters of the twentieth century is further illustrated by the qualifications that legal academics held. Wilson's survey found that 78% of those responding had professional qualifications to practise law whilst only 17% had a PhD (Wilson 1966: 30 and 29).[13]

The degree to which these academics would be isolated, both intellectually and physically, particularly in provincial law schools is easy to underestimate. They were often in practice but could never be wholly part of practice because of their academic commitments. As legal academics, their mode of work separated them out from their fellow academics. Moreover, it was difficult for them to turn to other legal academics for support. In his memoir, Neville Brown writes that when he joined the University of Birmingham in 1955, there were five full-time and five part-time academic staff in the Faculty of Law (Neville Brown 2004: 69).[14] This was an era decades before easy transport or communication.[15] Their isolation was exacerbated by the fact that there was very little staff movement between institutions. Wilson's survey found that the majority of legal academics had taught at only one institution and that 44% of his respondents were teaching at the university where they had taken their first degree (Wilson 1966: 30). The picture that results is one of a relatively small number of people with relatively little contact with each other living on the border between professional practice and academic life. However, by the mid-1960s, things were changing – 62% of Wilson's respondents who had been teaching for less than five years did not have a professional qualification (Wilson 1966: 30). The influence of practice was beginning to wane. At the beginning of the 1960s, Hood Phillips, then President of

12 See also Wade's enigmatic comment that full-time teachers of law when he was writing were 'happily … not shut off from all contact with practice' (Wade 1951: 418).

13 The survey found that the majority of legal academics responding had two degrees, although 24% had only one degree. A total off 9% had an LLD or its equivalent (Wilson 1966: 29).

14 Jenks published figures for the number of academics in law schools in the 1933–1934 academic session, but he did not indicate whether or not these figures included both full-time and part-time staff. Only London, Oxford, Cambridge and Manchester had staff sizes that went into double figures (Jenks 1935: 179).

15 The building of the first motorway in the UK, the M1, did not begin until 1958 and by 1960 only 126 miles of motorway had been built (Drake 1969: 46 and 47).

the Society of Public Teachers of Law, is reported as commenting on what he saw as the new phenomenon of the 'career law teacher' (Mulholland nd: 22).[16]

By 1975, less than a decade after the publication of Wilson's report, law degrees were offered in 30 universities and 19 polytechnics, and other educational institutions (Wilson and Marsh 1975: 243). By this time there were 745 academics in university law schools, of whom 118 were part-time, whilst there were a further 411 academic staff in the polytechnics (Wilson and Marsh 1975: 269 and 271). Wilson and Marsh's report notes that the ratio of part-time to full-time staff had fallen from 1:4 at the time of the 1966 survey to 1:6 at the time of the 1975 survey (Wilson and Marsh 1975: 270). The Wilson and Marsh survey did not look at the qualifications held by academic staff in law schools. This was also true of two subsequent surveys (Wilson and Marsh 1978; Harris and Bellerby with Leighton and Hodgson 1993). It was not until 1995 that a survey once more mapped the academic qualifications held by staff in law schools. This revealed that 35% of the respondents had attained a taught postgraduate degree in law, 22% had either an MPhil or a PhD in law and 4% had either an MPhil or a PhD in a non-law subject (Leighton, Mortimer and Whatley 1995: 18). By this time there were 83 universities with law schools (Harris and Jones 1997: 44). The Harris and Jones survey estimated that there were approximately 2,440 academic staff members in those law schools (Harris and Jones 1997: 82). If the early 1960s had seen the first development of the career academic in university law schools, by the 1990s there was a sizeable community of such people holding higher academic qualifications and working full-time in British university law schools. Leighton, Mortimer and Whatley (1995: 20) noted that, notwithstanding the numbers of staff holding higher academic qualifications, 32% of their respondents were qualified as barristers and 21% were qualified as solicitors. Whilst this was a considerable fall from the percentage reported by Wilson in his 1966 survey, it still represented slightly over half of all legal academics. However, attitudes to the notion of being a full-time academic and, at the same time, being a practitioner were changing rapidly. Although academic lawyers held practice qualifications, this did not mean that they were, or at least that they should be, in practice as well as working as a legal academic. In 1989 the Committee of Heads of University Law schools issued a report which said, *inter alia*, that 'anyone spending significant time on outside activities instead of teaching, research and administration would be failing in his or her duty to the university' (CHULS 1989: 8). By 2004, a study of the websites of 10 out of the 11 top university law schools showed that amongst lecturers, the most junior grade in British universities and therefore normally the youngest academics, only 10–20% had practising qualifications for the jurisdiction they were working in

16 Although the notion of a career for at least some academics is rather different from that found in most other areas of employment (Bradney 2011).

(Bradney 2004: 5).[17] The academic legal profession, once small, often part-time and frequently practice-oriented, but now a sizeable body of people working full-time in the universities, had become academic.[18] In the conclusion to her study of contemporary legal academics, Cownie comments that:

> law is a culture which thinks of itself, to an increasing extent, as 'academic', with distinctive values and norms, separate from those of the legal profession. Academic lawyers become university lecturers because they want to be part of academia; many of them have contemplated (or actually tried) working as a practising lawyer first, and they are clear that this is not what they want to do … The culture of academic law is firmly embedded in the university. (Cownie 2004: 199)[19]

The Role of Contemporary British University Law Schools

The role of British university law schools was for a long time a contentious matter within those law schools. A memorandum by Goudy, then Professor of Law at Oxford, apparently expressing the views of all of the Professors of Law and Readers in Law at Oxford, quoted in a note published in the *Law Quarterly Review* by Pollock in 1896, revealed the divisions about the role of university law schools. The memorandum contended variously that university law schools should only concern themselves with the 'teaching of law on its *theoretical* side', that 'stress … should be principally laid upon Roman Law, Jurisprudence, History of Law, and Constitutional Law' and finally that '[the] evil of the present system [of teaching law in some universities] is that the theoretical and practical study are not kept distinct' (Pollock 1896: 1–2). The disagreement between those who saw the law school's role as purely academic and those who saw it as, at least in part, vocational was to continue for most of the twentieth century. In the volumes of the *Journal of the Society of Public Teachers of Law* for the first six decades of the twentieth century, articles arguing for law as a liberal education predominate

17 The website of the University of Oxford did not, at the time of the study, provide the information necessary to assess the percentage there.

18 The various surveys referred to above show that part-time work still continues in law schools (see most recently Harris and Beinart 2005: 348–9). However, its significance has changed with the very large growth in the number of full-time academics. This is not to say that the use of part-time staff now has no impact on law schools. The presence of staff on short-term contracts or part-time staff can have a detrimental effect on any department within a university (Dearing 1997a: 221–2). At the time of the Dearing Report, 11% of non-research academic staff in universities were part-time (Dearing 1997b: 116). Equally, there has been concern for some years about whether part-time academics in universities are properly treated (Knight et al. 2007: 436).

19 Twining, basing his comments on unpublished data from the survey that Halsey undertook for his book *The Decline of Donnish Dominion*, has said that British legal academics are now much like any other academic (Twining 1994: 201–4).

(see, for example, Haggen 1933; Stallybrass 1946; Wade 1951; and Llewelfryn Davies 1956).[20] However, the fact that so many law schools during this time employed significant numbers of part-time staff, taken together with the fact that so many full-time staff were in part-time practice, suggests that the actual nature of legal education in many law schools was somewhat removed from the liberal educational ideal. Equally important is the fact that at various times during the twentieth century, some university law schools taught professional courses as well as academic degrees (Cownie and Cocks 2009: 25–6). In an article on the history of legal education, Jenks calculated that in the 1933–34 academic year many provincial law schools had more students on professional courses than they had studying at degree level, although neither London nor Oxford had any students studying professional courses and Cambridge had only nine (Jenks 1935: 179). Given these figures, it is perhaps not surprising that there is some evidence of a division between provincial universities and the law schools in Oxford, Cambridge and London on the role of the university law school. In 1932 Professor Eastwood from the University of Manchester wrote to the Society of Public Teachers of Law's secretary to complain that the then President Hughes from Oxford did not represent 'the point of view held by many of us that legal education in a city should be the result of the co-operative efforts of the local legal profession and teachers' (Cownie and Cox 2009: 54). However, in the latter years of the twentieth century, the balance of opinion amongst legal academics as to the role of the university law school began to change.

Prompted perhaps by their general, increasingly more academic orientation, the majority of British legal academics no longer see the law school's role in vocational terms.[21] Most legal academics in twenty-first-century British university law schools see themselves as providing a liberal education (Cownie 2004: 75–8); academic law schools, with very few exceptions, do not see their mission as being vocational.[22] Whether law schools should offer a vocational education, training students to be lawyers, is not germane to this chapter.[23] What is important to note here is the empirical point that whilst there is a long history of debating the role of the law school within the history of British university law schools, the current view of the vast majority of those working in academic law schools is that the school is a place where the ethos of a liberal education should prevail.

20 For an article arguing for a partially vocational approach, see Hughes 1932.

21 There are, of course, individual exceptions. See, for example, Brayne 2000.

22 There are a few British university law schools that do offer a vocational programme. Northumbria University's law school offers a range of undergraduate programmes that integrates academic and professional education (see www.northumbria.ac.uk/sd/academic/law/courses/?view=Standard), whilst the law school at the University of York offers both an undergraduate law degree with a liberal arts orientation and a programme with a vocational emphasis (http://www.york.ac.uk/law/undergraduate).

23 For a defence of liberal education in the law school, see Bradney 2003a.

The Culture of Contemporary UK University Law Schools

Whilst it is apparent that the character of university law schools in the UK has changed in a fundamental way, it is less clear what has taken the place of the old culture. Plainly doctrinal approaches to research no longer predominate in the way that they once did (Cownie 2004: 54–8). Nevertheless, some scholars in law schools still do research in a pure doctrinal mode (Cownie 2004: 55). Moreover, some would argue that the doctrinal past still has its influence on the present practices of some, and perhaps many, non-doctrinal scholars (Bartie 2010: 354–9). Finally, if the evidence of new editions of textbooks is to be believed, doctrinalism still finds a place in the law school's teaching. Yet, even with these doubts and hesitations, it is clear that British university law schools are very different places from what they once were (Bradney and Cownie 2000a). However, whilst doctrinalism was once a dominant paradigm, no new paradigm has now taken its place. British university law schools may now be, or may be in the process of becoming, socio-legal, as Cownie concludes in her study of contemporary English legal academics (Cownie 2004: 198).[24] The socio-legal approach to research and teaching is not, however, a paradigm.[25]

Socio-legal Studies

The meaning of the term 'socio-legal' is a contentious matter (Twining 2009a: 227–8). Harris begins a very early account of socio-legal studies by noting that 'there is no agreed definition of socio-legal studies' (Harris 1983: 315). It has sometimes been used in a relatively narrow manner. For example, Campbell and Wiles distinguish socio-legal work from work done within the sociology of law, seeing socio-legal work as being atheoretical and policy-oriented (Campbell and Wiles 1976). However, more frequently the term has been used very broadly. Thus, for example, Wheeler and Thomas describe socio-legal studies as an 'academic phenomenon' (Wheeler and Thomas 2000: 267) and go on to state that 'the word "socio" in socio-legal studies means to us an interface with a context within which law exists, be that a sociological, historical, economic, geographical or other context' (Wheeler and Thomas 2000: 270). In the ESRC's 1994 report on socio-legal studies, the section entitled 'What is Socio-Legal Studies?' begins

24 The interviews on which Cownie's analysis is based took place in English university law schools (Cownie 2004: 14). Cownie notes that, because there are variations across a range of factors between law schools in different jurisdictions, her results may not apply to law schools in Wales, Scotland or Northern Ireland (Cownie 2004: 25–6).

25 For a contrary view see Thomas 1997: 19. Although Hillyard uses the term paradigm with respect to socio-legal studies he also writes of a "huge diversity within the paradigm in terms of subject areas, theoretical orientations, and methodologies" (Hillyard 2002: 646) suggesting that he is not using the word in Kuhn's sense. Campbell writes of "competing paradigms" with respect to socio-legal studies (Campbell 1974: 28).

by saying that socio-legal studies is an 'umbrella' term and then goes on to spend two A4 pages describing what is done within socio-legal studies (ESRC 1994); no definition of the term is attempted. This breadth in socio-legal work has increased the longer it has existed in the legal academy. Harris, writing in the 1980s, suggested that socio-legal studies begins with academic lawyers turning to sociology and argued that sociology, social policy and social administration have had the greatest impact on socio-legal studies (Harris 1983: 315). Yet, even at this early stage in the development of socio-legal studies, Harris noted the potential importance of social history for socio-legal studies (Harris 1983: 331–2). From its very beginning, socio-legal studies has encompassed more than a use by academic lawyers of one of the social sciences and, writing in the present day, it is now difficult to think of any discipline in the social sciences or humanities that has not been used by scholars working in a socio-legal mode.[26] The very variety of the kind of work being done in socio-legal studies can be seen as being an intellectual advantage. Cotterrell has argued that 'an important reason for the vitality of the sociolegal community in Britain ... has surely been its rich, almost anarchic heterogeneity and its consistent openness to many different aims, outlooks, and disciplinary backgrounds' (Cotterrell 2002: 632–3). It is this ever-increasing diversity in what constitutes socio-legal studies that prevents it becoming a new paradigm; socio-legal studies is not a new starting point for enquiry into law but is, instead, a series of starting points. This means that law schools do not simply have a different culture to that which existed when doctrinalisnm prevailed; it has not only changed, it is also richer and much more complex.

Legal Pluralism

At the same time as socio-legal studies has taken the place of doctrinal studies as the dominant mode of working within law schools, so law schools have begun to reconsider the notion of what law they should be examining. Theories of legal pluralism arguing that different systems of law, whether emanating from the state or not, can and usually do exist alongside each other within a society have begun to be discussed within law schools.[27] There is no necessary intellectual link between these socio-legal studies and concepts of legal pluralism. Scholars working in a socio-legal manner can and often do confine themselves to examining the system of state law that has been the traditional focus of attention in British university law schools. Equally, those who concern themselves with legal pluralism have no necessary reason to delve into the wide variety of academic disciplines that have been used by socio-legal scholars. Yet the fact that the two movements

26 A number of writers have noted that those working in socio-legal studies in the UK have largely, although not entirely, come from university law schools. See, for example, Thomas 1997: 12.

27 Such theories have a long history. Ehrlich's *Fundamental Principles of the Sociology of Law* (1975), for example, was first published in 1936.

have become increasingly influential in law schools is not entirely coincidental. Closer inquiry into exactly how state law works almost inevitably raises the issue of in what significant way state law is different from other forms of regulation (Cotterrell 1995: 310–14).

As with socio-legal studies, the precise definition of and approach to legal pluralism is a matter for debate (compare, for example, Tamanaha 2001: Chapter 7 and Benda-Beckmann 2002). Whatever form it takes, it has yet to achieve the dominance that socio-legal studies has in British university law schools. Notions of legal pluralism have been used explicitly in some areas of analysis. Thus, for example, a number of authors have used theories of legal pluralism as a basis for their analysis of the relationship of religious minorities to law (Menski 1987; Bradney and Cownie 2000b; Shah 2005). Tie (1999: 48–50) has argued that the notion of legal pluralism is increasingly important in critical legal studies. However, neither Thomson (1987) nor Goodrich's (1992, 1999) historical accounts of critical legal studies in the UK uses the term. Nevertheless, the idea is perhaps implicit if not explicit in the work of at least some critical legal scholars including Goodrich himself (see, for example, Goodrich 1996). Nonetheless, despite these and other examples, there are still doubts about the place of legal pluralism in contemporary law school culture.

Cotterrell, himself an exponent of legal pluralism, has argued that the notion has had 'little long-term impact on [English] legal thought' (Cotterrell 2006: 39). Moreover, the utility of the concept has been questioned, even by scholars who have an interest in non-state law, with Roberts, for example, arguing that:

> it is inevitably problematic to attempt to fix a conception of law going beyond the robust self-definitions of state law. Where the project is to recover 'suppressed discourses', we should begin that process in their own terms, not by telling them what they 'are'. (Roberts 1998: 105)[28]

However, whatever the degree of impact that the concept of legal pluralism has had and whatever its substantive merit as a tool for analysis, the very fact that some legal scholars in British university law schools are now basing their work on the proposition that there is no significant difference between state law and non-state law in itself shows how far British university law schools have moved from their doctrinal past.

Contemporary British University Law Schools

Whilst the picture of the legal culture that emerges from the above is complex, it is clear that British university law schools are now happy to draw upon a variety of other academic disciplines and to challenge concepts that would have been seen as foundational in the law school's past. British university law schools are now

28 Roberts writes as a legal anthropologist (see, for example, Roberts 1979).

intellectually cosmopolitan places, eagerly taking on new ideas and approaches. However, this does not mean that there are no limits to what the contemporary law school can do.

The Limits of British University Law Schools

The Role of the University Law School

In *Being a University*, Barnett writes that 'there are boundaries to what a university might be' (Barnett 2011: 13). What precisely those boundaries are has long been the subject of debate. As Barnett himself immediately goes on to observe, those boundaries [to the university] have widened and are widening; and are becoming more open to negotiation' (Barnett 2011: 13). Nevertheless, the basic point is not contentious. There are some things which, although they are good in themselves, are manifestly not part of the business of the university. The question is what those boundaries to the proper business of the university might be. In looking at this question, Fish has argued that, with respect to students:

> the job of someone who teaches in a college is to (1) introduce students to bodies of knowledge and traditions of inquiry they didn't know much about before; and (2) equip those same students with the analytical skills that will enable them to move confidently within those traditions and to engage in independent research should they choose to do so. (Fish 2008: 18)

Other matters, in Fish's view, fall outside the purview of a university. A university is not there, for example, to instill moral goodness in its students (Fish 2008: 66–72). Fish's focus is on the university as an academic and intellectual institution; his boundaries are a wall round that role. Given the academic orientation of British university law schools described above, this provides a starting point for arguments about the limitations to what British university law schools can or should do.

The majority of present-day British legal academics would probably accept Fiss' contention that the job of a legal academic is simply 'to study law and to teach their students what they happen to discover' (Martin 1985: 26). The fact that British university law schools see themselves as academic institutions in this sense means that not all of the educational needs of those of their students, who will later find themselves in professional practice, will be met in the university. Purely vocational matters are dealt with elsewhere. Thus, arguments about why a British law school should move beyond text in its teaching practices have to be predicated on how such a move will benefit a law student qua law student not a law student qua nascent lawyer or professional. Moreover, they have to show how a law student benefits in terms of their knowledge of law, not in terms of any wider benefit such a move might bring to the students. Thus, for example, whether or not the ethical behaviour of students would improve if they were exposed to arguments beyond text is not relevant; in thinking about and studying law, the ethical behaviour of students is pertinent only insofar as it relates to their treatment of those around them in the law school or the wider university and their adherence to good scholarly practices such as not plagiarizing the work of others.[29] Morally bad people can be successful law students, achieving the highest grades possible. However, this is not to say that arguments about ethical issues raised elsewhere in this volume are irrelevant to the law school.

In thinking widely about law, it is impossible to avoid questions about ethical issues. Indeed, the abandonment of the doctrinal paradigm has meant that discussion of ethical issues has come much more to the centre of work in the law school. Within the law school, a wide range of theoretical perspectives now see matters of morality as being implicated not just in questions about what the law should be but also in questions about what the law is. However, teaching law students about the importance of reflecting on moral issues is not the same thing as trying to inculcate into students a particular set of moral values (Cownie 2003). The question then becomes: will engaging in arguments beyond text either assist British university legal academics in promoting the learning of British university law students with respect to the connection between moral issues and law or will such arguments help the academics in their own research? I would argue that the nature of British university law students and British university academics makes this unlikely.

British University Law Students

British university law students are not a cross-section of British university students. Only a limited amount of research has been undertaken on British university law students. However, such research as has been done shows law students to be very different from students in most other academic disciplines.

Some of the things that make law students different from their fellow students are well known. For example, academically they are better qualified for entry into university than any other group of students except those studying medicine and veterinary science (Halpern 1994: 27). However, other points of difference between law and non-law students may be less immediately apparent. Purcell and Pitcher's analysis shows that law students are much more likely than other university students to pursue their studies for largely pragmatic reasons related to future job expectations rather than from interest in their subject (Purcell and Pitcher 1996: 11).[30] Their career-oriented approach to their choice of studies does

---

29 This must be so even for those who argue that universities should put forward a particular moral schemata for students (see, for example, Stryker 1996). To argue otherwise would be to argue that universities should impose moral values on their students.

30 An Australian study suggests that British law students are not alone in this, with the law students surveyed being far less likely than other students to find their studies intrinsically interesting (Tani and Vines 2009: 24).

not mean that they are necessarily intent on becoming lawyers. A comparative study of law and medical students showed that whilst 62.8% of medical students in the study showed a very high level of desire to be a doctor, only 36.4% of law students evinced the same degree of desire to be a lawyer (Cavenagh, Dewberry and Jones 2000: 899); law students hope to have a successful career, whether as a lawyer or as something else. The vocational orientation of law students produces the paradoxical result that, whilst the majority of law students like being at university, only a minority enjoy studying law (Halpern 1994: 33).[31] This does not mean that law students are likely to leave their studies; it simply reflects the fact that, for the vast majority of law students, their studies are simply a means to an end.

Law students are taken into their law schools because of their achievements in learning various forms of largely text-based analysis. They need have no aptitude, skills, training or even taste for other approaches.[32] They are, as compared with other students in their respective universities, academically high-achieving and will probably wish to remain so in their legal studies so that they can pursue their career aspirations. Suggesting that such students will have any widespread desire to engage in non-text-based forms of learning, especially if these forms of learning are included in their assessments, seems implausible. The percentage of law students who would wish to engage in non-text-based forms of argument would seem likely to correlate fairly closely with the percentage who would like to join the university orchestra.

The characteristics that are peculiar to law students do not and should not determine what the law school does. Law students think that preparation for professional practice is the third most important thing that happens in a law school (Halpern 1994: 39), but, as we have seen above, law schools and legal academics continue to regard preparation for practice as being of little consequence in the life of the law school. Nevertheless, the nature of the student body is relevant when considering proposed reforms to the curriculum. If students are not a ready audience for the kind of reforms suggested elsewhere in this volume, this, at the very least, has an impact on the resources that will be required to show them that the work that they will be asked to engage in is 'relevant' to their studies.[33]

---

31 The precise percentages for both these things varies depending on the type of university the student is attending.

32 There will, of course, be students that have all of these things, but this will be coincidental, not because the admissions process to university law schools is designed to ensure it.

33 Halpern (1994: 38) notes that importance that law students attach to 'relevance', not necessarily construed in vocational terms, in their studies.

British Legal Academics

In some respects the work beyond text that is discussed in this volume may not seem that far removed from work already being done in the law school. Film and television series are, for example, already a resource that are used in teaching and research in a number of law schools (see further Bradney 2003b, 2006; Greenfield, Osborn and Robson 2008). Using drawing, cameras or the other media discussed in this volume might seem little different from work like this. However, it is the manner in which these media are to be used which separates it from previous work in law schools. Whilst non-textual material has been used in law schools in the past, the way in which it is used has largely been textual. Films and television series are analysed for the ideas about law and legal institutions that they contain or reflect; this analysis is thus textual in nature, even when it takes account of non-textual elements such imagery or music. Doing this work in these areas is in accordance with the intellectual tradition that has developed in British university law schools. Ideas about law are debated in an atmosphere that is increasingly alive to other debates within the university, but the debates are circumscribed by the context of being in the university.

Work that goes beyond text is not unknown in British university law schools. Thus, for example, Rush describes a performance that he gave at a Critical Legal Conference which involved, *inter alia*, the use of taped voices, mime and audience participation: '[a] few participated by leaving, most stayed' (Rush 1990: 21). More recently, Minkkinen concludes an analysis of various Crucifixion pictures with the observation that:

> In Grünewald's *Crucifixion*, the expressionless is the brutal experience of suffering that cannot be narrated … because even after every detail of the painting, after every element of attribute, composition and colour has accurately been depicted and account for, a residue remains, an ethical truth that cannot be appropriated but that nevertheless calls for a response. (Minkkinen 2008: 84)

Work of this sort is, however, comparatively rare within British university law schools. Moreover, in the case of Minkkinen, whilst his article both concludes with an observation about something that is seen as being beyond text and is centrally about something that is seen as being beyond text, the article itself is a textual analysis. Similarly, whilst Rush's performance might have been non-textual, his article commenting on that performance is textual. In the end it seems that even those few legal academics who look beyond text in the law school return to text.

Since the opening sections of this chapter above have shown the ever-widening intellectual horizons in British university law schools, it might be argued that calling for the law school to take on ways of thinking that are beyond text is to suggest no more than a new chapter in the law school's development. British legal academics once held rigidly to the doctrinal paradigm, but have learnt that there were other ways of thinking about law. Legal academics may now be focused on text-based approaches to law, but they need to learn, perhaps with the help of others with appropriate expertise, new ways of looking at law which do not depend on text. Stasis in legal education, as was argued at the very beginning of this chapter, is never desirable. However, such an argument misunderstands why the law school has developed in the way that it has and underestimates the constraints that law schools operate within.

The history of British university law schools shows both a widening range of intellectual interests within the law school and an ever-deepening focus on academic enquiry as opposed to other matters. Cownie's study of legal academics shows that academics regard the likelihood of being promoted to professor as being linked almost solely to success in publishing academic research, whilst they link the broader question of what it is to be a successful academic with teaching and research (Cownie 2004: 86–95). Very few of her respondents saw work done outside the university and reputation amongst non-academics as being important (Cownie 2004: 94). Similarly, Duxbury (2001: 105) notes that few academics in law schools, especially those outside of Cambridge, London and Oxford, see the possibility of collaborating with appellate judges in the creation of law as something that is of interest to them. Legal academics have their area of expertise and show an ever-increasing desire to focus on that expertise. In his call for legal academics to contribute more to improving the public understanding of law, Twining suggests that at present 90% of legal scholarship and teaching from British legal academics is directed to legal audiences (Twining 2009b: 528). There are of course many things that British legal academics could do, given their abilities. However, perhaps because of the intellectual complexity and difficulty of the academic task they are already engaged in, they show little desire to do those other things. Acknowledging that there is work beyond text and that this might be relevant to law and legal issues is one thing; for academics who work in the tradition described in this chapter to engage in producing such work is quite another; producing work that is beyond text lies outside what is and what is likely to remain the expertise of legal academics.

Conclusion

To ask British university law students and legal academics to think about the implications of the existence of non-text based forms of argument and thinking is to suggest an incremental reform in legal education; to ask them to engage in non-text based forms of arguments and thinking is to suggest a revolutionary reform in legal education. In the end, the final determinant of individual academic behaviour should be and will be the decisions of each individual academic. Academic freedom protects an academic's right to determine the direction of his or her research and teaching; the fact that, at least in the law school, research and teaching is largely part of the private life of the university makes it difficult to restrict that right.[34] However, the arguments above would suggest that although it would be profitable for law students and legal academics to consider the possibility of arguments that go beyond text in relation to law and legal institutions, for either students or academics to go further than this and themselves seek to engage in these arguments would be to go too far. Work done beyond text can be meritorious, but not everything that is good in the world is the province of either a university or its law school.

References

Abel-Smith, B. and Stevens, R. 1967. *Lawyers and the Courts*. London: Heinemann.

Atkinson, P. 1997. *The Clinical Experience: The Construction and Reconstruction of Medical Reality*. Aldershot: Ashgate.

Barnes, B. 1982. *T.S. Kuhn and Social Science*. London: Macmillan.

Barnett, R. 2011. *Being a University*. London: Routledge.

Bartie, S. 2010. 'The lingering core of legal scholarship'. *Legal Studies*, 30(3), 345–69.

Becher, T. 1989. *Academic Tribes and Territories*. Stoney Stratford, Milton Keynes: SRHE and Open University Press.

Becher, T. and Trowler, P. 2001. *Academic Tribes and Territories*. Buckingham: SRHE and Open University Press.

Benda-Beckmann, F. Von. 2002. 'Who's afraid of legal pluralism?' *Journal of Legal Pluralism and Unofficial Law*, 47, 37–82.

Bradney, A. 2003a. *Conversations, Chances and Choices: The Liberal Law School in the Twenty-first Century*. Oxford: Hart Publishing.

Bradney, A. 2003b. 'Choosing laws, choosing families: images of law, love and authority in "Buffy the Vampire Slayer"'. *Web Journal of Current Legal Issues*. Available at: http://webjcli.ncl.ac.uk/2003/issue2/bradney2.html [accessed 19 August 2012].

Bradney, A. 2004. 'University law schools and the legal profession: the academic legal profession – academic or legal?' *European Journal of Legal Education*, 1(2), 1–14.

34 The distinction between the private and public life of the university, the private life being 'what actually happens in the classrooms, the libraries, the laboratories, at the desks and in the offices', was first made by Trow (1975: 113). Whilst academics are now the subject of various forms of appraisal and audit, which they or may not take seriously, it remains the case that individual teaching is done in the privacy of the lecture theatre or seminar room and research only becomes public once it has been completed. External control of such work is therefore difficult. University law schools are a very long way from being Foucault's panopticon (Foucault 1979: 200–202).

Bradney, A. 2006. 'The case of Buffy the Vampire Slayer and the politics of legal education', in S. Greenfield and G. Osborn (eds), *Readings in Law and Popular Culture*. London: Routledge, 15–30.

Bradney, A. 2007. 'Can there be commensurability in comparative legal education?' *Canadian Legal Education Annual Review/Revue de l'enseignment de droit au Canada*, 1, 67–84.

Bradney, A. 2011. 'Instead of a career: work, love and art in university law schools', in C. Maughan and P. Maharg (eds), *Affect and Legal Education: Emotion in Learning and Teaching the Law*. Aldershot: Ashgate, 109–24.

Bradney, A. and Cownie, F. 2000a. 'British university law schools in the twenty-first century', in D. Hayton (ed.), *Law's Future(s)*. Oxford: Hart Publishing, 1–17.

Bradney, A. and Cownie, F. 2000b. *Living Without Law: An Ethnography of Dispute Avoidance and Resolution in the Religious Society of Friends*. Aldershot: Ashgate.

Brayne, H. 2000. 'A case for getting law students engaged in the real thing: the challenge to the saber-tooth curriculum'. *The Law Teacher*, 34(1), 17–39.

Bridge, J. 1975. 'The academic lawyer: mere working mason or architect?' *Law Quarterly Review*, 91(4), 488–501.

Brown, W. 1902. 'The purpose and method of a law school'. *Law Quarterly Review*, 18(1) and 18(2), 78–91 and 192–210.

Campbell, C. 1974. 'Legal thought and juristic values'. *British Journal of Law and Society*, 1(1), 13–30.

Campbell, C. and Wiles, P. 1976. 'The study of law and society in Britain'. *Law and Society Review*, 10(4), 547–78.

Cavenagh, P., Dewberry, C. and Jones, P. 2000. 'Becoming professional: when and how does it start? A comparative study of first-year medical and law students in the UK'. *Medical Education*, 24(11) 897–902.

CHULS (Committee of Heads of University Law Schools). 1989. *Academic Staff Recruitment and Retention*. London: Committee of Heads of University Law Schools.

Clark, E. 1885. 'Jurisprudence; its use and its place in legal education'. *Law Quarterly Review*, 1(2), 201–6.

Cocks, R. 1988. *Sir Henry Maine*. Cambridge: Cambridge University Press.

Collini, S., Winch, D. and Burrow, J. 1983. *That Noble Science of Politics: A Study in Nineteenth-Century Intellectual Politics*. Cambridge: Cambridge University Press.

Conant, J. and Haugeland, J. (eds). 2000. *The Road Since Structure: Thomas Khun: Philosophical Essays 1970–1993, with an Autobiographical Interview*. Chicago: University of Chicago Press.

Cotterrell, R. 1995. *Law's Community: Legal Theory in Sociological Perspective*. Oxford: Clarendon Press.

Cotterrell, R. 2002. 'Subverting orthodoxy, making law central: a view of sociolegal studies'. *Journal of Law and Society*, 29(4), 632–44.

Cotterrell, R. 2006. *Law, Culture and Society: Legal Ideas in the Mirror of Social Theory*. Aldershot: Ashgate.
Cownie, F. 2000. 'English legal education: from doctrinalism to pluralism', in P. Torremans (ed.), *Legal Convergence in the Enlarged Europe of the New Millennium*. The Hague: Kluwer Law International, 271–88.
Cownie, F. 2003. 'Alternative values in legal education'. *Legal Ethics*, 6(2), 159–74.
Cownie, F. 2004. *Legal Academics: Culture and Identities*. Oxford: Hart Publishing.
Cownie, F. and Cocks, R. 2009. *'A Great and Noble Occupation!': The History of the Society of Legal Scholars*. Oxford: Hart Publishing.
Dearing, Lord. 1997a. *Higher Education in the Learning Society (The Dearing Report)*. London: National Committee of Inquiry into Higher Education.
Dearing, Lord. 1997b. *Higher Education in the Learning Society (The Dearing Report): Report 3: Academic Staff in Higher Education: Their Experience and Expectations*. London: National Committee of Inquiry into Higher Education.
Drake, J. 1969. *Motorways*. London: Faber & Faber.
Duxbury, N. 2001. *Jurists and Judges: An Essay on Influence*. Oxford: Hart Publishing.
Duxbury, N. 2004. *Frederick Pollock and the English Juristic Tradition*. Oxford: Oxford University Press.
Editorial Notes. 1937. *Modern Law Review*, 1(1), 1–2.
Ehrlich, E. 1975. *Fundamental Principles of the Sociology of Law*. New York: Arno Press.
ESRC. 1994. *Review of Socio-Legal Studies: Final Report*. Swindon: Economic and Social Science Research Council.
Fish, S. 2008. *Save the World on Your Own Time*. New York: Oxford University Press.
Foucault, M. 1979. *Discipline and Punish: The Birth of the Prison*. London: Penguin.
Getz, F. 1995. 'Medical education in later medieval England', in V. Nutton and R. Porter (eds), *The History of Medical Education in Britain*. Amsterdam: Editions Rodopi, B.V., 76–93.
Glasser, C. 1987. 'Radicals and refugees: the foundation of the Modern Law Review'. *Modern Law Review*, 50(6), 688–708.
Goodhart, A. 1931. *Essays in Jurisprudence and the Common Law*. Cambridge: Cambridge University Press.
Goodhart, A. 1955. Foreword, in M. Gluckman, *The Judicial Process Among the Barotse of Northern Rhodesia (Zambia)*. Manchester: Manchester University Press, xiii–xvii.
Goodrich, P. 1992. 'Critical legal studies in England: prospective histories'. *Oxford Journal of Legal Studies*, 12(3), 195–236.
Goodrich, P. 1996. *Law in the Courts of Love: Literature and Other Minor Jurisprudences*. London: Routledge.

Goodrich, P. 1999. 'The critic's love of the law: intimate observations on an insular jurisdiction'. *Law and Critique*, 10(3), 343–60.

Greenfield, S., Osborn, G. and Robson, P. 2008. *Film and the Law*. Oxford: Hart Publishing.

Gwynedd Parry, R. 2010. *David Hughes Parry: A Jurist in Society*. Cardiff: University of Wales Press.

Haggen, G. 1933. 'The training of the practical man'. *Journal of the Society of Public Teachers of Law (OS)*, 14–21.

Halpern, D. 1994. *Entry into the Legal Professions: The Law Society Cohort Study: Years 1 and 2*. London: The Law Society.

Halsey, A. 1992. *Decline of Donnish Dominion: The British Academic Professions in the Twentieth Century*. Oxford: Clarendon Press.

Harris, D. 1983. 'The development of socio-legal studies in the United Kingdom'. *Legal Studies*, 3(3), 315–33.

Harris, P. and Beinart, S. 2005. 'A survey of law schools in the UK, 2004'. *The Law Teacher*, 39(3), 299–366.

Harris, P. and Bellerby, S., with Leighton, P. and Hodgson, J. 1993. *A Survey of Law Teaching: 1993*. London: Sweet & Maxwell.

Harris, P. and Jones, M. 1997. 'A survey of law teaching in the UK'. *The Law Teacher*, 31(1), 38–126.

Hart, H. 1953. 'Philosophy of law and jurisprudence in Britain (1945–1952)'. *American Journal of Comparative Law*, 2(3), 355–64.

Hazeltine, H. 1924. 'Forward tendencies in English legal education'. *Journal of the Society of Public Teachers of Law (OS)*, 1, 1–16.

Henkel, M. 2000. *Academic Identities and Policy Changes in Higher Education*. London: Jessica Kingsley Publishers.

Hillyard, P. 2002. 'Invoking indignation: reflections on future directions of socio-legal studies'. *Journal of Law and Society*, 29(4), 645–56.

Holland, H. 1922. 'The revision of the law tripos'. *Cambridge Law Journal*, 1(2), 193–7.

Holland, H. and McNair, Lord. 1970. 'Some Edwardian reminiscences'. *Cambrian Law Review*, 1, 41–4.

Hughes, J. 1932. 'Culture and anarchy in legal education'. *Journal of the Society of Public Teachers of Law (OS)*, 1–10.

Jenks, E. 1935. 'English legal education'. *Law Quarterly Review*, 51(1), 162–79.

Kirkpatrick, J. 1889. 'How law is taught in Italy'. *Juridical Review*, 1(2), 137–40.

Knight, P., Baume, D., Tait, J. and Yorke, M. 2007. 'Enhancing part-time teaching in higher education: a challenge to institutional policy and practice'. *Higher Education Quarterly*, 61(4), 420–38.

Kogan, M. and Hanney, S. 2000. *Reforming Higher Education*. London: Jessica Kingsley Publishers.

Kuhn, T. 1970. *The Structure of Scientific Revolutions*. Chicago: University of Chicago Press.

Lawson, F. 1968. *The Oxford Law School, 1850–1965*. Oxford: Clarendon Press.

Leighton, P., Mortimer, T. and Whatley, N. 1995. *Law Teachers: Lawyers or Academics?* London: Cavendish Publishing.
Llewelfryn Davies, D. 1956. 'Problems of legal education'. *Journal of the Society of Public Teachers of Law (NS)*, 3(4), 198–204.
Llewelfryn Davies, D. 1970. 'Foreword'. *Cambrian Law Review*, 1, 11.
Macmillan, Lord. 1937. 'Prefatory note'. *Modern Law Review*, 1(1), 3–4.
Martin, P. 1985. 'Of law and the river and of nihilism and academic freedom'. *Journal of Legal Education*, 35(1), 1–26.
Menski, W. 1987. 'Legal pluralism in the Hindu marriage', in R. Burghart (ed.), *Hinduism in Great Britain: The Perpetuation of Religion in an Alien Cultural Milieu*. London: Tavistock Publications, 180–200.
Minkkinen, P. 2008. 'The expressionless: law, ethics, and the imagery of suffering'. *Law and Critique*, 19(1), 65–85.
Mulholland, M. nd. *The Faculty of Law of Manchester University: A Brief History*. Manchester: School of Law, University of Manchester.
Murphy, W. 1990. 'Reference without reality: a comment on a commentary on codifications of practice'. *Law and Critique*, 1(1), 61–80.
Murphy, W. and Roberts, S. 1987. 'Introduction'. *Modern Law Review*, 50(6), 677–87.
Neville Brown, L. 2004. *Law Without Frontiers: Memoirs of a Comparatist*. Birmingham: Self-published.
Purcell, K. and Pitcher, J. 1996. *Great Expectations*. Manchester: Higher Education Careers Service.
Pollock, F. 1896. 'Notes'. *Law Quarterly Review*, 12(1), 1–5.
Raleigh, T. 1898. 'Legal education in England'. *Juridical Review*, 10(1), 1–11.
Reid, S. 1936. 'Education of solicitors' apprentices'. *Northern Ireland Legal Quarterly*, 1(1), 29–34.
Roberts, S. 1979. *Order and Dispute: An Introduction to Legal Anthropology*. Harmondsworth: Penguin.
Roberts, S. 1998. 'Against legal pluralism'. *Journal of Legal Pluralism and Unofficial Law*, 42, 95–106.
Rush, P. 1990. 'Killing me softly with his words: hunting the law student'. *Law and Critique*, 1(1), 21–37.
Shah, P. 2005. *Legal Pluralism in Conflict: Coping with Cultural Diversity in Law*. London: Glasshouse Press.
Simpson, S. 1946. 'Refresher education for lawyer veterans'. *Modern Law Review*, 9(1), 13–25.
Sinclair, S. 1997. *Making Doctors: An Institutional Apprenticeship*. New York: Oxford.
Stallybrass, W. 1948. 'Law in the universities'. *Journal of the Society of Public Teachers of Law (NS)*, 1(3), 157–68.
Street, H. 1979. 'The university law teacher'. *Journal of the Society of Public Teachers of Law (NS)*, 14(4), 243–52.

Stryker, C. 1996. 'The Holocaust and liberal education', in R. Brecher, O. Fleischmann and J. Halliday (eds), *The University in a Liberal State*. Aldershot: Ashgate, 7–20.

Sugarman, D. 1986. 'Legal theory, the common law mind and the making of the textbook tradition', in W. Twining (eds), *Legal Theory and Common Law*. Oxford: Basil Blackwell, 26–61.

Sugarman, D. 1991. '"A hatred of disorder": legal science, liberalism and imperialism', in P. Fitzpatrick (ed.), *Dangerous Supplements: Resistance and Renewal in Jurisprudence*. London: Pluto Press, 34–67.

Sugarman, D. 2005. 'Hart interviewed: HLA Hart in conversation with David Sugarman'. *Journal of Law and Society*, 32(2), 267–95.

Tamanaha, B. 2001. *A General Jurisprudence of Law and Society*. Oxford: Oxford University Press.

Tani, M. and Vines, P. 2009. 'Law students' attitudes to education: pointers to depression in the legal academy and the profession?' *Legal Education Review*, 19(1), 3–39.

Thomas, P. 1997. 'Socio-legal studies: the case of disappearing fleas and bustards', in P. Thomas (ed.), *Socio-Legal Studies*. Aldershot: Dartmouth Publishing, 1–22.

Thomson, A. 1987. 'Critical legal education in Britain'. *Journal of Law and Society*, 14(1), 183–97.

Tie, W. 1999. *Legal Pluralism: Toward a Multicultural Conception of Law*. Aldershot: Dartmouth Publishing.

Trow, M. 1975. 'The public and private life of higher education'. *Daedalus*, 104, 113–27.

Twining, W. 1974. 'Some jobs for jurisprudence'. *British Journal of Law and Society*, 1(2), 149–74.

Twining, W. 1979, 'Academic law and legal philosophy: the significance of Herbert Hart'. *Law Quarterly Review*, 95(4), 557–80.

Twining, W. 1980. 'Goodbye to Lewis Eliot – the academic lawyer as scholar'. *Journal of the Society of Public Teachers of Law*, 15(1), 2–19.

Twining, W. 1987. '1836 and all that: laws in the University of London 1836–1986'. *Current Legal Problems*, 40, 261–99.

Twining, W. 1994. *Blackstone's Tower: The English Law School*. London: Sweet & Maxwell.

Twining, W. 2009a. *General Jurisprudence: Understanding Law from a Global Perspective*. Cambridge: Cambridge University Press.

Twining, W. 2009b. 'The SLS centenary lecture: punching our weight? Legal scholarship and public understanding'. *Legal Studies*, 29(4), 519–33.

Unsigned. 1938. 'The Solicitors Act (Northern Ireland) 1938: provisions relating to education, apprenticeship and qualifications'. *Northern Ireland Legal Quarterly*, 2(3), 117–30.

Veblen, T. 1919. *The Higher Learning in America*. New York: August M. Kelly, Bookseller.

Vick, D., Murray, A., Little, F. and Campbell, K. 1998. 'The perceptions of academic lawyers concerning the effects of the United Kingdom's Research Assessment Exercise'. *Journal of Law and Society*, 25(4), 536–61.

Wade, E. 1947. 'The aim of legal education'. *Cambridge Law Journal*, 9(3), 286–91.

Wade, E. 1951. 'Legal education: the changing scene'. *Journal of the Society of Public Teachers of Law (NS)*, 2(6), 415–24.

Wheeler, S. and Thomas, P. 2000. 'Socio-legal studies', in D. Hayton (ed.), *Law's Future(s)*. Oxford: Hart Publishing, 267–79.

Wilson, J. 1966. 'A survey of legal education in the United Kingdom'. *Journal of the Society of Public Teachers of Law (NS)*, 9(1), 1–139.

Wilson, J. and Marsh, S. 1975. 'A second survey of legal education'. *Journal of the Society of Public Teachers of Law (NS)*, 13(4), 239–331.

Wilson, J. and Marsh, S. 1978. *A Second Survey of Legal Education in the United Kingdom*. London: Institute of Advanced Legal Studies.

Chapter 5
'Associated Life': Democratic Professionalism and the Moral Imagination

Paul Maharg

Introduction

As Abel demonstrates so well, the complex relationship of democracy and the politics of professionalism is highly contested within the legal profession (Abel 2003). In legal education, the relationship between democracy and professionalism has been underdeveloped, not just in theory but in educational practice as well. It should come as no surprise: both domains are historically contingent and highly problematic, and there is no foundational body of theory bridging them. Mainstream undergraduate programmes will contain analyses of the place of law in democratic societies, and there are of course syllabi on professionalism, often in modules that focus on the place of the legal profession in society. In postgraduate vocational courses generally, there is by contrast a focus on technical aspects of legal practice, often dealing quite narrowly with a set of regulations as they apply to technical practice – conflict of interest, confidentiality and the like. But very few undergraduate and vocational programmes, for a range of complex reasons, give a broad view of professionalism and democracy. While there is critique (see, for instance, Boon, Flood and Webb 2005; Flood 2011) the subject, it could be said, is unregarded and as a result becomes invisible to students. Nor is it sufficient to say of the constellation of values around professionalism and democracy that it can only be 'caught' within professional practice rather than learned and taught within educational programmes. If we are introducing students to legal professional and ethical values as an essential to the practice of justice in society, it might be legitimately asked of us where concomitant values appear in our programmes and methods. It could be argued that we should critique and practise versions of the values of critical professionalism in our programmes and in our educational practices.

In the literature of professionalism there is a movement to begin to analyse why and how this invisibility might have come about. In addition to the work of Larson (1977), Nelson and Trubek (1992) and Abel (2003) on professionalism, commentators such as Pellegrino, Veatch and Langan (1991), Dzur (2002) and above all Sullivan (1995) have shown how normative assumptions concerning the relationship of ethics and professionalism need to be rethought, and not just with regard to the profession, but also in educational processes. Sullivan identified the importance of integrity, security and democracy to the whole professional project – integrity, in terms of personal fulfilment and public recognition; security, in terms of the ever-evolving pact struck with society as regards remuneration, trust and social good; and democracy, in terms of the interface that can be developed between technical processes in society generally and the political and moral processes that underlie them. Sullivan contrasts technocratic professionalism (concerned with technical self-interested practices and motivations driven by commercial profit only) with civic professionalism, which invests professional practice with moral meaning and with democratic value.

Dzur goes further and in a helpful comparison of de Tocqueville, Dewey, Sullivan and Fischer analyses what democratic professionalism might consist of. He defined its values over against its shadow, namely technocratic professionalism. His critique is worth quoting in detail:

> If the ideal of democratic professionalism is so beneficial, then why is it losing to the technocratic model? An obvious reply is that the latter fits neatly into the rationalized procedures and needs for predictability and control found in modern economic and political organization. Further, those trained for professions currently have minimal instruction in the democratic consequences of their professional domains. Applied ethics instruction abounds, of course, and more so with every passing year. Yet the explicitly democratic values of lay participation and task-sharing discussed in this paper are rarely part of the ethics seminars required in nearly all professional training curricula. (Dzur 2002)

What is interesting about Dzur's approach here, though, is the lack of what one might term pragmatic or situationist approaches to democratic professionalism within an educational context. Dzur talks here of ethics and seminars without reference to the whole stream of educational literature (stemming ironically enough from Dewey) which argues, broadly, that talk about ethics is, educationally, important but insufficient: much more needs to be done to enact ethics within educational contexts.

Just what could be done, and the place of the moral imagination in the project, is the subject of this chapter. I would like to examine some of the issues involved in dealing with moral imagination with reference to professionalism and how we might approach the transformation of professionalism into democratic professionalism by taking the approach summarized in Figure 5.1.

In this chapter we shall start with some of the values described generally at level one and work our way down; however, as I hope to show, the approach is the opposite of a one-way street. Educational intention and performances are always in-tension activities, moving constantly and inescapably between the three levels of Figure 5.1. Aspirational values are central to almost all educational implementations. Biggs' (1999) concept of alignment is one metaphor for this.

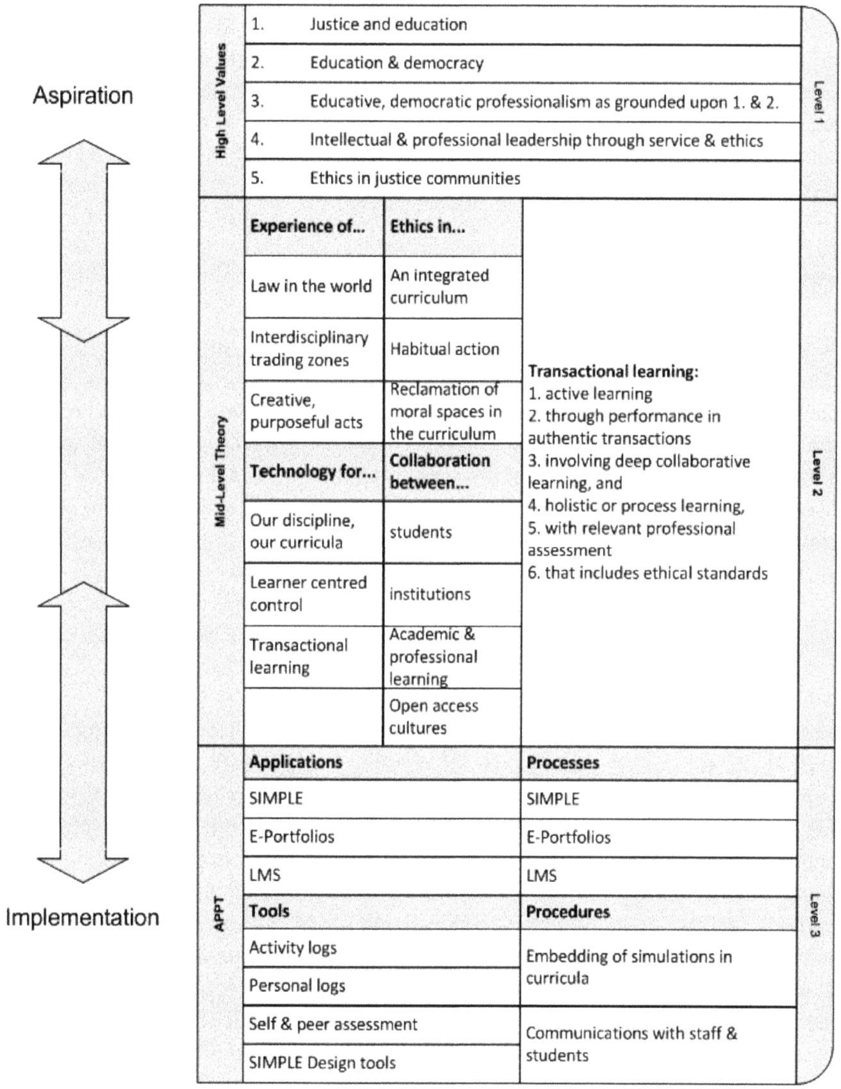

Figure 5.1 Three levels of engagement

I prefer the more organic one of ecological balance, which can include aspects of values, culture and intellectual history. An ecology is never static and it is often dependent not on the survival of what might be regarded as the higher entities, but on the survival and evolution of all entities in the ecosphere (see, for example, Nardi and O'Day 1999). Choose the wrong tools or procedures at the lower end of level 3, for instance, and the higher level values begin to be eroded. Ignore the values at the top end, and the tools at the lower end become the perfect instruments of a value-neutral approach to lawyering that is replete with values (often corporatist or consumerist), critiqued in so much of the literature on lawyering and legal education, particularly in the USA. A central figure in this approach is the educationalist and philosopher John Dewey, for whom philosophy and education were almost synonymous.

The Deweyan Educational Praxis

What is particularly appealing about Dewey's oeuvre to any analysis of moral imagination and education is the primacy he gives to experiential learning. For Dewey, learning is a social process, as he points out in *Experience and Nature*; the achievement of social ends cannot be reduced to prior rational self-interest alone. Human learning is inevitably drawn to the social sphere where it enacts itself and becomes more sophisticated and at the same time more open to change and improvement:

> Experience is the result, the sign, and the reward of that interaction of organism and environment which, when it is carried to the full, is a transformation of interaction into participation and communication. (*LW* 10: 28)[1]

Learning is experience, then, and throughout his career Dewey returned again and again to explore the nexus of learning, experience, participation and communication. In legal education experiential learning (something of a tautology for Dewey) can be the foundation for the development both of professionalism and a commitment to democratic behaviour, whether in clinic, simulation or in some other pedagogy. But, as Dewey realized, commitment to democracy means embodying that commitment in the educational forms and values we use every day within education. Ralph Sleeper makes this point well: what mattered for Dewey in all human activity, he observed, was 'the emergence of logical forms from the practice of inquiry' (Sleeper 1986: 202). Dewey's radical form of Pragmatism possessed a 'ground-map whereby [social] inequities could be identified and diagnosed, as well as a method for resolving them' (Sleeper 1986: 202). It is also a map for educational transformation, as radical now as it was over a century ago in Dewey's Chicago Laboratory School.

As Laurel Tanner (1997) shows in her fine study of the origins and practices of the Laboratory School, Dewey recognized the importance of collaboration and of mutuality – and he expressed this himself many times:

1 All references to Dewey's work are to the standard critical edition, *The Collected Works of John Dewey*, edited by J.A. Boydston and published as *The Early Works* (*EW*), *The Middle Works* (*MW*) and *The Later Works* (*LW*).

> Individuals will always be the centre and consummation of experience, but what the individual actually *is* in his life experience depends upon the nature and movement of associated life. (Dewey *LW* 14: 91)

The School's teachers played key roles in developing Dewey's curriculum plan: their 'associated life' stemmed from their 'associated thought' as professionals within an organization, and the relationship was deeply democratic. Dewey was well aware of the effect that organizations have upon our ability to develop associated lives. As he put it:

> All those who are affected by social institutions must have a share in producing and managing them. The two facts that each one is influenced in what he does and enjoys and in what he becomes by the institutions under which he lives, and that therefore he shall have, in a democracy, a voice in shaping them, are the passive and active sides of the same fact. (*LW* 11: 217–18)

Linked with the associated life is 'associated thought' (Dewey *LW* 5: 10), which, as Dzur interprets it (2002: 16), is collaborative working, particularly the collaborative problem solving that Dewey especially prized as a heuristic in the Laboratory School (Tanner 1997: 83). Dewey's interest in the social context of learning was one aspect of a more general interest among American commentators in the 1890s in the nature and function of sympathy. J.H. Mead's theory of the self was, as he acknowledged, a theory of sympathy (Leys 1993), while Addams and William James also explored this. It is the basis of Mead's social interactionism (Joas 1985, 1997), as it was for Dewey.[2] As we shall see in the next section, the intellectual and cultural history of associated thought and its effects on moral imagination are grounded in Scottish Enlightenment values, as are a number of important elements of the concepts used in the debates surrounding professionalism.

Moral Imagination and Associated Thought

The moral imagination plays an important role in associated thought for it is critical to the sympathetic construction of the other. The concept of associated thought derives, at least in the modern period, from the Scottish Enlightenment debates concerning the nature and function of the moral sense. We can see this in the work of Adam Ferguson, Francis Hutcheson and Adam Smith, amongst others. Ferguson's view of the moral imagination was linked to the moral

2 As Dewey put it in a piece entitled 'The Ethics of Democracy', and commenting on those who would focus on individual human traits only, 'the non-social individual is an abstraction arrive at by imagining what man would be if all his human qualities were taken away' (*EW* 3: 227–49).

sense. He agreed with other *literati* on the Stoic position, *contra* Hobbes and Rousseau: civic virtues were central to society and emanated from knowledge of duty, conscience and social position (Haakonssen 1990).[3] More than most, he emphasized that individual virtue contributed to the wider social good: 'the immediate uses of moral law are choice, practice and conduct' (Ferguson 1978: 6). Ferguson therefore recommended social activism, participation in public and political life and, remarkably, the development of education in civics in schools (Hill 2006: 216, 219–20). Ferguson's view of moral cognitivism is highly social, but as with much of his thought it exists in tension. He emphasizes that social action is the result of moral agents acting on the world and he held that, as moral agents, we act through self-discovery and self-emergence in daily practices, habits and interaction (Hill 2006: 143; Maharg 2007: 107).

Ferguson's view of social action was grounded in the concept of Hutcheson's 'moral sense', which was not merely a philosophic and cognitive category but an aesthetic one too.[4] Hutcheson's moral sense, literally a sense, may appear to be merely a version of eighteenth-century faculty psychology, but it is more subtle than that. Hutcheson held that beneficence and the perception of virtue are acts of cognition and affect primarily, but they are also, inevitably, legal and political in their nature and consequences. That they are so is promoted in society because, according to Hutcheson, all our civil institutions, including legal institutions and universities, require us to contribute to the virtue and self-fulfilment of all.[5] This belief Hutcheson would have encountered in Stoic sources, though as Hannah Arendt pointed out, there is an earlier source in Plato.[6]

Contradicting Rousseau, Hutcheson defined the moral sense as a key sense for the apperception of the link between learning and virtue (Hill 2006: 199, n. 1278). The aesthetic quality is important: as Kivy points out, Hutcheson's understanding of the nature and role of the *sensus communis* in aesthetic matters pre-dates Kant's treatment of 'aesthetic idea' and the fusion of aesthetic form and content, and is more subtle in his resolution of the difficulty in accounting for the source of

3 For further comment, see Marshall 1984.

4 I discuss an example of this in detail in the sister volume to this book (Barton, Garvey and Maharg 2012).

5 As Mautner points out, Hutcheson does not deny the importance of rights in discussions of moral positions – this is clear from his treatment of jurists such as Pufendorf and Grotius. However, Hutcheson does suggest, regarding these and other jurisprudential commentators, that their context is too narrow and that the structure and operation of rights needs to be seen within a wider moral and ethical context. Mautner put this well: 'His complaint, one which he seems to have been the first to articulate, and which has often been heard subsequently, is directed against the tendency to identify moral theory with a theory of rights, and against the view that respect for a person's rights is the only important kind of moral consideration' (Mautner 1993: 53).

6 As she put it, Plato reproached Pericles 'because he did not "make the citizen better" and because the Athenians were even worse at the end of his career than before (*Gorgias*, 515)' (Arendt 1958: 188).

aesthetic pleasure (Kivy 2003: 280–82). It is so partly because of Hutcheson's treatment of the imagination as the power by which the moral sense operates – to a considerable degree, it is still imaginative and aesthetic feeling that impels the moral sense. The imagination operated by ideas such as fitness – a key term for eighteenth-century aesthetics and metaphysics – which included the perception of qualities in an object such as proportion, design, aspects of beauty and the like.[7]

It is interesting that, as Brown observes, in Hutcheson's early work the moral sense springs from a disinterested impulse to do good for its own sake, while in later work it becomes more social, affected by the responses from others. Later still, Hutcheson emphasizes the link between the moral sense and conscience, with the sense of judgement – ethical, moral and religious judgement – that that may entail (Brown 1994: 63–4).[8] In this we can see possible origins for Smith's description and analysis of the bond between morality and accountability. As he put it (Smith 1976), '[a] moral being is an accountable being. An accountable being, as the word expresses, is a being that must give an account of its actions to some other, and that consequently must regulate them according to the good-liking of this other'.[9]

It is relatively easy to grasp the idea of a moral sense; but part of its problem is how imagination operates in actuality to develop it. Hutcheson's responses to his critics, John Clark and Archibald Campbell, on the subject describe how sympathy plays a key role (Turco 1999). The issue is, as Hutcheson, Ferguson and Smith realized, not merely one of cognition; it also involved our awareness of how the imaginative narratives (of motive, cause, event, character and the like) that we create in part out of our moral sense and sympathy can affect others. In the twentieth century, Arendt pointed out how speech and narratives, much more than philosophy and political economy tracts, can engage others in a critical argument precisely because they deal in situations, in particular circumstances, and can persuade listeners and readers to come to complex moral and ethical decisions (Arendt 1958: 175–88).[10]

For Smith, one of the problematics of sympathy was how one might be at one and the same time both inside oneself and yet the impartial spectator of whom he approves (Smith 1976: III.3.25). Brady saw in Smith's discussions of

7 Kivy points to the link between association of ideas and the perception of fitness as an aesthetic category (Kivy 2003: 184–8). See also Darling (1989) and Sheridan (2007).

8 To a considerable degree, though, it is still imaginative and aesthetic feeling that impels the moral sense. See Harrison (1995) for the link between imagination and aesthetics in Smith, and evidence of Smith's debt to Hutcheson in this regard.

9 As Dubnick (2010) points out, the textual history of the concept expressed in Smith's words is complex. The words appear in the first edition of *The Theory of Moral Sentiments* (1759, Pt III, Chapter 1), are adapted in the second (1761), and in the sixth and final edition (1790, commonly regarded as the definitive) they do not appear at all. I agree with Dubnick, though, that the link between morality and accountability is retained implicitly in the sixth edition of the book.

10 See also Gottsegen (1994: 180–84).

sympathetic imagination a cognitive turn where the self regulates itself and its moral judgements on nature and humanity (Brady 2011). Yet, as Brown points out, Smith's philosophical voice is 'unable to achieve a complete resolution in which the sympathetic construction of the impartial spectator achieves a state of moral wholeness for the moral agent' (Brown 1994: 75). I agree with her that in Smith as in Hutcheson we see less of the calm and generous Stoic citizen and more of a 'fractured and struggling moral being' (Brown 1994: 75). It is a moral being that is familiar from the work of Ferguson, too; and not because of the difficulty of the Stoic position per se. As Hill (2006: 11) put it, Ferguson was concerned about the new economic and moral conditions rapidly taking hold in Scotland: he 'fretted about the increasingly important role of prudential reasoning, bureaucratic rationality and centralised planning in the running of societies and, in particular, their effects upon the moral strength of nations'.

Hutcheson's central idea of the moral sense mutated in the later eighteenth and nineteenth centuries in the hands of Stewart and Reid into forms to which he would not have assented, but which were nevertheless influential in their own right.[11] The flexible links between moral theory and lived practice advocated by Hutcheson, however, became formalized in undergraduate courses on Moral Philosophy and Ethics. The Hutchesonian legacy also lived on in a migrated form. Hutcheson's ideas on beatific moral theory were significantly influential in university and political circles in North America (Norton 1976). John Dewey first encountered them while a student in the Department of Philosophy at the University of Vermont, and he would have been familiar with constellations of Stoic and Enlightenment thinking around the moral sense, sympathy and the association of ideas.[12] While he moved well beyond them in his own philosophical and educational thinking, there were some ways in which he was, paradoxically, moving towards Hutcheson, particularly in his idea that learning is a social process. As he writes in *Experience and Nature*, the achievement of social ends cannot be reduced to prior rational self-interest alone (any more than it could be for Hutcheson). Human learning, including learning in morals, is inevitably drawn to the social sphere where it enacts itself within a social context, and becomes more sophisticated and at the same time more open to change and improvement:

11 As Cairns points out (1992: 169), by the mid-eighteenth century, natural law thinking had come to dominate the moral philosophical curriculum in the Universities of Edinburgh and Glasgow. Barton, Garvey and Maharg (2012) describe some of influences of Hutcheson's thinking in the nineteenth century, as does Ward (2002).

12 For example, in addition to reading the basic texts, he read John Stuart Mill's analysis of Hamilton (Mill 1865). See Feuer (1958). Dewey may even have borrowed the phrase from Dugald Stewart, who analysed the effects of 'perceptible objects' on 'associated thoughts and associated feelings' (Stewart 1854: II, 256).

> The principle of continuity of experiences means that every experience both takes up something from those which have gone before and modifies in some way the quality of those which come after. (Dewey *LW* 10: 35)

Learning, including learning in moral imagination, is also experience, then, and throughout his career Dewey returned again and again to explore the nexus of learning, lived experience and participation in imaginative action. It was for him the foundation for the development both of professional behaviour, ethical commitment and indeed the ground of democratic action for individuals and institutions. It can be so for us in legal education, whether in clinic, simulation or in any similar experiential pedagogy, where there is commitment to democratic and ethical behaviour in the everyday educational ideas, gestures, physical environment and abstract structures we surround ourselves with.

How might these Deweyan values be explored and used in legal education? The next section, the first of two case studies, is a study in regulatory change, one based not just on Deweyan concepts but also on the analysis of key Enlightenment ideas such as fitness, accountability and learning via narrative.

Case Study One: Professional Legal Education and Regulation in Scotland

If the values of professionalism and the interface between moral values and professionalism are becoming an issue of key concern to educators, it is even more so for regulators of professions, and not just because of high-profile cases such as Enron in business, the recent cases of financial services fraud or the case of Harold Shipman in medical practice. Research is focusing on what professionalism might be, how it might be taught and learned, and how it might be measured. Papadakis et al. (2004b), for instance, set out to determine if medical students who demonstrated unprofessional conduct in medical school were more likely to be disciplined by their State Board. Their study set out possible correlative factors, including gender, grade point average, Medical College Admission scores, school grades, National Board of Medical Examiner Part 1 scores and negative excerpts from evaluation forms. The study subjects were alumni graduating between 1943 and 1989. They revealed correlations between unprofessional behaviour at medical school and practitioners who had been disciplined by their profession. As they reported:

> We found that UCSF School of Medicine students who received comments regarding unprofessional behaviour were more than twice as likely to be disciplined by the Medical Board of California when they become practicing physicians than were students without such comments. The more traditional measures of medical school performance, such as grades and passing scores on

> national standardized tests, did not identify students who later had disciplinary problems as practicing physicians. (Papadakis et al. 2004b: 248)[13]

What this and similar research reveals is the misalignment between professional values and educational methods and assessment processes. However, it also reveals two significant issues in the educational structure of professions. First, the questions that arise in reading research findings such as this – what constitutes 'unprofessional behaviour'? Who determines that? What are the normative performance baselines for such a concept? – need answering by regulatory bodies in dialogue with other stakeholders in the profession and with reference to research on professionalism. For example, Selznick (1992) has pointed out the need for professionals to be 'genuinely other-regarding and constructively self-regarding'. Selznick (1992: 227) goes on to characterize the 'responsible self' as being manifested in three ways: character-defining choice, self-affirming participation and personal statesmanship.' His traits of the moral self, strikingly similar to those outlined by Ferguson in his *Institutes* and quoted earlier, go to the heart of the regulatory enterprise and compel us to ask searching questions: what is regulation? What is being regulated? Can regulation enforce moral conduct?[14]

Second, the critical literature on professionalism itself analyses the deep structures of the term as a social construct, and this needs to be brought into educational processes and inform the regulatory process. Stronach et al. (2002), for instance, has explored the nature of professionalism, caught between an 'economy of performance' and various 'ecologies of practice', with professionals themselves located in the 'nexus between policy, ideology and practice'. They go on to critique the 'reductive typologies and characterizations of current professionalism' and they argue for the construction of professional identities that arise from the 'local, situated and indeterminable nature of professional practice, and the inescapable dimensions of trust, diversity and creativity' (Stronach et al. 2002: 109). As they observe, 'excellence can only be motivated, it cannot be coerced' (Stronach et al. 2002: 138).

The Law Society of Scotland is an example of a regulatory body that is coming to terms with these issues of professional values. The Diploma in Legal Practice, the current primary professional programme it has regulated for over 30 years, has undergone review in a wide consultation on the future of legal education in Scotland, with proposals for a programme to be called Professional Education and Training (PEAT) 1 to replace it. Before we examine this process and its outcome, it would be helpful to describe briefly the current Diploma programme and the process of change.

13 See also Papadakis et al. (2004a).

14 Ferguson's words are quoted above: 'the immediate uses of moral law are choice, practice and conduct' (Ferguson 1978: 6). Selznick's work on the moral content of social theory is based firmly in Dewey's and Mead's epistemological analyses.

Context of the Diploma in Legal Practice

In Scotland until 2011, there were a number of routes to qualification as a solicitor or advocate. It was possible to sit examinations held by the Law Society of Scotland in what were known as the 'qualifying subjects', a pass in which qualified the candidate to proceed to a postgraduate course in professional subjects, called the Diploma in Legal Practice. The commonest route to the legal profession, however, was via university study. In their undergraduate years, most students studied for their LLB degree in one of a variety of routes stretching from two to four years, depending on their previous experience and pattern of study. This was followed by the postgraduate Diploma, which lasted for around seven months – effectively a full academic year. All students then entered a traineeship of two years in a legal office, during the course of which the Law Society of Scotland required them to undertake a Professional Competence Course and, during their traineeship, to undertake the Assessment of Professional Competence.

The Diploma programme consisted of eight subjects and one option – at the Glasgow Graduate School of Law (a joint graduate school between the universities of Glasgow and Strathclyde – GGSL) we added another, namely the first in the following list:[15]

1. Foundation Course in Professional Legal Skills.
2. Civil Court Practice.
3. Criminal Court Practice.
4. Financial Services and Accountancy.
5. Private Client.
6. Professional Ethics.
7. Conveyancing.
8. Practice Management.
9. *Either* Company and Commercial *or* Public Administration.

In the late 1990s, as a result of dissatisfaction from students, trainees and legal service employers, the Diploma curriculum underwent revision by the Law Society, with the result that a number of skills were identified as being crucial to legal practice which had hitherto not sufficiently been the focus of the curriculum. The Society was keen to see the Diploma develop from what it was before, namely yet another academic course focusing on substantive and procedural law, into a programme of study where attributes, values and knowledge are integrated. The Society therefore required providers to focus on a number of professional skills areas, namely:

15 The GGSL was a joint graduate school between the law schools of the Universities of Glasgow and Strathclyde; and existed from 1999 to 2010. In the future, PEAT 1 will be hosted separately by each of the two law schools.

1. interviewing;
2. negotiation;
3. advocacy;
4. legal writing;
5. drafting;
6. research.[16]

From Diploma to Professional Education and Training (PEAT) Programmes

Quite soon after this review process was concluded, however, it became clear that little real change was taking place in the Diploma. One of the many lessons learned from this first attempt at changing the Diploma curriculum was the central paradox of curriculum design and change culture: inside-school reform needs to start with outside-school reform. A second, and much more ambitious, process of change was therefore embarked upon, one that was inclusive of the undergraduate programme, the traineeship experience, practitioner Continuing Professional Development (CPD) and stakeholder views.

Early in this change process, a Working Party was tasked with drawing up a set of learning outcomes for a new Diploma. The macro-design envisaged a core consisting of professionalism statements that would define the professional standards that lay at the core of the professional legal educative process (see the Appendix to this chapter). Around this were other professional standards: 'Professional Relationships' focused largely on professional relations in the programmes and traineeships (effectively one form of Deweyan 'associated thought'), while 'Professional Communications' was subdivided into areas such as interviewing, negotiation, advocacy, etc.

The outcomes, particularly Professionalism, were drafted with much of the research into professionalism outlined above. It was not sufficient that we outlined *what* skills or knowledge components were going to be the focus of PEAT 1 or *how* they would be taught and learned within the programme of study; we also needed to consider the moral and ethical context of the programme, and the values underpinning the skills and knowledge of the substantive curriculum. Instruction without moral context implicitly teaches our students the impoverished and value-neutral model of legal practice referred to above, and many commentators, educational as well as legal, have pointed out the dangers of this approach to skills learning.[17] As Ronald Barnett has pointed out:

16 For more information, see Maharg 2004b.

17 See, for example, Toddington 1996. The problem of course is inherent in any professional programme – see Stenhouse 1983. See also Maharg 2007, particularly Chapter 4, '"By the end of this module ...": the intimate dimensions of ethical education', 99–118.

> A higher education designed around skills is no higher education. It is the substitution of technique for insight; of strategic reason for communicative reason; and of behaviour for wisdom. (Barnett 1994: 61)

The first value statement in the Scottish list is an attempt to find a common ground to what is otherwise incommensurable in the values of democratic commitment. Just what that commitment might entail on the PEAT 1 programme is set out in the positive indicators and could be detailed for various future educational stages. It is not defined: the debate is left for the profession to engage in, and in the porous nature of the statement lies both its strength and its weakness. In that debate, however, is the attempt to escape a self-referential professionalism, the values of which are 'mostly unremarkable and unobjectionable, not least because they coincide with the commitments and objectives of lawyers' traditional professionalization project' (Webb and Nicolson 2005: 168). Instead, a commitment to democracy reaches out to the fundamental values of our society and in its recognition of the tension in those values rejects 'the possibility of the conventional monistic approach capturing the complexity of ethical life' (Webb and Nicolson 2005: 169).

The Working Party therefore needed to define the value-context within which skills would be learned.[18] At the outset, there were a number of key issues to be addressed. We refined these as the following statements:

1. *Knowledge and skills must be taught* critically *within the value system of the profession.* Values such as integrity, industry, service and duty, wisdom, compassion, accountability and responsibility, all of which underpin professional relationships and activities – these values were part of the essential context of knowledge and skills, and had to be acknowledged as such. Where there was a dissonance or clash of values, this needed to be explored honestly – indeed, such dissonance formed a critically important 'learning moment' in the construction and understanding of professional values as described by Stronach et al. (2002).
2. *Knowledge and skills are part of professional behaviour*, and professional behaviour can never be taught in classroom activities alone. It required the presence of practitioners, and often the setting of the office or the court in order to deepen the learning process, even if such settings were proxy, e.g. in simulations. Even in office and court, however, the process of learning professional behaviour is not only taught overtly – it is caught in trainees' observations of practitioners at work, in conversation and at leisure. Similarly, on the PEAT 1 programme, professional behaviour is 'caught' in the interstices of the curriculum. It is in this sense that the 'hidden curriculum' and the 'null curriculum' of the Diploma are useful

18 Maharg was one of the Working Party, as well as a member of the Society's Education & Training Committee.

concepts – that is to say, the unintentional lessons that students learn from a curriculum and what is unofficially labelled as irrelevant or unimportant by its absence in a curriculum (Jackson 1968: 353; Eisner 1985). Law students learn professional behaviours by observing and imitating peers, tutors and other role models, not just in the classroom but in hallways, cafeterias and lifts. As the literature suggests, the process of learning professional skills can be greatly enhanced by active engagement with professional issues in the classroom and in simulations where models of behaviour can be discussed to bring out the issues involved.

3. If we were to take experiential learning seriously, then we needed to acknowledge that there is a *substantial difference between teaching and learning*. What a teacher teaches may not be what a student learns from a teaching event. Any approach to experiential education must start from this fundamental point (Wolf and Turner 1989).
4. *New practices on the PEAT 1 programme would need to be developed and shared among all*. We were not starting a course *de novo*, but there needed to be change in educational practices. The relation between old and new practices made change a highly complex process. There was a considerable body of existing practice at each existing Diploma centre that needed to be taken account of in the development of skills for the future. The course directors of these centres had a body of design experience and knowledge of their tutor base. The tutors had experience of teaching and communicating with students, and they would probably have taught with a high degree of autonomy in their classes. The Society needed to facilitate change in educational practices, but also enable the shared experience within centres to thrive and develop effectively, while at the same time ensuring that models of good practice were being carried out by all providers, both new and old, and were applied with reasonable consistency across the range of different providers.
5. *Quality of education: 'good, fast, cheap – choose two'*. So goes the engineering saying, pointing out the common-sense relationship between these qualities. The challenge for providers was to become genuinely more innovative in their design of teaching and learning. The challenge for the Law Society as a regulator was to enable ways for this to come about, and to do so bearing in mind the financial costs of high-quality professional education and the words of Stronach in the epigraph 'excellence can only be motivated: it cannot be coerced'.
6. *Student perceptions of their skills development*. It is fair to say that many students believe that they are reasonably well skilled when they graduate, and this is true of many (though not all) of them as regards academic skills. However, it is also true that the vast majority of them will not have undertaken intensive skills training or have used professional resources to help them learn the professional practice of law. They needed to develop new perceptions of training and education, of legal skills and of their

own changing identities if they were to learn effectively from the PEAT 1 programme. Just as a culture change was required among teaching staff, it would also be required among students.

If PEAT 1 really were to be a 'bridge' course, then the foundations of that bridge to professionalism were the core modules Ethics and Standards, and Professional Communications. These modules should declare to students and others that ethics are regarded as critical to professional practice by the Society, and that effective communication is a critical part of the ethical dimension of professionality. Other professions recognize this – see, for example, the work of Hickson et al. (1992) and others in medical education and ethics.[19] It was also proof that professionalism was held as a key educational quality by the Society – and again, there was good evidence from the Working Party's research that other professions had similar perspectives.[20] As regards communications outcomes, two points were borne in mind:

1. The list of learning outcomes generated by the Working Party and the Consultation was a definition of the minimum or threshold experience that students should have had on PEAT 1. In other words, students should have had the opportunity to practise every minor domain on this list at least once and preferably twice or more, with feedback. Providers were encouraged to innovate imaginatively and go beyond the threshold skill set, ideally in the form of Bruner's spiral curriculum.
2. Because there is a difference between teaching and learning as we have said, the list was not to be regarded as prescriptive of the skill or knowledge set for a capable trainee. Students themselves were to be encouraged to develop beyond the outcomes. In this regard, providers were encouraged to use portfolio learning in order to enable students to develop not merely the skills or the fundamental values of ethics and communications alone, but also the student's own developing sense of professionalism – the *Bildungsroman* of professionalism. It was suggested that the portfolio could link to an undergraduate personal development file and the forms of work-based assessment that trainees were required to undertake as part of PEAT 2.[21]

---

19 The medical educational literature is extensive. See also Frank et al. (2000), who explored the patient perspective: 'patients who feel ignored, deserted, or who suspect that there is a "cover up" by the medical profession, may be more inclined to sue. Failure to understand the patient and family's perspective and devaluing their point of view have also been identified as common triggers for lawsuits' (2000: 268).

20 See, for instance, in medical education Ginsburg et al. 2000; Brownell and Côté 2001; Ginsburg and Stern 2004; Papadakis et al. 2004a; and Papadakis et al. 2004b. See also, in the teaching profession, Breger, Calabrese and Hughes 2004.

21 The development of this functionality is not a trivial task. A special Working Party was set up under the aegis of the Society's Education & Training Committee to develop software and educational guidelines around the use of the software by staff, students and trainees.

Approaches to Good Practice

The development of professionalism in a course of study is never an easy task, and general guidelines were drafted for providers on the following topics:

- the ways in which the teaching environment and the available resources could be used to structure student activity;
- types of teaching and learning, and how the mix of learning styles contributed to knowledge acquisition and professional development;
- how tasks and transactions could be interleaved and integrated with each other;
- the acquisition and development by students of the shared set of terms, external representations that provide a common ground for communication and shared understanding between trainees and training firms, and between client and lawyer.

There is extensive literature on this in medical education. In a series of experiments on the role of biomedical knowledge in clinical reasoning, for instance, Boshuizen and Schmidt (1992) have shown that experts acquire a robust knowledge base that integrates situated and general knowledge. Knowledge integration is an active process that involves articulating a global framework (the biomedical knowledge), reflecting on situated experiences (individual cases as they are encountered) and actively making connections between situated knowledge and the global framework.

This is also true of the legal domain. A lawyer in private practice will see something in the order of many thousands of cases in a working life. Through the experience of casework, she gains an extensive stock of what might be termed mental schemas and performance knowledge. Solicitors know this implicitly. When presented with a set of facts within their area of practice, they are able quite quickly to invoke a schema and can test this initial schema against the evidence. Lesgold et al. (1989) suggest that, in the process of becoming an expert, a trainee acquires fragments of automatized procedure that gradually become integrated into extended sequences that guide performance. These sequences can be formed quite slowly from practice through the composition of fragments of activity, but the process can be made much more efficient if students are taught the procedures explicitly, as a list of steps towards problem identification and solution, and also taught to begin the process of case pattern recognition. These two forms of learning can bring trainees to a practical knowledge of a transaction much more efficiently if learning is carried out via simulation and transaction. In this respect, what is true of biomedicine and radiology and many other professional domains is equally true of legal practice. And as Selznick (1992) and Stronach et al. (2002) have both pointed out, the ability and the freedom that professionals require in order to make the link between local and global is a critical function of professionalism.

The practice of this function should begin in the domain of the academy, where its education in the moral imagination can be constructed.

What are the best ways to bring this about? There is no one royal road and there is much literature about which methods are effective for which skills and in which teaching environments and stages of learning.[22] Whatever method is used, it ought to be highly experiential and include elements such as role-plays, case studies, simulations, structured interviews, prompted recall, detailed analysis of achievements and performance problems in skills practice and the like.

Great benefit can be derived from intensive coaching sessions at any stage in PEAT 1, where such sessions focus on feedback and review. It is also the case that development in professionalism is greatly enhanced if skills are embedded across the curriculum in realistic transactions. Much of the medical literature on clinical skills emphasizes the importance of immediate feedback, of opportunities for practice following review and of practice within different contexts (Kneebone et al. 2002). Local course providers are therefore best placed to know where to embed skills within their courses, given their knowledge of their tutors and other conditions pertaining to the course. However, there is always a tension between local innovation and standards within the jurisdiction and across jurisdictions.[23] As stated above, the problem can be resolved if jurisdiction-wide standards exist as threshold or minimum standards, and best practice is shared collaboratively among providers.

Above all, we need to return to the Deweyan value of professional life as associated life, and embed that within our teaching and learning. If the discussion in the first few sections of this chapter have been at the aspirational level one of Figure 5.1, the boxes at level two describe examples of the mid-level theory by which this can be achieved, and in particular the relations that need to be strengthened between students (where learning, trust and responsibility are built into collaborative activities), between institutions in the market, and between academic and professional learning. Given the role that any regulatory body plays in setting not just rules and benchmarks but also tone, culture and relationships, it is therefore essential that key professional concepts such as fitness and accountability are defined, not in terms of the narrow technicism of the policy-audit culture, but in terms of trust, openness to experience and critical responsibility.

In its recognition of this, and in its attempt to view legal education as a democratic process, one where associated life is of the essence in the creation of educational values, the Law Society has encouraged a unique experiment. A number of providers came together to plan collaborative inquiry and resource

22 See, for example, Eaton and Cottrell (1999); and Taverner et al. (2000).

23 In a wider context, this is precisely what a number of bodies in medical education are setting out to explore and improve. The work of the Institute for International Medical Education is crucial in this regard (www.iime.org). See, for instance, World Health Organization/Education Commission for Foreign Medical Graduates (1995); World Federation for Medical Education Task Force (2000); and Schwartz and Wojtczak 2002.

design. Current providers of the Diploma met informally with the Society in 2009 to examine how resources, methods and approaches to professional learning could be licensed as Open Educational Resources (OER) to determine the best approaches to the use of technology, the development of ethical learning and to consider many other components of learning in associated lives. To what extent the initiative thrives depends greatly on the relations between providers, of course, and this will take time, but it is significant that the regulator has encouraged its existence and dynamic.

Associated Thought and Social Software

So far we have been discussing pedagogical approaches only to the development of democratic professionalism. But – and bearing in mind Figure 5.1 above – let us take this down to a further level of granularity – to applications, approaches to learning in detail. Can technology play a role in enhancing democratic professionalism? If so, how might it do so, and should this be part of the regulatory project?

Recall the use of the moral imagination to develop the moral sense in the work of Hutcheson and Ferguson, the link between associated thought and associated life, and how this was, as Tanner observed, essential to Dewey's creative problem-solving method in the Laboratory School. What Dewey created, for both students and teachers, was what James Paul Gee in recent years has called 'affinity spaces'. These are informal learning spaces where, *inter alia*, common endeavour is primary, where novices and masters share common space, where intensive and extensive knowledge are encouraged, as well as both individual and distributed knowledge. Gee goes on to define this in more detail (Gee 2004: 83–9) using the examples of video games. Many more studies attest to this quality of game genre – the research of Nick Yee, for example, or Constance Steinkuhler, or the research of Henry Jenkins. Taylor (2006: 81) in her fine study of the userbase of Sony's EverQuest notes the plethora of sites associated with such games, describing them as 'a kind of "collective intelligence", an idea Henry Jenkins (2002) picks up from Pierre Levy's (1997) work on the reconfigurations occurring in contemporary society around technology and knowledge'.

Video games and social software are examples of such affinity spaces. Facebook can of course be used for purely commercial purposes (and it goes without saying that video games themselves are hugely commercial undertakings), but like in-world texting, simulations, blogs, tweets, wikis and many other new genres of textual production in the social software revolution, they are exemplars of how Deweyan 'associated thought' can be combined with new technologies to bring about a significant shift in the method and content of professional learning. What are the lineaments of this transformation for legal education in particular? They are characterized by the level two categories of Figure 5.1, particularly the four boxes to the left, under the headings Experience, Ethics, Technology and Collaboration (Maharg 2007). All four concepts (which of course express value-laden approaches to legal education) can be significantly enabled and enhanced by the use of appropriate technology, allied to educational, moral and ethical theory on level one, and when embedded in applications such as those outlined at level three.

In the next section I shall briefly outline how this might come about in one particular application, namely simulation. In the process of examining how such an approach works in practice, we shall see how the moral imagination works in detail at this level of implementation and how it can be enabled by the mid-level theory at level two.

Case Study Two: Professionalism and SIMPLE – Associated Thought in Action

This case study is a curriculum-wide implementation of simulation activities within the Diploma in Legal Practice. It involves learning face to face using conventional print resources and involves online digital resources. While the use of the web to simulate a professional environment is nothing new in itself, our implementation of it and on this scale is fairly unique. In addition, the design and use of the online learning environment has led to the redesign of face-to-face interventions, derived from other disciplines, which are unusual in legal education. Accompanying the implementation is a developing body of theory called transactional learning (Maharg 2007; level two in Figure 5.1 above), which aims to describe and analyse forms of learning based upon all professional interactions and which is relevant to both undergraduate and postgraduate courses. To do all this, we developed a simulation engine, called SIMPLE, which would enable forms of Deweyan education to be enacted within a regulatory structure – one where forms of professional learning could also, conceivably, be enacted, via 'associated thought', as forms of democratic professionalism.[24]

SIMulated Professional Learning Environment (SIMPLE)

The simulation environment has two primary software outputs, in the form of the SIMPLE platform and SIMPLE tools, collectively known as the SIMulated Professional Learning Environment, or SIMPLE. Both products are finished to beta user stage. Each of these products is aimed at different areas of the teaching eco-system: the platform is targeted towards students and staff, and is there to provide the day-to-day systems for engaging with and managing simulations. The tools, on the other hand, are targeted towards academic or professional educators, and allow them to design professional simulations and manage all of the resources that are required to provide an engaging learning experience. Both open-source products are available to the further education (FE) and higher education (HE)

24 For more information on SIMPLE as an application, see http://simplecommunity.org.

communities free at point of use at http://simplecommunity.org, with appropriate open-source licence structures in place.

The SIMPLE platform is web-based, allowing access from anywhere in the world where staff and students have an Internet connection. This allows for flexibility in the student learning environment as well as flexible options for staff management of student simulations (enabling more efficient multi-tasking in administration and learner support). We have made plans for extensive further development of both tools and platform.

What do users do with the environment? Figure 5.2 is an example of the environment, seen from a tutor point of view. Staff see what students see, but with added functionality (staff would click on 'Staff Tools' in the left-hand column to access staff-specific communication tools and information). Students use the environment as a professional working environment. They can receive, send and store documents, graphics, video and other file formats by uploading them to the environment. They can communicate with real or fictitious persons and institutions, and receive feedback on their work in-role. They have access to any resources that staff may wish to make available to them; they can share tools and resources. They have access to a map of a fictional town and a directory. Using the environment, students can build up the correspondence and drafts of an entire transaction and either use the environment as a single student or as part of a collaborative grouping.

It is difficult to describe briefly the scale of the simulation activities undertaken by students in this programme-wide simulation. For background information and further comment, see Maharg 2004a, 2006; Barton and Westwood 2006; Barton and Maharg 2007; Maharg 2007; and Maharg and Owen 2007.

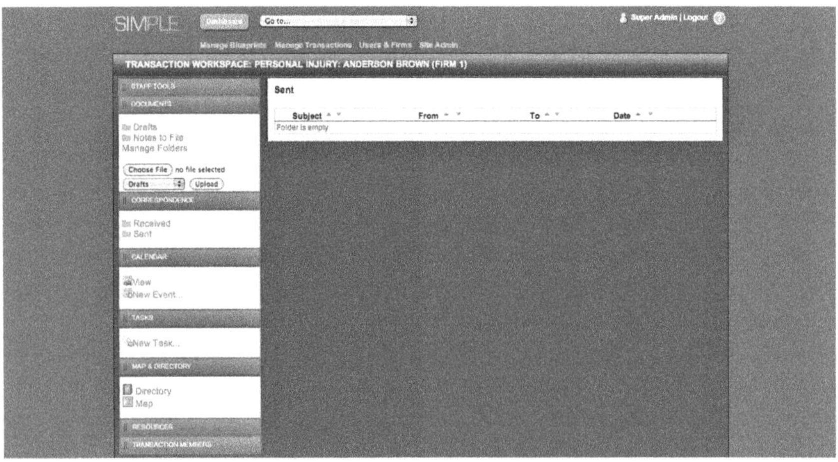

Figure 5.2 SIMPLE environment

Currently at Strathclyde, students on the Diploma are formed into groups of four at the start of the academic year, each one being a simulated law firm. Sited on the south bank of the Clyde, the town acts as a complex simulation of the reality that surrounds actual legal transactions. For example, in the Personal Injury Negotiation Transaction (PI), the firms act for clients, as either the injured claimant or as the insurance company's solicitors, in a personal injury negotiation that lasts almost a full semester (12 weeks in total). In order to negotiate the case, they need to engage in fact-finding by contacting characters and institutions within the virtual community, pooling the information they obtain. They then need to carry out legal research on issues such as liability and quantum, set out their negotiation strategy and perform the negotiation, either by email or through a face-to-face meeting. Discussion forums for both sides support students in the complex process of carrying out this legal transaction – a visiting professor, who is a solicitor specializing in personal injury practice and who is on both forums, answered student queries and provided information. Postgraduate students, trainees and newly-qualified solicitors are trained to answer emails in the guise of any one of around 12 different fictional characters and to give the appropriate information to students. They are supported by an online forum where the PI practitioner is present (the author of the scenario and many resources). If they wish, students can meet as a firm with either this tutor or another negotiation tutor to discuss strategy and performance before they negotiate with the other side. This meeting is in effect a form of small-group, salon learning. It is voluntary: there are no face-to-face interventions at all, apart from an introductory and general feedback lecture (students can also, if they wish, obtain feedback on performance from file assessors at the end of the project).

This is only one of a number of simulations that use the SIMPLE environment. There are at least another six transactions on the programme. Nor is this form of learning applicable to legal professional programmes only. It has been used successfully in undergraduate law programmes at Warwick, Northumbria and Glamorgan University Law Schools, and in postgraduate Masters programmes and vocational programmes. It is not jurisdictionally specific: it is currently being used by the Law Workshop of the Australian National University and the University of New Hampshire Law School in the USA. It has also been used successfully, in the initial JISC/UKCLE SIMPLE project, in postgraduate Architecture and undergraduate Management Science modules.

Associated Thought and Simulation

What is the point of this form of learning and what part does the moral imagination play in its implementation? On a surface level, it simulates the reality of actual transactions. Note that the aim is not the *replication* of reality, which would be an impossibility, but *simulation* of aspects of it. This allows staff to focus on the transactional elements that students may learn – in the PI transaction, for instance, these included problem-identification and solving, the integration of different bodies of substantive legal knowledge (delict (including liability and quantum), tax, welfare law), the skills of negotiation formation within the transaction, specific forms of letter-writing and time management of the transaction, negotiation performance and client-centred lawyering.

In addition, it also allows staff to create open-field transactions (such as the PI transaction) which are in effect powerful problem-based learning environments, and bounded-field transactions (such as conveyancing, where we supply students with template documents and the transaction is much more linear and bounded by custom and statute) – see Barton and Maharg (2007) for more information on this, and the table below for more detail of the distinction we make.

Further, it allows staff to create environments that are both zones for learning and assessment where the environments are powerful learning and testing grounds for contested value-constellations such as professionalism. Such values, as we have seen from research into the forms of education that best fit cultures of professional activity, do not fit easily into the structures of academic assessment (Stern and Papadakis 2006). Above all, this approach avoids the damaging separation of learning from assessment that often occurs in conventional academic learning.

Next, in examining the work of professionals it is clear that real professional life is about the integration of knowledge into contexts that are changing continuously. This knowledge becomes valuable when it is contextualized in the narratives of professional experience. There is a considerable difference in emphasis in the notion and techniques required for professional development as compared to a technical approach to training. Professional education requires judgement rather than simple answers. This has been well articulated by Bevis and Watson (1990), who compared a technical model against a professional model for clinical nurse education (see Table 5.1). The language of their comparison is similar to that of Dzur and is close to the antinomies of Stronach et al., and to the anxieties about the nature of professional society that go back to Ferguson and Scottish Enlightenment discourse. We would argue that approaches such as SIMPLE simulations allow us to shift educational practice much more to the professional end of the spectrum than to the technical end.

Table 5.1 Technical and professional models

Technical model	Professional model
The only learning worth evaluating can be seen as behavioural changes.	Worthwhile learning is often personal, obscure and private. Only some learning appears as behavioural changes.
Everything that exists do so in some quantity, and therefore can be counted and measured.	Many things that exist are not externally verifiable.
The teacher-selected goals are the important ones and are therefore the evaluated ones.	Both teacher- and student-selected goals are important, as is learning attained without goals.
Comparing behaviours to some objectively held criteria or comparing to the progress of other students determines how well something is learned.	Educative learning cannot be rated on a scale. Most learning cannot be compared either to some 'objectively' conceived criteria or to the progress of other students.
The teacher–student relationship is hierarchical and the teachers assess students by how well they have met specific objectives.	The teacher–student relationship is egalitarian. Learning requires a process of trusting grades to exploration among expert and novice learners and thrives on constructive criticism.
The quality of rigour of a course can be determined by how well it helps its students meet the discipline requirements as reflected by test scores, attainment of behavioural objectives and accreditation requirements, since these reflect the agreed-upon discipline content.	The quality of rigour of a course can be determined by how well it helps students collect paradigm experiences, develop insights, see patterns, find meanings in ideas and experiences, explore creative modes of enquiry, examine assumptions, form values and ethics in keeping with the moral ideal of the caring scholar-clinician, respond to social needs, live fully and advance the profession.

Source: Bevis and Watson 1990, cited in Maharg and Owen 2007.

How does simulation manage to do this? Put simply, it allows for a creative space, a middle domain of playful activity where the moral imagination is, in a Hutchesonian sense, encouraged to play. Students *play* roles, have the space to take up traits and characters that are not (yet) disciplined by the Weberian cage of professional practice reality, and can develop the play of imaginative sympathy, amongst other emotions, within their learning and their work.

Or not. For there is a body of work carried out by Barton and Westwood that analyses how, in terms of learning and trust, the collaborative relationship is enacted in the simulation environment, how the ecology of that environment can shape student learning and how students themselves shape it (Barton and Westwood 2006, 2011).

Type 2: Legal Eagles **Low Trust High Learning** **Culture** Suspicious, blame, independence, me first, team second **Task** Task focused: debate about details, my way; high engagement, exhausting **Relationships** Insular, abrasive, reluctant, limited listening, suspicious **Work styles** Inflexible, rigid, majority, one-upmanship	**Type 1: Learning Community** **High Trust High Learning** **Culture** Inclusive, fair, interdependence, team first, win-win **Task** Task focussed: our way; high engagement to get things done, good communications **Relationships** Open, value each other, mutually supportive, honest, shared responsibility, respect **Work styles** Flexible, adaptive, learn from mistakes, consensus, responsive, resilient	
Type 4: Dysfunctional **Low Trust Low Learning** **Culture** Suspicious, blame, ego-centred, me first, firm nowhere **Task** Not task focussed; low engagement **Relationships** Blame, victimisation, polarised, abrasive, no self-awareness **Work styles** Inflexible, superficial, dictatorial, rigid	**Type 3: Friendly Societies** **High Trust Low Learning** **Culture** Inclusive, cosy, dependence, friends first, firm second **Task** Not task focussed; low engagement **Relationships** Like minded, sociable, nice, supportive **Work styles** Superficial, majority, avoid conflict	**Trust**

Figure 5.3 Learning/trust matrix
Source: Barton and Westwood 2006.

Analysing individual reflective reports that GGSL students wrote on their experience of working in firms, they drew up a matrix the axes of which were composed of learning and trust, with student firms plotted into one of four quadrants – high learning, high trust ('Learning Communities'); high learning, low trust ('Legal Eagles'); low learning, high trust ('Friendly Societies'), and low learning, low trust ('Dysfunctional' firms).[25] The traits of the quadrants are illustrated in Figure 5.3.

According to their analyses, the student firms achieved most in terms of academic and professional practice when they were in the Type 1: Learning Community quadrant, but the first study in 2003/2004 revealed a relatively high proportion of problematic traits in the formation of group dynamics, the emotional

25 For examples of dissonant behaviour and problematic learning, see Maharg 2007: Chapter 7.

resilience of group work and many other issues (see Figure 5.3). Clearly, GGSL staff wanted as many students as possible to be in the Learning Community. In our view, and given our concept of Deweyan civic professionalism as well as our sense of the role of sympathy and feeling in collaborative work, this was where not only the most significant achievement took place, but where students learned best the ideals of a democratic professionalism. Correspondingly, we wanted Legal Eagles to be less suspicious with each other and more trusting, the Friendly Societies to be less friendly and more task-focused, and the Dysfunctional firms to give more time to the intra-firm relationship itself and seek help where required.

As a result, the GGSL team implemented a number of changes to the context of the firm environment on the programme. One of the changes was the development of a partnership contract amongst the firm members. Early in the programme the contract was drawn up on a template, but the firms were asked to choose at least four values from a total of 31 that they would espouse in their workings with each other in the firm, and to insert these into the document. The document was then executed formally and witnessed by their Practice Manager, a member of staff. The values chosen by firms were tracked by staff. The most popular was *reliability*, with *work-life balance* second, and *integrity* and *quality* the third. What was interesting, however, was the next most popular constellation: *democracy*, *happiness*, *challenge* and *excellence*, particularly when balanced against the values that were unused by any agreement, namely *change*, *competition*, *freedom*, *friendships*, *independence*, *leadership*, *privacy* and *status* (Barton and Westwood 2011). When given the choice, students chose what must surely be regarded as a more Hutchesonian constellation of values.

The partnership agreement, formed and executed during the initial Foundation Course of the Diploma, was used in subsequent sessions with Practice Managers (staff who had been given special training to be coaches, rather than tutors, to the student firms). Students and Practice Managers found it a helpful document because it clarified the commitment the firm's members had made to themselves and to each other. It also functioned, in Gee's terms, as part of the 'affinity space' and, as such, contributed to the play of the aesthetic and the moral imagination precisely because it was part role-play, part reality, a mesocosmic area where learning was enhanced precisely because it took place neither in one zone nor the other entirely. In this sense the whole approach of the simulated firm environment, with its values chosen in part by students, replicates the situations of players in online games who choose their character – dwarf, elf, healer and warrior, for instance. The latest games are more sophisticated. In *The Secret World*, for example, players are not species-specific: they are given the choice of seven active and seven passive abilities, and reorganize these when they wish. As has often been observed, these games are powerful tools for imaginative play (Gee 2004; Juul 2005; Taylor 2006; de Freitas and Maharg 2011).

The partnership agreement and other tools also helped students to focus on the local as the ground of professional value – a process that is identified in at least some of the literature on professionalism as an important influence upon the development of ethical practice. Discussing the whole process by which the American Bar Foundation had developed its Model Rules for Professional Conduct, for instance, Schneyer argued against earlier critical theories about the provenance and significance of professional ethics codes, and for a view of the Model Rules as an instance of *de facto* law-making by a private group. He constructed what he termed 'professionalism-in-fact' – a matrix of common themes by which lawyers thought about the field of legal ethics – and sited this in the diversity and pluralism of lawyers' practices, arguing that the roots of lawyers' ethical preoccupations could be found in the circumstances of their particular practices.

The results of the changes, charted in 2005/2006 (Table 5.2 below), showed the significant improvement in student achievement. Compared against 2003/2004, the results of 2005/2006 showed fewer Legal Eagle and Friendly Society types of firms, a significant reduction in the number of Dysfunctional firms and a corresponding increase in the number of Learning Community firms. It is significant that the results of 2004/2005, the year when the interventions (including the partnership agreement) were being planned, broadly replicated the results of the previous year in type 1 and 4 firms. Since then, the 2005/2006 results have been maintained.

Table 5.2 Comparison of firm characteristics

	2003/2004 (N=51 firms)	2004/2005 (N=64 firms)	2005/2006 (N=66 firms)
Type 1 Learning Community	41%	42%	56%
Type 2 Legal Eagles	27%	14%	18%
Type 3 Friendly Society	20%	31%	18%
Type 4 Dysfunctional	12%	13%	8%

Source: Adapted from Barton and Westwood 2011.

Conclusion

In this chapter I have argued for situated forms of educational praxis as one way in which we can exercise the play of imagination and direct it towards some of the critical debates about professionalism in our society. It might be thought that professionalism is too narrow a concept for the expansive values of Hutcheson, Dewey and others I have cited in this chapter, and it is certainly the case that much of the literature is sited in variants of professional technicism. However, I would argue that as the ground of the professional classes, it requires recuperation and renewal along the lines set out in this chapter. The alternative, as Dzur and others point out, is the triumph of narrow technocratic definitions of the concept by those with powerful interests to affect legal education, such as regulators and policy makers.

As we have seen, the debate about an expansive version of professionalism is nothing new. It only appears new because we have forgotten the sense of the term's larger cultural, social and philosophical context – a context that we can appreciate in the discourse of Enlightenment critiques of social theory and praxis, where imagination, through aesthetic activity in everyday life, impels the moral sense.

In the forms of situated learning described above, students learn much more than the mere mechanics of professional practice. They also learn about their own developing associative life in a profession. The immersive group work of the virtual firm in SIMPLE becomes a microcosm, a sandbox for working practices, habits and attitudes that can function as a critique of legal practice. The affinity space of SIMPLE is a profound example of the use of technology as a form of education in the cause of democratic professionalism, advocated by Dewey, practised in his Laboratory School and throughout his work. It is also an educational initiative that attempts to go beyond text-focused heuristics by providing collaborative learning spaces that enable students to explore and engage in imaginative ways with identity, fitness, responsibility, decision-making, ethics and many other concepts vital to their learning of what it is to be fully professional.

References

Abel, R. 2003. *English Lawyers Between Market and State. The Politics of Professionalism*. Oxford: Oxford University Press.

Arendt, H. 1958. *The Human Condition*. Chicago: University of Chicago Press.

Barnett, R. 1994. *The Limits of Competence: Knowledge, Higher Education and Society*. Milton Keynes: Open University Press.

Barton, K. and Maharg, P. 2007. 'Simulations in the wild: interdisciplinary research, design and implementation', in C. Aldrich, D. Gibson and M. Prensky (eds), *Games and Simulations in Online Learning*. Hershey, PA: Idea Group Ltd, 115–48.

Barton, K. and Westwood, F. 2006. 'From student to trainee practitioner – a study of team working as a learning experience'. *Web Journal of Current Legal Issues*, special issue on Legal Education, edited by M. Spencer. Available at: http://webjcli.ncl.ac.uk/2006/issue3/barton-westwood3.html [accessed 22 August 2012].

Barton, K. and Westwood, F. 2011. 'Developing professional character – trust, values and learning', in P. Maharg and C. Maughan (eds), *Affect and Legal Education. Emotion in Learning and Teaching the Law*. Aldershot: Ashgate, 235–56.

Bevis, E.O. and Watson, J. 1990. *Towards a Caring Curriculum: A New Pedagogy for Nursing*. New York: National League for Nursing.

Biggs, J. 1999. 'What the student does: teaching for enhanced learning'. *Higher Education Research & Development*, 18(1), 57–75.

Boon, A., Flood, J. and Webb, J. 2005. 'Postmodern professions? The fragmentation of legal education and the legal profession'. *Journal of Law and Society*, 32(3), 473–92.

Boshuizen, H.P.A. and Schmidt, H.G. 1992. 'On the role of biomedical knowledge in clinical reasoning by experts, intermediates and novices'. *Cognitive Science*, 16, 153–84.

Brady, E. 2011. 'Adam Smith's "sympathetic imagination" and the aesthetic appreciation of environment'. *Journal of Scottish Philosophy*, 9(1), 95–109.

Breger, M.L., Calabrese, G.M. and Hughes, T.A. 2004. 'Teaching professionalism in context: insights from students, clients, adversaries and judges'. *South Carolina Law Review*, 55, 303–47.

Brown, V. 1994. *Adam Smith's Discourse: Canonicity, Commerce and Conscience*. London and New York: Routledge.

Brownell, A.K.W. and Côté, L. 2001. 'Senior residents' views on the meaning of professionalism, and how they learn about it'. *Academic Medicine*, 76(7), 734–7.

Cairns, J. 1992. 'The influence of Smith's jurisprudence on legal education in Scotland', in P. Jones and A.S. Skinner (ed.), *Adam Smith Reviewed*. Edinburgh: Edinburgh University Press, 168–89.

Darling, J. 1989. 'The moral teaching of Francis Hutcheson'. *Journal for Eighteenth-century Studies*, 12(2), 165–74.

De Freitas, S. and Maharg, P. 2011. 'Digital games and learning: modelling learning experiences in the digital age', in S. de Freitas and P. Maharg (eds), *Digital Games and Learning*. London: Continuum Press, 17–40.

Dewey, J. 1969–1972. *The Early Works of John Dewey, 1882–1898*, edited by J.A. Boydston. Carbondale, IL: Southern Illinois University Press.

Dewey, J. 1976–1983. *The Middle Works, 1899–1924*, edited by J.A. Boydston. Carbondale, IL: Southern Illinois University Press.

Dewey, J. 1981. *The Later Works, 1925–1953*, edited by J.A. Boydston. Carbondale, IL: Southern Illinois University Press.

Dubnick, M.J. 2010. *'A Moral Being is an Accountable Being': Adam Smith and the Ethical Foundations of Accountable Governance*. Paper presented at the 68th Annual Meeting of the Midwest Political Science Association, The Palmer House, Chicago, 22– 25 May 2010. Available at: http://mjdubnick.dubnick.net/papersrw/2010/mwsmith2010.pdf [accessed 22 August 2012].

Dzur, A.W. 2002. *Civic Participation in Professional Domains*. Paper delivered at the Annual Meeting of the American Political Science Association, Boston, August–September 2002. Available at: http://muse.jhu.edu/login?uri=/journals/good_society/v013/13.1dzur01.html [accessed 22 August 2012].

Eaton, D.M. and Cottrell, D. 1999. 'Structured teaching methods enhance skill acquisition but not problem-solving abilities: an evaluation of the "silent run through"'. *Medical Education*, 33(1), 19–23.
Eisner, E.W. 1985. *The Educational Imagination: On the Design and Evaluation of School Programs.* New York: Macmillan.
Ferguson, A. 1978. *Institutes of Moral Philosophy*. New York: Garland Publishing Company.
Feuer, L.S. 1958. 'John Dewey's reading at college'. *Journal of the History of Ideas*, 19(3), 415–21.
Flood, J. 2011. *Legal Education in the Global Context. Challenges from Globalization, Technology and Changes in Government Regulation.* Report for the Legal Services Board, University of Westminster School of Law Research Paper No. 11-16. Available at: http://papers.ssrn.com/sol3/papers.cfm?abstract_id=1906687 [accessed 1 September 2012].
Frank, V. et al. 2000. 'A survey of physician training programmes and communication skills for malpractice prevention'. *Journal of Law, Medicine and Ethics*, 28(3), 258–66.
Gee, J.P. 2004. *Situated Language and Learning. A Critique of Traditional Schooling*. New York and London, Routledge.
Ginsburg, S., Regehr, G., Hatala, R., McNaughton, N., Frohna, A., Hodges, B., Lingard, L. and Stern, D. 2000. 'Context, conflict, and resolution: a new conceptual framework for evaluating professionalism'. *Academic Medicine*, 75(10 Supplement), S6–11.
Ginsburg, S. and Stern, D. 2004. 'The professionalism movement: behaviours are the key to progress'. *American Journal of Bioethics*, 4(2), 1–14.
Gottsegen, M.G. 1994. *The Political Thought of Hannah Arendt*. New York: State University of New York Press.
Haakonssen, K. 1990. 'Natural law and moral realism: the Scottish synthesis', in M.A. Stewart (ed.), *Studies in the Philosophy of the Scottish Enlightenment*. Oxford: Clarendon Press, 61–85.
Harrison, J.R. 1995. 'Imagination and aesthetics in Adam Smith's epistemology and moral philosophy'. *Contributions to Political Economy*, 14, 91–112.
Hickson, G.B. et al. 1992. 'Factors that prompted families to file medical malpractice claims following perinatal injuries'. *Journal of the American Medical Association*, 267, 1359–63.
Hill, L. 2006. *The Passionate Society. The Social, Political and Moral Thought of Adam Ferguson*. Dordrecht: Springer.
Jackson, P. 1968. *Life in Classrooms*. New York: Holt, Rinehart and Winston.
Jenkins, H. 2006. *Convergence Culture. Where Old and New Media Collide*. New York and London: New York University Press.
Joas, H. 1985. *G.H. Mead. A Contemporary Re-Examination of His Thought*, translated by R. Meyer. Oxford: Polity Press.

Joas, H. 1997. 'George Herbert Mead and the renaissance of American pragmatism', in C. Camic (ed.), *Reclaiming the Sociological Classics. The State of the Scholarship.* Malden, MA: Wiley-Blackwell, 262–81.

Juul, J. 2005. *Half-Real. Video Games Between Real Rules and Fictional Worlds.* Cambridge, MA: MIT Press.

Kivy, P. 2003. *The Seventh Sense. Francis Hutcheson and Eighteenth-century British Aesthetics*, 2nd edn. Oxford: Clarendon Press.

Kneebone, R. et al. 2002. 'An innovative model for teaching and learning clinical procedures'. *Medical Education*, 36, 7, 628–34.

Larson, M. 1977. *The Rise of Professionalism: A Sociological Analysis*. Berkeley, CA: University of California Press.

Lesgold, A., Glaser, R., Rubinson, H., Klopfer, D., Feltovich, P. and Wang, Y. 1989. 'Expertise in a complex skill: diagnosing X-ray pictures', in M. Chi, R. Glaser and M. Farr (eds), *The Nature of Expertise*. Hillsdale, NJ: Lawrence Erlbaum, 311–42.

Leys, R. 1993. 'Mead's voices: imitation as foundation, or, the struggle against mimesis'. *Critical Inquiry*, 19(2), 277–307.

Maharg, P. 2004a. 'Virtual communities on the web: transactional learning and teaching', in A. Vedder (ed.), *Aan Het Werk met ICT in het Academisch Onderwijs*. Nijmegen: Wolf Legal Publishers, 75–93.

Maharg, P. 2004b. 'Professional legal education in Scotland'. *Georgia University State Law Review*, 20, 947–77.

Maharg, P. 2006. 'On the edge: imagining ICT and professional legal learning'. *Web Journal of Current Legal Issues*, special issue on Legal Education, edited by M. Spencer Available at: http://webjcli.ncl.ac.uk/2006/issue3/maharg3.html [accessed 22 August 2012].

Maharg, P. 2007. *Transforming Legal Education: Learning and Teaching the Law in the Early Twenty-First Century*. Aldershot: Ashgate.

Maharg, P. 2011. 'Affect and legal education', in P. Maharg and C. Maughan (eds), *Emotion in Learning and Teaching the Law*. Aldershot: Ashgate.

Barton, K., Garvey, J. and Maharg, P. 2012. '"You are here': learning law, practice and professionalism in the academy', in Z. Bańkowski, M. Del Mar and P. Maharg (eds), *The Arts and the Legal Academy*. Aldershot: Ashgate.

Maharg, P. and Owen, M. 2007. 'Simulations, learning and the metaverse: changing cultures in legal education'. *Journal of Information Law & Technology*, 1. Available at: http://www2.warwick.ac.uk/fac/soc/law/elj/jilt/2007_1/maharg_owen [accessed 22 August 2012].

Marshall, D. 1984. 'Adam Smith and the theatricality of moral sentiments'. *Critical Inquiry*, 10(4), 592–613.

Mautner, T. 1993. *Francis Hutcheson: Two Texts.* Cambridge: Cambridge University Press.

Mill, J.S. 1865. *An Examination of Sir William Rowan Hamilton's Philosophy*, 2 vols, Boston: William V. Spencer.

Nardi, B. and O'Day, V.L. 1999. *Information Ecologies. Using Technology with Heart.* Cambridge, MA: MIT Press.
Nelson, R. and Trubek, D. 1992. 'Arenas of professionalism: the professional ideologies of lawyers in context', in R. Nelson, D. Trubek and R. Solomon (eds), *Lawyers' Ideals/Lawyers Practices: Transformations in the American Legal Profession.* Ithaca, NY and London, Cornell University Press, 176–95.
Norton, D.F. 1976. 'Francis Hutcheson in America', in T. Besterman (ed.), *Studies on Voltaire and the Eighteenth Century*, 154, 1547–68.
Papadakis, M.A., Loeser, H. and Healy, K. 2004a. 'Early detection and evaluation of professionalism deficiencies in medical students'. *Academic Medicine*, 76(11), 1100–106.
Papadakis, M.A., Hodgson, C.S., Teherani, A.P.D. and Kohatsu, N.D. 2004b. 'Unprofessional behaviour in medical school is associated with subsequent disciplinary action by a state medical board'. *Academic Medicine*, 79(3), 244–79.
Pellegrino, E.D., Veatch, R.M. and Langan, J. (eds). 1991. *Ethics, Trust and the Professions.* Washington, DC: Georgetown University Press.
Schneyer, T. 1989. 'Professionalism as Bar politics: the making of the Model Rules of Professional Conduct'. *Law & Social Inquiry*, 14(4), 677–736.
Schwarz, M.R. and Wojtczak, A. 2002. 'Global minimum essential requirements: a road towards competence-oriented medical education'. *Medical Teacher*, 24(2), 125–9.
Selznick, P. (1992). *The Moral Commonwealth: Social Theory and the Promise of Community.* Berkeley, CA: University of California Press.
Sheridan, P. 2007. 'The metaphysical morality of Francis Hutcheson: a consideration of Hutcheson's critique of moral fitness theory'. *Sophia*, 46(3), 263–75.
Sleeper, R. 1986. *The Necessity of Pragmatism. John Dewey's Conception of Philosophy.* New Haven, CT and London: Yale University Press.
Smith, A. 1976. *The Theory of Moral Sentiments*, edited by D.D. Raphael and A.L. Macfie, 6th edn, *The Glasgow Edition of the Works and Correspondence of Adam Smith, Vol. 1.* Oxford: Oxford University Press.
Stenhouse, L. 1983. *Authority, Education, Emancipation.* London: Heinemann.
Stern, D. and Papadakis, M. 2006. 'The developing physician – becoming a professional'. *New England Journal of Medicine*, 354, 1794–9.
Stewart, D. 1854. *The Collected Works of Dugald Stewart*, edited by W. Hamilton. Edinburgh: Constable.
Stronach, I., Corbin, B., McNamara, O., Stark, S. and Warne, T. 2002. 'Towards an uncertain politics of professionalism: teacher and nurse identities in flux'. *Journal of Education Policy*, 17(1), 109–38.
Sullivan, W. 1995. *Work and Integrity. The Crisis and Promise of Professionalism in America*, 2nd edn. New York: John Wiley & Sons.
Tanner, L.N. 1997. *Dewey's Laboratory School. Lessons for Today.* New York and London: Teacher's College, Columbia University.

Taylor, T.L. 2006. *Play Between Worlds. Exploring Online Game Culture*. Cambridge, MA: MIT Press.

Taverner, D. et al. 2000. 'Comparison of methods for teaching clinical skills in assessing and managing drug-seeking patients'. *Medical Education*, 34(4), 285–91.

Toddington, S. 1996. 'The emperor's new skills: the academy, the profession and the idea of legal education', in P.B.H. Birks (ed.), *What are Law Schools For? Pressing Problems in the Law*, vol. 2. Oxford: Oxford University Press, 69–91.

Turco, L. 1999. 'Sympathy and moral sense: 1725–1740'. *British Journal for the History of Philosophy*, 7(1), 79–101.

Ward, I. 2002. 'The echo of a sentimental jurisprudence'. *Law and Critique*, 13(2), 107–205.

Webb, J. and Nicolson, D. 2005. 'Public rules and private values: fractured profession(alism)s and institutional ethics'. *International Journal of the Legal Profession*, 12(2), 165–72.

Wolf, F.M. and Turner, E.V. 1989. 'Congruence between student and instructor perceptions of clinical teaching in paediatrics'. *Medical Education*, 23(2), 161–7.

World Federation for Medical Education Task Force. 2000. 'Defining international standards in basic medical education. Report of a Working Party, Copenhagen'. *Medical Education*, 34(8), 665–75.

World Health Organization/Education Commission for Foreign Medical Graduates. 1995. 'Towards a global consensus on quality medical education: serving the needs of population and individuals'. Proceedings of the 1994 WHO/ ECFMG Consultation in Geneva, Switzerland. *Academic Medicine*, 70(7), Suppl.

Appendix 5.1

Table 5A.1 PEAT 1 Professionalism Learning Outcomes (Law Society of Scotland)

The full set of learning outcomes for PEAT 1 is available at http://www.lawscot.org.uk/media/39767/peat_1_guidelines_-_final.pdf.

Major domain	**1. Professionalism**		
Minor domain	*Throughout the programme, a student should demonstrate a commitment to:*	*Positive indicators*	*Appropriate forms of assessment*
1.	The interests of justice and democracy in society	Displays an interest in the workings of justice in society; has an ethical awareness of legal practice, and a developing sense of the regulatory framework of professional ethics. Shows awareness of his or her responsibility to improve the capacity of legal institutions and process.	Best assessed longitudinally throughout the programme, by more than one assessor and in more than one assessment, so that a variety of views are obtained under different conditions. Providers should be under an obligation to inform the Society of students who obtain problematic scores in any of the minor domains. Forms of assessment could include: Client-based long case Case file review of simulated client file Portfolio – self-assessment Log book/activity log/confidential file Critical incident review Peer review Transactional assessment Tutor reports
2.	Effective and competent legal services on behalf of a client	Updates and expands knowledge of the law, knowledge of legal practice, client-centred practice and management of client service. Pays careful attention to standard of detail in legal work; evaluates own client care; appraises new forms of client care and adopts improvements; acts quickly to protect clients and the public from risk.	
3.	Continuing professional education and personal development	Is aware of own strengths and weaknesses and forms plans to develop character, values, knowledge and skills throughout the course.	
4.	Diversity and public service	Shows an awareness of the importance of equality of access to and participation in legal services regardless of culture, race, religion, gender or disability; assists in the training of new lawyers through peer learning and training of undergraduate students or other groups in society.	
5.	Personal integrity and civility towards colleagues, clients and the courts	Is honest with all others on the course; relates to colleagues on the programme with civility; treats tutors, administrative staff and others with respect.	

Chapter 6

Challenging the Primacy of Text: The Role of the Visual in Legal Education[1]

Clare Sandford-Couch

Introduction

It has been suggested that 'western thought has traditionally conceived of images as inferior and deceptive substitutes for written communications' (Were 2005: 659). Arguably, this statement finds clear application in relation to legal education. Law is often seen, and indeed often presents itself, as an image-less, completely rational language, a text-based discourse. Most students, if asked, would probably tend to regard law as a text-based subject, referring to textbooks, statutes, case reports, etc. And yet the culture outside the ideal world of the legal text is relatively saturated with images (Wagner and Penack 2006). Arguably, in contemporary society, the dominant media or technology of communication is increasingly visual. Contemporary attitudes of and towards the law are often shaped by its representation in film and television. Rarely do these representations or images accord with the experiences of legal professionals or those engaging with law on an academic level.[2] Law students may well have absorbed these images of law and lawyers and have had their understanding both reflected and shaped by popular culture, without necessarily making a connection between such images and the written sources of law they meet in the course of their studies. Students today may engage more readily and more comprehensively with images, such as graphs and other visuals, than texts: 'They enhance the classroom experience for students that have grown up in a multi-media environment and seem to be less receptive to black and white text than former generations' (Berger-Walliser and Haapio 2010). There may be, inherent in the manner of much legal education,

---

1 Earlier versions of aspects of this chapter were delivered at the SLS Annual Conferences in 2010 and 2011. I am grateful to those participants at the conferences for their comments and suggestions, especially Fiona Cownie, who encouraged me to further research this area. I should also like to thank my PhD supervisor at the University of Edinburgh, Dr Claudia Bolgia, for her ongoing patience.

2 These issues, amongst many others, were explored by articles posted to 'Picturing Justice: The Online Journal of Law and Popular Culture', which ran from 1997 to 2006. Its archives are still accessible at http://usf.usfca.edu/pj/ [accessed 22 August 2012].

a disconnect between the impression of the law students gain from everyday life and from their studies.

Within the space available, this chapter aims to explore some of the reasons why legal education may be so resistant to the use of images, to consider some of the arguments in favour of doing so and to address possible examples of how this might be achieved. The first part attempts to consider some of the reasons why legal education generally does not make use of images and also offers possible reasons why it should. The next part considers some alternative approaches to a 'text-only' experience for students, looking at the role film and television may have to play in legal education, and exploring concepts of legal visualization and the use of digital games in learning. The subsequent part offers several case studies to explore how images have been incorporated in the law classroom. Finally, in the concluding part, I offer some suggestions as to how images could be relatively painlessly included into the early years of an undergraduate law degree. A study of the English legal system, for example, could provide a suitable forum to encourage students to go beyond text by considering what we can learn of the law from looking at legal architecture and the image of justice. In this chapter, I express the view that incorporating or referencing aspects of visual culture in legal education may encourage students to reflect critically upon legal and moral issues. Studying and unpacking images of justice, or of law, lawyers or lawyering, for example, may enable students more readily to explore complex notions such as the connection of law and society, or their understanding of the concepts of 'right' and 'wrong' and the moral dimension of law. Further, in utilizing the creative effects of intersections between law and visual culture, we may also acknowledge the role of imagination in learning, for 'imagination is that which allows us both to express and to understand ideas' (Warnock 1976: 72).

Why Legal Education Does Not Make Use of Images, and Why it Should

The packed curriculum of today's qualifying law degree and the increasing pressures upon providers of higher education mean that there are undoubted practical difficulties to taking such steps to encourage creative thinking in law students, such as increased staff workloads, or staff reluctance to change their teaching, or departmental reluctance to move away from tried-and-tested teaching methods; class sizes, contact time and the availability of suitable resources will also be contributory factors. These should also be considered in light of the difficulties one must acknowledge in attempting to engage with students' moral imagination; many would agree that 'a discussion of the moral content of law in a world in which religious and other metaphysical certainties are no longer so self-evidently persuasive is … an uphill struggle' (Gurnham 2009: 1).

In addition, perhaps the general reluctance to incorporate the visual into the teaching of law could be attributed to the legal education of our legal educators, which is likely to have been heavily text-based; alternatively, perhaps the reluctance may lie partly in a lack of confidence in their value as sources, and yet studies suggest that 'visual data does not have more problems to do with trustworthiness than does text-based data' (Cousins 2009: 213). Perhaps it may be attributable to a fear of the unknown: lawyers, legal academics and law students are so used to the primacy of text that the visual may seem to be at best a source of 'illustration' rather than 'explanation', but to see images only as ornaments to text-based sources is overly reductive. Images remain underused, despite the fact that they have intrinsic qualities which should make them a valuable resource in legal education: it appears that 'unlike language and writing, visual forms access parts of our brains which have been in gear since we appeared on the earth' (Cousins 2009: 214). Possibly for this reason, anthropology in particular has made extensive use of and conducted studies into visual sources of data, which suggest that thinking through images is a process that 'evidently relates to the way in which people formulate and shape concepts about their world' (Were 2005: 660): 'much of the way we learn – as well as the intuitive means by which we form conclusions or solve problems – involves thinking through images' (Were 2005: 659).[3] It would seem that these skills – to form conclusions and to solve problems – are of particular relevance to legal education. It is possible that the general reluctance to include images in legal education may in fact be failing to make use of a resource which could help students to learn.

Many studies have raised a concern that the ways in which we teach (and in many cases are possibly, because of financial considerations, constrained to teach) are not ones under which students flourish and learn to become active and independent learners.[4] When considering some of the desirable, even essential, skills required for 'self-learning, competent lawyers and citizens for life' – those whose reasoning abilities will promote 'courage, humility, curiosity, independence, stability, order, faith, fair-mindedness and other attributes of a responsible and wise citizenry', academics have identified analytic reading, conceptualizing, critical reasoning and energetic and creative thinking (Miller and Charles 2009–2010). It is perhaps this notion of creative thinking which may be of especial interest in relation to the arguments surrounding the use of images in legal education.

3 Perhaps judges seek to tap into this innate human ability to think through images, and the fact that images may well provoke a more emotional response than words alone could achieve, when their judgments involve an often quite lyrical verbal creation of an image. I am grateful to Geoffrey Samuel for this observation.

4 'University education in its widest sense is a whole-person process, where the focus is not so much on the teaching and learning of specific skills or training as it is on the cultivation of personal autonomy, intellectual independence and the development of life-long critical perspectives' (Sam Banks 1999).

A 2006 research report, *Facilitating Creativity in Higher Education: The Views of National Teaching Fellows*,[5] found that 'Most National Teaching Fellows believe that the capacity to be creative helps people to be successful and that developing students' creativity is important. Most National Teaching Fellows see creativity as a capacity that can be developed rather than as a rare gift' (Fryer 2006a). Given that the concept of 'creative thinking' is capable of many definitions, the survey suggested that 'the four aspects of creativity most congruent with the National Teaching Fellows' definitions of creativity are: "imagination", "seeing unusual connections", "original ideas" and "combining ideas"' (Fryer 2006a). Arguably, encouraging law students beyond traditional text-based sources may be more likely to lead to greater originality or the ability to forge unusual connections. And yet it would seem unreasonable to expect greater creativity of students if those involved in legal education are not prepared to similarly embrace greater creativity in teaching. Again, the views of National Teaching Fellows in the survey would appear to support this: 'creativity is integral to the self-identity of most NTFs and there is a widely held belief that creative teaching facilitates creative learning' (Fryer 2006a).

For if 'the mind is excited by the necessity to overcome obstacles in thinking' (Warnock 1976: 39), innovative teaching methods may provoke creativity in learning. When we consider how students learn, it seems that 'learning occurs when the student is confronted with something new or different from what they have known before' (Grantham 2005).[6] Further, it has been argued that 'the degree of brain activity is directly related to the level of stimulation in the learning environment' (Grantham 2005). Studies into positive impacts on student learning have suggested that most innovations have positive effects on student achievement (Hattie 2009). This evidence would propose that there may be benefits for those involved in legal education – both students and academics – through embracing the new or unexpected. This may also be the best means of developing the moral imagination of students, for in attempting to do so, we must appeal beyond intellectual responses alone; whilst legal texts may appeal to reason, images or aspects of visual culture may also appeal to the senses or the emotions. Encouraging refection on those responses may help to bridge the gap between intelligible thought and emotion, leading students towards a deeper, more nuanced understanding or appreciation of the moral aspects of the law. If one accepts the philosophical view that 'it is the representational power of the imagination, its power actually to form images, ideas or likenesses in the mind, which is supposed to contribute to our awareness of the world' (Warnock 1976: 33), it is at least arguable that the issue of incorporating images in legal education in

5 http://www.heacademy.ac.uk/resources/detail/resource_database/id589_facilitating_creativity_in_he_ntf_views [accessed 22 August 2012]. Now see also Fryer 2006b.

6 http://www.ukcle.ac.uk/resources/teaching-and-learning-practices/grantham2 [accessed 22 August 2012].

developing a wider engagement with legal and moral issues is worthy of further consideration.

Alternative Approaches to a 'Text-Only' Experience for Law Students

Suggestions to expand the horizons of legal education are legion, in the face of what many regard as an increasingly narrow technical, legal practice emphasis in legal education. Many current social, political and economic trends may have combined to produce a more systemic legal environment, and those factors may have also encouraged the same restrictions in the field of legal education (Slorach 2007). It is likely that the educational environment may well become more restrictive if current trends continue. As well as the increasing financial pressures facing higher education, legal education in particular is facing calls to include a study of legal ethics into the qualifying law degree syllabus to aid the development of more ethically aware legal practitioners. This has prompted criticism that it could be seen as taking a law degree a further step away from a liberal education.[7]

The view that it is time to see law as an interdisciplinary subject requiring an interdisciplinary approach taps into the debate surrounding the notion of a law degree forming part of a liberal education.[8] 'Contextualizing' law is capable of several meanings, but can generally be taken as attempts to set the law within a wider agenda, looking into historical, socio-economic and political considerations.[9] While this is not a novel approach – indeed, there is now perhaps a presumption that much legal education would attempt to encourage students into debate and analysis on issues falling outside the narrow scope of legal 'rules' – conceptualizing can be taken further in what can be termed 'law +' courses, which combine law with some other aspect of the humanities or social sciences. One example is the connections between law and literature;[10] even so, relatively few UK law schools offer law and literature as part of their law degree, a situation which may be attributable, at least in part, to a narrowing of focus. It would appear

7 Much has been written on the notion of a law degree as part of a liberal education, and the tensions between those advocating a narrower professional, skills-based focus as opposed to a broader conception of higher education; see, for example, Bradney and Cownie 1998; Maharg 2007; Bradney 2008; and http://www.transforming.org.uk [accessed 22 August 2012]. Further examples include, for the UK, Sam Banks 1999; and Boon and Webb 2008; for the USA, Miller and Charles 2009–2010; and for Australia, Kift 2008.

8 On interdisciplinarity, see, for example, Berard 2009. On law as part of a liberal education, see footnote 4 above.

9 For discussion of this point, see Twining 1997. See also entries on 'Law and Literature', 'Law and Film', 'Law and Television' in Cane and Conaghan 2008.

10 On law and literature, see, for example, Posner 2009. See also the journal *Law and Literature* by the Cardozo School of Law, Yeshiva University. For a discussion of the benefits of the study of literature for legal education, see Reichmann 2006 and Nussbaum 2006.

that even less has been done in the field of law and poetry (Lister 2007), say, or law and music (Levinson and Balkin 1991).

Film and Television

The primacy of the text has been challenged in some degree programmes which require students to engage with the debate on the representation of law in film and television.[11] Considering what can be learned of the law from how it looks has been explored in connection with political science; for example, at the University of Massachusetts, Amherst, a course in Political Science entitled 'Visualizing Law' addresses 'images in/and law' (Brigham 2007).[12] In the US, many university law degrees offer courses on law + film/television, and so address this nexus between law and image. In the Law School at Griffith University in Queensland, an elective course entitled 'Legal Fictions: Representations of Law in Cinema, Literature and Philosophy' investigated the ways in which the various images of law in high and popular culture depict, distort and critique the legal process and lawyers.[13] The course aimed to introduce students to a range of literary, cinematic, televisual and philosophical representations of the law in popular culture, and to equip law students with the necessary techniques of close textual analysis to enable them to 'read' a popular cultural text – whether film, TV or literature – as a kind of legal fiction and to enrich their understanding of both cultural studies and law, developing an interdisciplinary approach to their study. In the UK, the University of Greenwich offers a 'Law through Film and Literature' option to final-year students on its LLB (Honours) degree. Those running the course sought 'to show how law-related film and literature can be a useful tool in the legal classroom' (Pawlowski and Greer 2009: 49).[14] Student feedback indicated that many felt they had gained a wider perspective on law, lawyers and justice from the course (Pawlowski and Greer 2009: 60). The objectives of such courses would appear to address many of the concerns about the need to broaden legal education, and the possibilities of non-traditional sources to stimulate greater creativity in students.

In fact, it is possible to use film and television to explore the application of the law in an innovative way without necessarily making it the subject of an entire module or course. Some interesting work has been done on this. Many courses make reference to films such as *To Kill a Mockingbird* (Robert Mulligan, 1962), but one could expand this to include films such as *My Cousin Vinny* (Jonathan

11 The issue of law and film was the subject of *Journal of Law and Society*, March 2001, 28(1).

12 http://works.bepress.com/john_brigham/17/ [accessed 22 August 2012]. See also Van Belle and Mash 2010, which aims to introduce political science through books, movies and popular culture, and addresses courts and law through the same media.

13 Available at: http://www.griffith.edu.au [accessed 22 August 2012].

14 The emergence of law and film in the curricula of UK law schools was examined in Osborn 2001. See also Knowles 2008 on the role of video.

Lynn, 1992). There is an analysis of the number and variety of laws broken by Ferris Bueller in the 1986 film *Ferris Bueller's Day Off* (John Hughes, 1986);[15] colleagues at Northumbria University have encouraged students into a close analysis of the variety of legal issues raised throughout the film *Shrek* (Andrew Adamson, 2001) and, in a similar vein, students in one US law school conducted a mock trial of the Dr Seuss character Yertle the Turtle (Joseph 2000). Students at the University of Sheffield even produced a silent movie, *Mrs Carlill and her Carbolic Smokeball Capers.*[16]

Encouraging law students to engage with such images of law, lawyers and lawyering may act as a necessary corrective to the impressions gained from an unmediated consumption of these notions in popular culture, but may also act to stimulate learning; the more such images are incorporated into legal education, the more it may be possible to encourage a questioning attitude. In this way, incorporating aspects of visual culture into legal education could provide a means of encouraging critical thinking.

Legal Visualization

There may also be interesting possibilities in 'visualization', using 'visual communication tools to convey information in a way that makes the information easily accessible and understandable for the intended audience' (Haapio 2010). One possibility is perhaps to draw upon the stylings of comics and graphic novels. This is a notion which has been used in the field of medicine to explain medication or treatments in accessible form to patients and their families. There are a number of adult-themed graphic stories which address medically relevant themes and even an interdisciplinary conference on *Graphic Medicine: Visualizing the Stigma of Illness* (Williams 2011).[17] The medium of comics and graphic novels has also been used to share medical experiences; for example, a webcomic, *Mom's Cancer*, was intended by its creator, Brian Fies, to convey the experiences of his family following his mother's diagnosis and treatment in part to help their assimilation of their experiences, but also to share those experiences for the benefit of others.[18] His reasoning for doing so in comic form is interesting in the context of the discussion over the inclusion of images in legal education: 'something about the combination of one picture with a few words told more than either the picture or the words alone would have been able to'. At Northumbria University, the possibility of extending this use of an approach drawn from the comic strip or graphic novel into

15 Available at http://m.jezebel.com/5810927/the-criminal-lessons-of-ferris-bueller [accessed 22 August 2012].

16 Available at http://www.youtube.com/watch?v=ABZeKvAIyEc&feature=related [accessed 22 August 2012].

17 Available at http://graphicmedicine.org [accessed 22 August 2012].

18 Details of the webcomic and the interview with its creator are available at www.guardian.co.uk/science/blog/2010/jul/14/medical-comics-patients [accessed 22 August 2012].

legal education has been explored by students in the Student Law Office, which focuses on clinical legal education as part of an exempting degree programme, for example, deploying a comic-style format to offer prison inmates advice on their legal rights. The fact that the stories in many comics and graphic novels have as their sub-text a battle between good and evil or relate someone's struggle to achieve justice or to right some wrong may suggest that these formats could be particularly effective media for adaptation for use in legal education.[19]

Although visualization is a relatively new area, there are further possibilities of using it in relation to law; for example, it has been explored in connection with attempts to make contracts in business more readily understood (Berger-Walliser and Haapio 2010; Haapio 2010).[20] In Central Europe, visualizing legal information has developed into a research field in its own right.[21] The legal profession is also increasingly prepared to acknowledge and harness the power of visual rhetoric. Some have even argued that lawyers may face competitive disadvantage if they do not utilize the effect that visual tools may have on their audiences' perceptions, thoughts and emotions (New York Law School 2011).[22] One such example is the use, particularly in the US in personal injury cases, of 'Day-In-The-Life' films as victim impact evidence; a further example aims to improve client well-being by integrating multi-sensory law and therapeutic jurisprudence into lawyer/client relations (Brunschwig 2011);[23] another field is the use of strategic graphics and other visual communication tools in courts and other areas of legal practice to supplement traditional methods of legal reasoning (Hoogwater 2011).[24]

The notion of 'legal visualization' could be incorporated into education, drawing upon innovative and visual approaches to help explain or explore legal concepts, or make complex legal rules more accessible. The Visual Persuasion Project of the New York Law School has been exploring how to integrate new visual tools into more traditional legal approaches to legal analysis.[25] Encouraging visual literacy, or critical visual intelligence, could appeal to part of students' imaginations that may not have otherwise been engaged by their legal education,

---

19 There is a growing awareness of the possibilities offered by comics studies; for example, a conference on *Interdisciplinary Methodology: The Case of Comics Studies* was held in October 2011 at the University of Bern. A useful resource is the website run by Dr M. Gibson of Northumbria University: http://www.dr-mel-comics.co.uk [accessed 22 August 2012].

20 I should like to thank Helena Haapio for bringing to my notice several references in this area.

21 See, for example, the work of Dr Colette R. Brunschwig at the Legal Visualisation Unit of the Department of Law at the University of Zurich.

22 The 'Visual Persuasion Project' of New York Law School: www.nyls.edu/centers/projects/visual_persuasion [accessed 22 August 2012].

23 www.rwi.uzh.ch/oe/zrf/abtrv.html [accessed 22 August 2012].

24 www.legalvisuals.nl [accessed 22 August 2012].

25 www.nyls.edu/centers/projects/visual_persuasion [accessed 22 August 2012].

encouraging fresh insights, including greater critical engagement with legal and moral issues.

'Gamification'[26]

Another possibility for including visual culture into education may be that of 'gamification': the term, pithily described as 'as elegant as a teenager jawing a mouthful of bubble gum' (Corcoran 2010),[27] refers to a relatively new concept of using online gaming, social and location-based digital games and game-like mechanics and systems to increase engagement and motivation in teaching and learning (Annetta et al. 2006). Its proponents suggest that its advantages may include providing instantaneous feedback, encouraging competition and allowing for progress to be rewarded; the possibilities may be indicated by this response to an article on using gamification in education:

> What if kids were proud of their A's in school and they wanted to earn more of them because they'd unlock the next level? What if teachers could engage students in quests to study a chapter and unlock secrets instead of giving them boring homework? You would see completion of homework increase and just like a game they'd want to solve every problem and unlock every secret. I've been dreaming about this ever since I was a kid.[28]

However, there are certain drawbacks inherent in this approach, which are partly resource-based, but that are also due to the varying appeal of gaming to different student groups.

But while these are interesting possibilities, they do not address the fundamental fact that images should not need words to add depth. So, for this reason, I would suggest that while including film, television, etc. in legal education, or making use of comic strip-style formats are interesting and creative means of moving beyond the traditional text-based sources used in legal education, they may not go far enough. Text remains present, via the script or dialogue or even a soundtrack. Legal education should challenge students to attempt to move 'beyond text'.

---

26 For further discussion, see Annetta et al. 2006 and Oblinger 2006: www.educause.edu/EDUCAUSE+Quarterly/EQVolume292006/EDUCAUSEQuarterlyMagazineVolum/157419; De Freitas and Maharg 2011.

27 http://www.forbes.com/2010/10/28/education-internet-scratch-technology-gamification.html [accessed 22 August 2012]

28 Ibid.

Further 'Beyond Text'?

The 'Beyond Text in Legal Education' project sought to examine how the visual and movement arts could help in promoting the ethical imagination and creativity needed when law and lawyers encounter certain situations. Many scholars have commented on what has been termed a 'moral vacuum in the law curriculum'. How to integrate and encourage ethical awareness is of particular interest at Northumbria University, given its emphasis on clinical legal education. However, it is an area which may also be of wider interest, given the current thinking of professional bodies towards requiring an element of education on legal ethics to be an essential part of a qualifying law degree. The possibility of using the visual and movement arts to promote ethical imagination seems to resonate with the notion that the visual may connect with an emotional dimension that the text-based often does not; if 'images evoke deeper elements of human consciousness than do words' (Cousins 2009: 213), it is at least arguable that incorporating aspects of visual culture into legal education may help to develop awareness of an emotional or ethical dimension beyond that which text-based sources may reach. However, the 'Beyond Text in Legal Education' project envisaged consciousness-raising exercises taking place outside the law classroom, either in an art gallery or in a properly equipped open space. The question is whether it may be possible to extend a 'beyond text' approach to the law classroom, at least to some extent.

One possibility is to focus on the non-verbal aspects of law and lawyering. The Learning in Law Conference 2009 heard a paper from academics at the University of Warwick on how a 'critical issues in law and management' module had adopted an interdisciplinary approach to helping law and business students develop both their critical thinking and interpersonal skills. This involved, amongst other sessions, a 'presence and presentation' workshop by a theatre director/tutor which considered non-verbal communication and the reading of still images (Heron, Lambert and Palmer 2009).[29] Currently, the Law School at Northumbria is investigating collaborations with the University's Department of Performing Arts to look at the non-verbal aspects of law and lawyering, and to explore the possibilities of 'forum theatre' to enhance students' appreciation of the issues raised in certain famous trials.

Alternatively, one could consider the possibilities offered by a study of the connection between law and art. Sir Basil Markesinis sought to explore this in his extended essay *Good and Evil in Art and Law* (Markesinis 2007), which looked at how each area understood these notions. In part this was motivated by his concern that, in a time of increased and increasing demand for specialized knowledge, few students have the time to undertake wider reading, even where this could enhance their understanding of the law and society generally (Markesinis 2007: 7). However, it is noticeable that even he found more to discuss in connection with

29 www.ukcle.ac.uk/resources/teaching-and-learning-practices/palmer [accessed 22 August 2012].

literature than pictorial art. And yet there may be good reasons why incorporating artistic images into legal education may be a means of encouraging critical engagement with legal and moral issues; there is a view that imagination and understanding are made to work together when we look at a single object and concentrate on its form, how it looks (Warnock 1976: 48–9), which would suggest that the intersections between law and images should be further explored. Although comparatively little has been written on the interconnection of law and art, a key text is *Law and the Image: The Authority of Art and the Aesthetics of Law* (Douzinas and Nead 1999), which looked at the diverse relationships between law and the artistic image. The possibilities of connections between law and art were further explored in *Law and Art: Ethics, Aesthetics and Justice* (Ben-Dor 2011), where the intention was to take an interdisciplinary approach to address the relationship between law and art in many areas, including literature and poetry as well as film, theatre, music and fine art.[30] It suggested that the uneasy relationship which exists between art and law may be attributable at least in part to the increasing specialization of legal expertise. I would suggest that this in turn impacted upon legal education, leading to the primacy of the text we recognize today. Further, I would suggest, this is an unnecessary restriction on legal education and one which can be challenged. Markesinis criticized much interdisciplinary work for its failure to show 'in concrete terms and by means of specific examples how the study of one branch of intellectual creativity can aid the work of the others' (Markesinis 2007: 9). I will attempt to avoid such criticism by considering some examples of how images can be included in legal education.

Case Study: Teaching Students to Compare and Contrast Cases through Art

Recognition that some students may find visual comparisons easier than word or concept comparisons led one academic at New York Law School to use fine-art imagery to explain to first-year students how to compare and contrast cases. The method involved comparing and contrasting two portraits, and using this process to guide students through the similar process they undertake in relation to legal cases. Although not effective for all students, the exercise suggested that 'the use of art gives some students an ability to "see" what is happening in the law school classroom for the first time' (Gross 1999).[31]

Case Study: Teaching Property through Art

In the School of Law at Indiana University, William C. Bradford sought to expand his teaching methods by encouraging property law students to discuss their

30 The issues were also discussed in a symposium, *Law and Art: Ethics, Aesthetics and Justice*, 23 March 2010, Tate Modern, London.

31 http://lawteaching.org/lawteacher/1999fall/lawteacher1999fall.pdf [accessed 22 August 2012].

responses to an original piece of art created by his wife, a professional artist, as her interpretation of a seminal US case in property law (Bradford 2004).[32] The optional exercise went sufficiently well for him to commission his wife to produce paintings illustrating several further themes, cases and doctrines addressed by the syllabus. The student responses to the artworks and the teaching approach were enthusiastic, leading Bradford to conclude that the use of art to teach property was enhancing student interest and participation in their legal education; these impressions were largely confirmed by student feedback at the end of the semester. While he acknowledges his was not an exercise from which it is easy to draw general conclusions, it is interesting that some students saw the exercise as an opportunity to express their own ethical, moral and legal judgments.

Case Study: The Trials of Christ

In the context of specific examples, I should like to consider my experiences of using visual images in an undergraduate module of the trials of dissenters at Northumbria University.[33] The intention was not to explore the nexus of art and law; rather, it was to encourage active engagement with artistic images – painting, sculpture, photography, etc. – during legal education. In the module, students study the trials of those accused of various types of dissent; following a presentation which introduced the particular trial or type of dissent to be discussed, students are then encouraged to independently research the area to prepare and deliver their own presentations on their findings. In the context of a discussion of Christ as a religious or political dissenter, students were encouraged to consider how His trials had been represented in art and sculpture, and how they too could use artistic images in the context of that module. In the case of each image, students were encouraged to try to set it in its context: who commissioned it? When? Where? Why? What contemporary social, cultural or political factors could have influenced how the trials were depicted?

Clearly, few if any law students would have had any grounding in reading visual images.[34] However, I am not advocating that such an indepth approach is necessary; the quality of the visual analysis is almost immaterial. What the approach sought to achieve was to widen the scope of the students' appreciation of the trials they studied by encouraging them to access sources which might provoke new levels of understanding or enquiry. The aim was that this could be an

---

32 http://lawteaching.org/lawteacher/2004fall/lawteacher2004fall.pdf [accessed 22 August 2012].

33 This module has been developed by Sarah Barbour-Mercer and Chris Rogers, colleagues in the School of Law at Northumbria. The module and the feedback obtained from students are discussed in Mercer, Rogers and Sandford-Couch 2011.

34 For a grounding in visual theory, there are number of sources, including Mitchell 1986; Berger 1990; Barthes 1993; Mirzoeff 1998; Cartwright 2001; Manguel 2001; and Burnett 2005.

effective means of increasing or enhancing their understanding of the law and the legal process and its application to the trials of political and religious dissenters. In addition, a further aim was to try to encourage students to think beyond the usual sources. I think there is educational value in including images in their own right, but there may also be a parallel benefit, in that it may help students with the interpretation of other, possibly more traditional legal texts; the new experience of studying artistic images may provoke or stimulate new or unusual connections for the students. So, for this reason and to help students find a way into an approach many seemed to find challenging, simply because in many cases they had not encountered artistic images in the course of their legal studies previously, students were introduced to the notion that images of the trials could be read as a form of 'text' and thus subjected to a form of the type of close textual analysis with which they were already familiar. Comparing the visual interpretations of the trials of Christ could be helpful in making students aware of the need to contextualize their sources and, as with written texts, could reinforce the need for students to be alive to the possibilities of bias in those sources. By this means, studying images could also reinforce students' research skills. It was probably significant that the students realized that the many differing representations of the trials of Christ came from the same limited sources to which they had access – largely the Biblical accounts and two non-Christian accounts – and so the images were clearly the result of a process of interpretation. This may have encouraged an appreciation that a level of scepticism may be in order when using a source, which is a valuable lesson for those engaging in research. Hopefully, this type of awareness should inform their methodologies when undertaking larger-scale research projects, such as final-year dissertations.

There are many artistic treatments of the trials of Christ to which students could be referred.[35] For example, students addressed themselves to an image of a fourth-century Roman sarcophagus[36] and were encouraged to consider the impression they gained from the image of the trial faced by Christ before Pilate. The consensus among the students was that the scene appeared to depict an ordered, calm procedure. In fact, it appeared difficult to see who was on trial at first glance. The students noted that the judge, in this case Pontius Pilate, appeared to adopt an attitude of contemplation, entirely suitable for one in a judicial role. To raise the issue of context, or to alert the students to the possibility that this may be a biased impression, the students were made aware that the sarcophagus was commissioned by or for a Roman who had held a similar governmental position to Pilate. In addition, given the date, this was commissioned by or for an early Roman convert to what had previously been a persecuted religion – factors which could

35 The selected images referred to here are available online on Wikimedia Commons: http://commons.wikimedia.org/wiki/Category:Pictures_and_images, by searching under 'trials of Christ'.

36 Marble relief, 359, Rome. Column sarcophagus of Junius Bassus. *Christ is led before Pilate*.

lead students to consider whether this might have affected the style of depiction of the trial of Christ before Pilate.

Another image discussed was from a sixth-century illuminated manuscript, again of the trial before Pilate.[37] Students could note how the impression the artist sought to give was of a procedurally correct judicial hearing: there even appears to be a stenographer! But there were also differences from the previous image to note; for example, students were asked to consider the gestures of the surrounding crowd and the fact that Christ as the accused was guarded at sword-point. This was then contrasted with a fourteenth-century image from a chapel in Padua, northern Italy, which showed a different trial – that before the Jewish High Priests.[38] The impression given of the trial in this image could not be more different: in a chaotic and claustrophobically crowded room, the accused, bound and huddled, cowers from imminent physical attack and faces a judge, Caiaphas, who rends his clothing in a traditional gesture of anger. By offering the students a brief summary of the contemporary social and political background to the artwork, which addressed the impact of the Inquisition and a rise in anti-semitism in Italy at the time, the students were encouraged to consider what may have led the artist to depict the trial in this way or why his patron chose this trial to be depicted, as well as considering what impression they gained of the type of trial and the type of prisoner being depicted.

The approach revealed quite a lot about how initially reluctant law students seemed to be to engage with visual sources, and of the need to create an environment in which they feel sufficiently comfortable to offer their suggestions. What do I think the students learned? This is probably quite difficult to quantify. After their initial reluctance – subsequent feedback interviews suggested that they had felt what almost seemed to be 'culture shock' at having been asked to consider visual images when they had not previously addressed or thought of these in connection with the study of law – students seemed to engage with the approach. Interestingly, some students subsequently used visual images in their presentations in relation to other trials studied in the module (Mercer, Rogers and Sandford-Couch 2011). In addition, the approach served to encourage awareness in students of the wealth of sources available beyond written media when studying the law, legal systems, legal history, etc. I think this is important – it is too easy to see law and the legal process as a body of words, and to overlook the ways in which visual images can be seen to engage with legal norms, notions of justice and injustice, of right or wrong. Studying images may reveal these issues to students in different ways, including a moral or ethical dimension, encouraging discussion of the interconnectedness of law and society and increasing awareness of the moral aspects of law.

37 Rossano Gospels, c.550–575. Illumination, *Christ before Pilate*.

38 Giotto, *Christ before Caiaphas*, c.1306, Scrovegni Chapel, Padua.

Incorporating Images into Legal Education: Some Suggestions

However, some of the above examples are relatively limited in their application. What is needed, I think, is the incorporation of images, whether sculpture, painting or photography, into core elements of a qualifying law degree. If introduced in the early years of undergraduate study, students may more readily access and utilize images throughout their course of study. This may also help to alleviate the possible (over)emphasis in first-year courses on learning legal rules, or case method and analytical thinking which can stultify imagination and marginalize moral reasoning, as discussed in the essay by Randy Gordon in this volume (Gordon 2012). Perhaps, therefore, an introductory module on the English legal system could provide an ideal forum. Might students' appreciation of aspects of the legal profession, the role of the judiciary and juries and the civil and criminal justice systems, or their willingness to discuss the same, be enhanced by some form of visualization? This may inspire and encourage the development of their moral imagination and may provide them with skills they could take with them into legal practice; in addition, in a multimedia age, when many receive news and information from television and the Internet, an ability to reach a more nuanced appreciation of the images appearing onscreen may be seen as a valuable tool for life, not just legal education.

Legal Architecture

A possibility of referencing the visual in legal education is to look at legal architecture. Linda Mulcahy has done much work in this area, including her book *Legal Architecture*, which addresses how the environment of the trial can be seen as a physical expression of our relationship with the ideals of justice (Mulcahy 2010). In part, her motivation was to move away from what she describes as 'lawyers' obsession with the word' (Mulcahy 2010: 3). In her book, she explores how 'legal architecture can associate law with tradition and conservatism or can equally well symbolise a commitment to change and innovation'. Her aim was to 'explore what the use of space in the courthouse and courtroom tells us about the respect afforded to participants and the social order of the courthouse over time' (Mulcahy 2010: 5). Interestingly, given earlier comments about the increased and increasing specialization of law, she notes the gradual containment of the public and the increasing amount of space allocated to advocates. Such an approach could be utilized and adapted; for example, by encouraging students to locate images of courtrooms and courthouses – whether collected in person or from an Internet search – and to subject them to a visual analysis. The tutor could frame the discussion around certain set questions or could prefer to encourage students to offer their own critiques. At Northumbria, students in the first year of an undergraduate law degree are expected in their own time, and in a location of their choosing, to undertake a court visit and to prepare a report on their visit, addressing certain questions. Many students comment without prompting upon the clothing or postures of those in the court, or the room layout, and it should then be possible by the nature of follow-up questions to encourage students to consider in greater detail the implications of not only the court proceedings but also their visual impressions.

Image of Justice – Justitia

A further possibility is a visual analysis of the image of Justice. Much interesting work has been done in relation to the image of Justice, for example, by US academics Judith Resnik and Dennis Curtis (Curtis and Resnik 1987; Resnik and Curtis 2011). It is unlikely that many law courses do not include some consideration of the image of Justice, but possibly more could be drawn from the image. For the purposes of legal education, students may find conducting a visual analysis of the image of justice a relatively painless introduction to the notion of referring to images, as well as to certain fundamental legal concepts, including the evolving relationship between law and morality.

The image of Justice from the Old Bailey in London seems to offer all the attributes one would expect of such an image.[39] By encouraging students to visually analyse the image, it may be possible to encourage discussion about the principles or values underpinning a justice system. One could, for example, consider its location, a point which could be further explored by looking at the use of images of justice in other locations. Alternatively, worthy of reflection with or by students is how far the representation of Justice as a woman is emblematic of our current justice system; this may raise many interesting questions. The attribute of the sword is also capable of analysis. In the Old Bailey image, for example, the sword is raised and unsheathed, which could be interpreted as Justice ready to act in the interests of society. It is double-edged, traditionally supposed to symbolize the power of Reason and Justice. Yet, the raised sword also carries with it the unspoken implication that justice must be prepared to administer punishment. Perhaps this implicit threat of violence inherent in the image is often overlooked, but it remains nonetheless. One could compare this to other, older images of justice, which make this aspect more explicit, and consider why that might be so.[40]

Moreover, one could compare such images with those where the sword is either non-existent or hidden, or where the sword points towards the ground; might these images offer differing meanings of the contemporary notion of justice? Alternatively, one could visually analyse an image which shows justice not only as

39 Frederick William Pomeroy (1900–1907), *Justice*, Old Bailey, London.

40 For example, one might consider *Ambrogio Lorenzetti, Distributive Justice, detail of The Good Government*, 1337–1340, fresco, north wall, Sala dei Nove, Palazzo Pubblico, Siena, a complicated allegory in which justice is revealed using the sword to decapitate a wrongdoer.

incorporating punishment via the sword but also a concept of reward.[41] As we seem to have lost the notion of reward as the counterpoint to punishment in contemporary interpretations of the image of justice, this may require students to engage their moral imagination to discuss interesting questions on the interrelationship of right and wrong or what society expects of its citizens. In this way, an older image may also possibly reveal something of our contemporary notion of justice.

Another aspect of the justice imagery – the scales or balance – offers much scope for unpacking the image. The link between justice and a balance is an old one – it can be traced back at least as far as the ancient Egyptian goddess Ma'at – and yet this attribute of Justice goes to the heart of how images can be seen to engage with legal norms. For the purposes of legal education, this could encourage students to engage with notions of justice and injustice, or right and wrong. So, for example, that the scales are empty may suggest that Justice is ready to serve society, for example; it also carries an implication of impartiality. Similarly, the scales held in equilibrium can convey a potent statement of the underlying values of a justice system: that all who appear before Justice will receive a fair trial, each case being judged on its merits. Through these features, the image carries meaning, indicative of the understanding of the contemporary notion of justice in a society. However, a discrepancy in the angle of the pans of the scales could convey a substantially different meaning. This type of analysis can lead students to discussions on the nature of justice operative where and when the image was created or more specifically as revealing contemporary perceptions of the state of the justice system. Alternatively, taking another angle, what does the fact that the image of Justice is blindfolded convey? This could suggest a reassuringly principled message of impartiality (Jay 1999: 24), but could the lack of sight seem to be a negative quality? Many earlier images of the personification of Justice do not feature a blindfold,[42] and the Old Bailey Justice similarly lacks this feature. When did this change occur? And, a question of more possibly interest to those teaching law students, why?[43]

Putting these attributes together in one image conveys a powerful message. Clearly, the image of Justice can play an active role in propagandizing for a particular viewpoint; for example, as in a six-metre statue of Justice erected on Clerkenwell Green, London, which wore thigh-high boots and a gown, open to the waist, revealing a thong and a garter with a dollar bill. Its presumed creator, Banksy, described it as 'the most honest depiction of British justice currently on

41 Ambrogio Lorenzetti, *Distributive Justice, detail of The Good Government*, 1337–1340, fresco, north wall, Sala dei Nove, Palazzo Pubblico, Siena, where justice uses the sword to decapitate a wrongdoer but simultaneously places a crown on the head of another individual.

42 See, for example, Giotto di Bondone, *Justitia* c.1306, fresco, south wall, Scrovegni Chapel, Padua.

43 Discussed in Jay 1999.

display in the capital' (BBC 2009).[44] The reception of an image can also reveal contemporary attitudes to the notion of law and justice; the Banksy image was removed within days by the local authorities. Also, if an image is attacked or defaced, the specific nature of the graffiti can be revealing. When a fourteenth-century image of justice was defaced, the images of those receiving punishment were attacked, while the personification of Justice remained intact.[45] Compare this to the obliteration of the face of Saddam Hussein depicted as the personification of Justice to reveal more modern views of the notion of justice prevalent in a society.[46]

Much like changing the wording of a document, a change to the iconography of an image can convey a significantly different meaning. It may be possible to encourage law students to discuss whether such significant and intentional changes in iconography can be linked to the ideology of the period – whether the change in iconography was prompted by changes in society, which in turn influenced what that society sought from its justice system. In this sense, images of justice may actively engage with socio-political and socio-legal issues; so, in this way, the image of Justice may convey to law students as much about expectations of a justice system and its relationship to a society as any other legal text. Imaginative engagement with the image can lead to a critical engagement with legal and moral issues. A simple Internet search can reveal many images of justice, both ancient and modern, for use in legal education.[47] Encouraging students to study the image of justice, or other images or aspects of visual culture, could be as useful as many texts to improve or enhance students' perception of the law and how legal systems work. Situating artworks, or other images or aspects of visual culture like film or TV, plays, graphic novels or comics, photographs, drawings or plans, in their wider context can be revealing of the society and the times in which they were created; this in turn could help to develop critical awareness and moral imagination in law students. By accessing visual culture, students could be encouraged towards a more nuanced, multi-layered appreciation of the law – developing their critical awareness of the possibility of a 'disconnect' between the 'ideal, textual world of law' and the world outside (Wagner and Pencack 2006: 269), offering a different perspective for understanding the interrelationship of law with a society's culture and beliefs or to encourage a greater awareness of the connection between law and society, or social values, or people's perceptions of the justice on offer. Visual analysis could be a means of encouraging students to engage with what are relatively complex concepts.

---

44 BBC 2009.

45 Giotto di Bondone, *Justitia* c.1306, fresco, south wall, Scrovegni Chapel, Padua.

46 *New York Times*, 27 April 2003. Photograph: *Mural of Saddam Hussein with the Scales of Justice*.

47 Copyright-free images can be accessed from certain databases, including Corbis Images, Google Images, Creative Commons, Flikr, etc.

Conclusions

Although the educational environment may become more restrictive if current trends continue, that does not mean the notion of encouraging greater creativity or expanding horizons in legal education should be abandoned. Those in legal education should not be afraid to cross or challenge disciplinary boundaries and explore new areas of enquiry. Encouraging law students beyond traditional text-based sources could lead to greater creativity or the ability to forge unusual connections. Referencing or studying artistic images may improve or enhance students' perception of the law and how legal systems work, offering a different perspective for understanding the interrelationship of law with ideology, culture and society. In utilizing the creative effects of intersections between law and culture, for example, we may also acknowledge the role of imagination in learning. Mary Warnock discussed a concept of imagination as 'that which creates mental images' (Warnock 1976: 10); incorporating some level of visual imagery may provide a possible means of encouraging law students out of their comfort zone of text towards more creative and imaginative thinking by accessing new sources and aspects of visual culture. The inclusion of the visual in legal education may benefit students, particularly those who prefer graphic to text-based material or whose learning style responds more readily to the visual (Bradford 2004; Grantham 2005); and perhaps at a time when there are concerns over the literacy and language skills of many students, greater engagement with visual sources would appear to be of increased relevance. It may also meet at least some of the concerns raised about the increasingly specialized direction in which legal education seems to be moving: an interdisciplinary approach connecting law with the liberal arts could help develop students' appreciation of and skill with language and broaden their cultural awareness; imaginative engagement with the arts and humanities could enhance legal education. If 'lawyers are trained to be good with words, not pictures' (Wagner and Pencack 2006: 269), now may be the time to challenge why that should be so, when there appear to be so many reasons why legal education should be prepared to adapt to and embrace the opportunities offered by the visual.

References

Annetta, L. et al. 2006. 'Serious games: incorporating video games in the classroom'. *Educause Quarterly*, 29(3), 16–22. Available at: http://www.educause.edu/EDUCAUSE+Quarterly/EQVolume292006/EDUCAUSEQuarterlyMagazineVolum/157419 [accessed 22 August 2012].

Barthes, R. 1993. *Camera Lucida: Reflections on Photography*. London: Vintage.

BBC. 2009. 'Guerilla artist in statue stunt', 4 August. Available at: http://news.bbc.co.uk/1/hi/3537136.stm [accessed 22 August 2012].

Ben-Dor, O. (ed.). 2011. *Law and Art: Ethics, Aesthetics and Justice*. London: Routledge-Cavendish.
Berard, T.J. 2009. 'The relevance of the social sciences for legal education'. *Legal Education Review*, 19, 189–216.
Berger, J. 1990. *Ways of Seeing*. London: Penguin.
Berger-Walliser, G. and Haapio, H. 2010. *Promoting Business Success through Proactive Contracting and Visualization*, paper to the Academy of Legal Studies in Business (ALSB) Conference: 2010 Annual Conference, Richmond, Virginia, 5 August.
Boon, A. and Webb, J. 2008. 'Legal education and training in England and Wales: back to the future?' *Journal of Legal Education*, 58, 79–121.
Bradford, W.C. 2004. 'Reaching the visual learner: teaching property through art'. *The Law Teacher*, Fall 2004, 12–13. Available at: http://lawteaching.org/lawteacher/2004fall/lawteacher2004fall.pdf [accessed 22 August 2012].
Bradney, A. 2008. 'Elite values in twenty-first century UK law schools'. *The Law Teacher*, 42, 291–301.
Bradney, A. and Cownie, F. 1998. *Transformative Visions of Legal Education*. Oxford: Blackwell.
Brigham, J. 2007. 'Visualizing law'. Available at: http://works.bepress.com/john_brigham/17/ [accessed 22 August 2012].
Brunschwig, C. 2011. 'Enhancing client well-being, integrating multisensory law and therapeutic jurisprudence'. Available at: http://www.rwi.uzh.ch/oe/zrf/abtrv/brunschwig/NYpresentation2009 [accessed 22 August 2012].
Burnett, R. 2005. *How Images Think*. Cambridge, MA: MIT Press.
Cane, P. and Conaghan, J. (eds). 2008. *The Oxford Companion to Law*. Oxford: Oxford University Press.
Cartwright, L. 2001. *Practices of Looking: An Introduction to Visual Culture*. Oxford: Oxford University Press.
Corcoran, E. 2010. 'The "gamification" of education'. Available at: http://www.forbes.com/2010/10/28/education-internet-scratch-technology-gamification.html [accessed 22 August 2012].
Cousins, G. 2009. *Researching Learning in Higher Education*. London: Routledge.
Curtis, D. and Resnik, J. 1987. 'Images of justice'. *Yale Law Journal*, 96(8), 1727–72.
De Freitas, S. and Maharg, P. (eds). 2011. *Digital Games and Learning*. London: Continuum.
Douzinas, C. and Nead, L. 1999. *Law and the Image: The Authority of Art and the Aesthetics of Law*. Chicago: University of Chicago Press.
Fryer, M. 2006a. 'Facilitating creativity in higher education: the views of National Teaching Fellows'. Higher Education Academy. Available at: http://www.heacademy.ac.uk/resources/detail/resource_database/id589_facilitating_creativity_in_he_ntf_views [accessed 22 August 2012].

Fryer, M. 2006b. 'Facilitating creativity in higher education: a brief account of National Teaching Fellows' views', in N.J. Jackson et al. (eds), *Developing Creativity in Higher Education: An Imaginative Curriculum*. London: Routledge-Falmer.

Gordon, R. 2012. 'Truth in context: sketching a (new) historicist legal pedagogy', Chapter 8, this volume.

Grantham, D. 2005. *Understanding Student Learning Styles and Theories of Learning*, paper presented at the UK Centre for Legal Education event on enhancing academic practice. Available at: http://www.ukcle.ac.uk/resources/teaching-and-learning-practices/grantham2 [accessed 22 August 2012].

Gross, K. 1999. 'Visual imagery and law teaching'. *The Law Teacher*, 7(1), 8. Available at: http://lawteaching.org/lawteacher/1999fall/lawteacher1999fall.pdf [accessed 22 August 2012].

Gurnham, D. 2009. *Memory, Imagination, Justice: Intersections of Law and Literature*. Aldershot: Ashgate.

Haapio, H. 2010. 'Visualising contracts and legal rules for greater clarity'. *The Law Teacher*, 44(3), 391–4.

Hattie, J. 2009. *Visible Learning; A Synthesis of Over 800 Meta-analyses Relating to Achievement.* London: Routledge.

Heron, J., Lambert, C. and Palmer, G. 2009. *Helping Law Students via Spaces and Performance*, paper presented to the Learning in Law Annual Conference: Concepts of Culture in Legal Education, University of Warwick, 23–4 January. Available at: http://www.ukcle.ac.uk/resources/teaching-and-learning-practices/palmer [accessed 22 August 2012].

Hoogwater, S. 'Legal visuals'. Available at: http://www.legalvisuals.nl [accessed 22 August 2012].

Jay, M. 1999. 'Must justice be blind? The challenge of images to the law', in C. Douzinas and L. Nead (eds), *Law and the Image: The Authority of Art and the Aesthetics of Law*. Chicago: University of Chicago Press, 19–35.

Joseph, P.R. 2000. 'Law and pop culture: teaching and learning about law using images from popular culture'. *Social Education*, 64(4), 206–11. Available at: http://m.jezebel.com/5810927/the-criminal-lessons-of-ferris-bueller [accessed 22 August 2012].

Kift, S. 2008. '21st century climate for change: curriculum design for quality learning engagement in law'. *Legal Education Review*, 18, 1–30.

Knowles, H.J. 2008. 'Cases, costumes, and civil concepts'. *Journal of Legal Education*, 58(2), 290–311.

Levinson, S. and Balkin, J.M. 1991. 'Law, music and other performing arts'. *University of Pennsylvania Law Review*, 139, 1597.

Lister, R. 2007. *Law and Literature and the LLB: An Apology for Poetry in the Curriculum*, Learning in Law Annual Conference, 4–5 January, University of Warwick.

Maharg, P. 2007. *Transforming Legal Education: Learning and Teaching in the Early Twenty-First Century*. Aldershot: Ashgate.

Manguel, A. 2001. *Reading Pictures: A History of Love and Hate*. London: Bloomsbury.
Markesinis, B.S. 2007. *Good and Evil in Art and Law: An Extended Essay.* Vienna: Springer.
Mercer, S., Rogers, C. and Sandford-Couch, C. July 2011. 'Teaching dissent in the law school: have students learned to disagree?' *Liverpool Law Review*, 32(2), 135–48. Available at: http://www.springerlink.com/openurl.asp?genre=article&id=doi:10.1007/s10991-011-9094-0 [accessed 22 August 2012].
Miller, N. and Charles, B. 2009–2010. 'Meeting the Carnegie Report's challenge to make legal analysis explicit – subsidiary skills to the IRAC framework'. *Journal of Legal Education*, 59, 192–220.
Mirzoeff, N. 1998. 'The subject of visual culture', in N. Mirzoeff (ed.), *The Visual Culture Reader*, 2nd edn. London: Routledge, 3–23.
Mitchell, W.J.T. 1986. *Iconology: Image, Text, Ideology*. Chicago: University of Chicago Press.
Mulcahy, L. 2010. *Legal Architecture.* London: Routledge.
New York Law School. 2011. *Visual Persuasion Project.* Available at: http://www.nyls.edu/centers/projects/visual_persuasion [accessed 22 August 2012].
Nussbaum, M. 2006. 'Reply to Amnon Reichmann'. *Journal of Legal Education*, 56(2), 320–29.
Oblinger, D. 2006. 'Games and learning'. *Educause Quarterly*, 29(3), 5–7. Available at: http://www.educause.edu/EDUCAUSE+Quarterly/EQVolume292006/EDUCAUSEQuarterlyMagazineVolum/157419 [accessed 22 August 2012].
Osborn, G. 2001. 'Borders and boundaries: locating the law in film'. *Journal of Law and Society*, 28(1), 164–75.
Pawlowski, M. and Greer, S. 2009. 'Film and literature in the legal classroom'. *The Law Teacher*, 43(1), 49–61.
Posner, R.A. 2009. *Law and Literature*, 3rd edn. Cambridge, MA: Harvard University Press.
Reichmann, A. 2006. 'Law, literature and empathy: between withholding and reserving judgment'. *Journal of Legal Education*, 56(2), 296–319.
Resnik, J. and Curtis, D. 2011. *Representing Justice: Invention, Controversy, and Rights in City-States and Democratic Courtrooms.* New Haven, CT: Yale University Press.
Sam Banks, N.K. 1999. 'Pedagogy and ideology: teaching law as if it matters'. *Legal Studies*, 19(4), 445–67.
Slorach, S. 2007. *Breaking the System? Creativity in Contemporary Legal Education*, Learning in Law Annual Conference, 4–5 January, University of Warwick.
Sturken, M. and Cartwright, L. 2001. *Practices of Looking: An Introduction to Visual Culture*. Oxford: Oxford University Press.
Twining, W. 1997. *Law in Context: Enlarging a Discipline*. Oxford: Clarendon Press.

Van Belle, D.A. and Mash, K.M. 2010. *A Novel Approach to Politics*. Washington, DC: CQ Press.

Wagner, A. and Pencack, W. 2006. *Images in Law.* Aldershot: Ashgate.

Warnock, M. 1976. *Imagination.* London: Faber & Faber.

Were, G. 2005. 'Thinking through images; *Kastom* and the coming of the Baha'is to northern New Ireland, Papua New Guinea'. *Journal of the Royal Anthropological Institute*, 11(4), 659–76.

Williams, I. 2011. *Graphic Medicine.* Available at: http://graphicmedicine.org [accessed 22 August 2012].

Chapter 7
Twyla Tharp Goes to Law School: On the Use of the Visual and Performing Arts in Professional Education

Thomas Wm. Mayo[1]

> Everything is raw material. Everything is relevant. Everything is usable.
>
> (Tharp 2003: 10)

Introduction

It was the beginning of our first class on euthanasia in my fall-semester 'Bioethics and Law' class, and I had passed out 'My Death', an arresting poem by Raymond Carver (Carver 1998: 122), as a discussion-starter. A third-year law student who had recently completed a summer clerkship with a small firm in Dallas spoke up: 'I get this whole "medicine is both an art and a science" thing, but what does art have to do with law? I've seen the practice of law: it's just plumbing.'

Setting aside the question of whether the student was being unfair to plumbers, his comment seemed to embody a dramatic failure – on his part or that of his teachers (or both) – a failure to understand the creative demands and possibilities within the practice of law. The same might be said about the teaching of it, as well, that the legal academy typically defines the enterprise in an excessively narrow and instrumentalist fashion that too often overlooks or diminishes the art of the practice of law.

My personal response to this perceived deficiency was to create a course that is currently taught under the title of 'Law, Literature, and Medicine'. It is designed for third-year law students and fourth-year medical students in their last semester of professional training. The course consists of 14 weeks of reading novels, plays, shorts stories and lots of poems. It concludes with the students creating works

---

1 I owe special thanks to Maksymilian Del Mar, Zenon Bańkowski and all the participants in the various workshops whose enthusiasm for the 'Beyond Text in Legal Education' project inspired me to probe the theoretical assumptions implicit in my teaching. I am also indebted to the research support of three law students at the SMU/Dedman School of Law: Virginia Welch '11, Jessica Edwards '12 and Meg Friess '12. I also thank the *Drexel Law Review* for their permission to use my description of an earlier version of 'Law, Literature and Medicine' as the basis for the description of the 2012 edition that appears here (Bard, Mayo and Tovino 2009).

of art for their final projects. This chapter is an attempt to describe exactly what we do in the course and, more importantly, why reading Shakespeare, Dickinson and Irving may make them better, more effective and happier lawyers (and physicians).

Two disclaimers are necessary at the outset. 'Beyond Text' may seem precisely the wrong rubric under which to consider a course that consists of almost nothing but texts, to which I offer two responses. My reading of 'Beyond Text' comes somewhat closer to 'Beyond [Traditional Legal] Text[s]', which opens up a world of fiction and poetry for our consideration. Moreover, the final projects that are described in greater detail below typically include, in addition to *texts*, paintings, sculptures, mosaics, weavings, photography, music and dance. These projects are not merely the last activities of the semester for these students; they are, for reasons I hope to make clear, the most important ones.

In addition, my reasons for offering such a course as 'Law, Literature and Medicine' do not rest upon assumptions as to whether any law-school or medical-school course is capable of improving the moral capabilities of their students. There is deep scepticism within the academy (and possibly in the world at large) that any such thing is possible, although developments in the field of moral psychology may provide a basis for some hope (Hamilton and Monson 2011). This is not a debate that will soon be resolved, and any claim that literature specifically or the arts in general can be useful in this regard adds a degree of difficulty that will make resolution in our lifetime even less likely.

Instead, the learning that occurs in 'Law, Literature and Medicine', and possibly beyond the course into the students' practising careers, turns on the importance of *empathy* in the learning and practice of law.[2] Exactly what I mean by this will take some development, but, as will become clear, my use of the word is an admittedly broad one. In brief outline, my theory for this course rests upon three propositions:

1. Empathy, broadly construed, is an important professional trait.
2. Law students, through their encounters with literature and the arts, can learn to model empathy.
3. Through an iterative process of encountering the arts in a professionally significant context, the empathic abilities of law students can be enhanced.

In the following section, I describe the 'Law, Literature and Medicine' course in some detail, with commentary on some of the more valuable aspects of various assigned readings. I will then go on to discuss the three propositions above, with particular emphasis being placed upon the broad range of artistic endeavours represented by the students' final projects.

---

2 I believe the same claim may be made for medical students and their development as practitioners after their formal training is over, but considering the focus of the larger work of which this chapter is a part, and for the sake of simplicity, the theory and claims that follow focus on the learning and practice of law.

Law, Literature and Medicine

'Law, Literature and Medicine' is advertised as a course about 'professionalism', although from the course 'Prospectus' (Mayo 2011), it should be clear that its focus is considerably broader than the traditional professional-school courses in 'professional responsibility', 'medical jurisprudence' or 'medical ethics':

- As much as anything, this course is about professionalism. Students will learn some important things about professionalism and about the profession they are about to enter. More specifically, the goals of this course include:
- to give future lawyers and doctors some insight into one another's profession, as well as to give them a chance to develop their own ways of talking to one another;
- to give each group a chance to gain insight into their own profession's values by taking a look at another profession;
- to introduce students to the study of literature as a way of gaining exposure to human experience and the ethical dilemmas of daily practice through the writings of master story-tellers;
- to underline the importance of a humane and humanistic professional education and outlook – to develop students' sensitivity to the human dimension of their professional lives;
- to introduce students to the notion that most of the information they will deal with in their professional lives is organized and transmitted in narrative form – judicial opinions, client and patient stories (in the form of complaints, histories, etc.), and practical clinical information (what worked the last time it was tried – in court or with a type of patient). In that vein, it is useful for students to sharpen their narrative skills by reading and discussing great stories; and
- to introduce students to a form of professional, case-based moral reasoning that resembles casuistry (as distinct from the dominant traditions of reasoning from first principles (deontology), consequentialism, and virtue ethics). We will consider the strengths and weaknesses of this approach through a variety of literary sources.

Mechanics

The hand-shake Each class begins with everyone walking around the seminar room, shaking everyone else's hand and exchanging greetings. Early in the semester, names are recalled. The past week may be briefly reviewed, or the next week previewed. I believe in the power of personal touch. It helps to break down barriers and facilitate mutual respect. It burns a few minutes of precious class time, but if it is good enough for the justices of the Supreme Court of the United States,[3] it is good enough for the participants in 'Law, Literature and Medicine'.

---

3 'Five minutes before conference time, 09:30 A.M. or 10:00 A.M., the Justices are summoned. They exchange ritual handshakes and settle down at the long table' (Supreme Court Historical Society 2012).

So far, no one has objected on the grounds that it is also an effective vector for the spreading of infectious disease.

Law-medical student pairings Throughout the semester, students choose readings for which they volunteer to lead one hour of class discussion. For most assignments, this means reading a 40-to-50-page segment from one of our anthologies and selecting five or six readings for class discussion. On the first day of class, the students are asked to volunteer for two or three such assignments. One medical student pairs with one law student and every effort is made to avoid pairing the same students twice. The result of this requirement is that law and medical students spend hours outside of class discussing the readings for their weeks, expressing their preferences and smoothing out their differences. If they are doing this right, they work out goals for the class and strategies for achieving those goals that are mutually acceptable. Then, of course, they get to lead the discussion as a team. They will be working in teams for the rest of their lives, some as small as the two-person student pairs, some as large as the 20-student seminar. For our 14 weeks together, the students have many opportunities to deal with group dynamics.

Journals Most years, students are required to keep a weekly journal. They can write about anything that relates to the course: the readings, the class discussion, or something that happened in the ambulatory-care or criminal-defence clinic that made them think of William Carlos Williams or Harper Lee. The content is not important. The goal here is to extend the readings and class discussion beyond the four walls of the classroom and to connect them with the students' 'real' lives. As much as we talk about making that connection in class, it is much more powerful when the students have to make the connection on a personal level. I collect the journals at the end of the semester simply to make sure they were kept. Everyone who turns in a journal passes this portion of the course. The journals are then returned to the students or destroyed in accordance with their instructions.

Writing assignments Students are given creative-writing assignments at approximately four-week intervals: a poem, a second poem and a set of three dramatic monologues. All of the assignments deal with some aspect of the course. At the end of the course, I collect all the writings in a single volume that each student receives at the class dinner.

For the poems, I give the students suggestions to get them started. None of the prompts are substantive in nature, but instead each one poses a writerly task and invites the students to come up with a writerly solution. For example:

- Write a short poem that begins and ends with the same line. The reader should feel differently about the line the second time he or she encounters it because of what happened in the poem.
- Describe a pair of shoes in such a way that a reader will think of a lawyer or a doctor. Do not mention lawyers or doctors in the poem.[4] (Mayo 2012a, 2012b)

Why do this? It is not to turn the students into competent poets. Throughout the semester, the class talks about craft, about respecting the tools of one's trade and the importance of honing one's skills across an entire career. 'The first kindness is competence', I say, quoting from a long-lost poem by Dr David Scheidermayer. We try to put craft and competence in context. Doctors, lawyers and poets all earn their living with their hands. The tools of their professions vary, but the need to master the tools is universal. The poetry assignments are intended to instil some respect for the craft of poetry.

The central challenge of the monologue assignment (which was minimally adapted from White 1973: 34–7) is simply to produce three narratives, one of which is by a doctor or lawyer, about a death (Mayo 2012c). The death can be one we read about in class, one that is plucked from the pages of a daily newspaper or one that is imagined. What matters is that the speaker in each monologue should be identifiable from his or her own words – vocabulary, syntax, diction, etc. In this exercise, the students have an opportunity to consider how language shapes identity and vice versa, as well as the impact of language upon the listener. The assignment gives students an opportunity to develop their 'narrative competency' and to consider the impact of language and perspective upon the narratives that are constructed around a single event.

Readings

The course readings have changed over time, with the exception of John Irving's *The Cider House Rules*, which has been the sole constant since 1986, the very first, embryonic year of this course. What follows is the reading list for the 2012 version of 'Law, Literature and Medicine', with some commentary about the way the different pieces work *in situ*.

First class The readings are three essays and three poems. The course generally shies away from essays out of what may be an excessive fussiness about the distinction between fiction and non-fiction, especially didactic non-fiction pieces. For the first class, however, there are some specific reasons for reading and discussing some essays.

4 Many of these prompts were taken or adapted from poetry workshops and workbooks. When I could remember the source, I have acknowledged my debt. In all other cases, I hereby thank the unnamed poetry workshop directors and poets for their contributions to 'Law, Literature and Medicine'.

We begin with Dr Rita Charon's 'Narrative and Medicine' (Charon 2004). This is the most eloquent and efficient exposition of 'narrative competencies' I have found. Dr Charon makes the case for attention to language (both the patient's and the clinician's), the inevitability of narrative-construction (for good or for ill) and the use of stories in medicine.

Next comes an excerpt from James Boyd White's essay 'Legal knowledge' (White 2002: 1396–402). This piece gives medical students an insider's view of what the law attempts to achieve (truth: not necessarily; justice: yes). For both sets of students, it seems helpful to expose them to White's distinctive approach to rhetoric and law. In what sense are lawyers storytellers? How does 'narrative competency' fit into the skill set of the lawyer or the judge? How is an opinion like a poem?

The first two pieces are offered to make the case to both the law students and the medical students that exposure to literature just might have some relevance to the practice of their chosen professions. The third essay is Benjamin DeMott's 'English and the promise of happiness' (DeMott 1991), which serves a quite different purpose. I am not a literary scholar, but this is a class that is built around literature. Therefore, in addition to my medico-legal goals for the course, I have certain literary goals as well. The classroom should be one where students understand their obligation to move their reactions to a piece of writing from the internal, personal sphere and into the classroom through participation in class discussion. Students should be willing to step outside of their carefully constructed professional personae and encounter the works we read in the spirit of honesty, openness and generosity. Their willingness to do this depends upon my ability to create a safe space in which students can let their guard down. DeMott addresses all of these issues in his essay and it has always seemed a good idea to put them on the table early on so that my expectations of the students (and their expectations of me) are explicit.

We finish this first class with three poems. Poetry plays a large role in 'Law, Literature and Medicine'. A few of the reasons for this are practical. More than half of the readings in the medical anthology we use are poems, undoubtedly because one of the editors – the cardiologist John Stone, MD – was a wonderful poet in his own right. Most of our poems are short (two pages or less), which allows us to read each poem out loud and to cover a wide range of subjects very efficiently.

In addition, there are few things on this planet more likely to strike fear into the hearts of most medical and law students than a poem. Faced with the task of leading a discussion of a poem, the students shed their veneer of professional competence and immediately look around the table for help. It has never been easier to create a collaborative learning environment than by throwing a poem into the middle of the room and watching the students reach out for assistance.

Almost any poem will do for this first class, but I have settled on these three: 'Introduction to poetry' by US Poet Laureate Billy Collins (Collins 2001), John Stone's 'The truck' (Stone 1980) and the classic 'The lawyers know too much' by Carl Sandburg (Sandburg 1922). Collins invites readers to play with a poem, to look at it from various angles and perspectives, and gently chides those who want to 'tie the poem to a chair with rope/and torture a confession out of it'. Stone's poem is a slightly challenging read (no punctuation and irregular spacing within lines) and it is about a serious topic (death), but its conversational tone and final joke are a winning combination. We spend some time considering how the poem 'works' as a technical matter and the poem also gives us a chance to think out loud about the differences between poetry and prose. Class ends with Sandburg's old chestnut ('tell me why a hearse horse snickers hauling a lawyer's bones'), an early example of a lawyer joke that is good as far as it goes and gives the class a chance to talk about what life would be like if all lawyers and the rule of law disappeared.

The rest of the semester *The Cider House Rules* (Irving 1985). None of the remaining readings is necessarily a permanent part of the course, although *The Cider House Rules* has always been on the list and I see no reason to drop it any time soon. In addition to being a glorious piece of writing, the novel has a deeply moral purpose through its multi-faceted exploration of life in America at a time when abortions were illegal. On one level, John Irving shows us the rules we write for public consumption – for example, 'Please don't go up on the roof [of the cider house] if you've been drinking – especially at night' (Irving 1985: 272) – almost every one of which is repeatedly broken, as opposed to the rules by which we actually lead our lives. The book also poses the question of whether someone (the young orphan, Homer Wells) with special skills (abortionist) has an obligation to violate the law as long as his services are needed and, because of legal prohibition, are scarce, expensive and dangerous to obtain. The students predictably resist the logic of Dr Larch's argument, which is far from foolproof, that until abortions are legal, safe and affordable, Homer has no choice but to provide abortions that are illegal, safe and affordable. Larch's argument provides a prelude to an in-class discussion of his argument in the context of the current prohibition (except in Washington, Oregon and Montana) against physician-assisted suicide. When, if ever, does a physician have an obligation to assist a terminally ill patient who wants to commit suicide? In states where it is still illegal, is refusal to assist a patient in such an endeavour tantamount, as Timothy Quill has argued, to abandonment (Quill 1991)? More generally, is there ever a moral obligation to disobey the law, and how should a professional – especially one with a unique relationship to the law – respond to the assertion of such a duty?

On Doctoring (Stone 2001) is a strong collection of stories, poems and essays on various aspects of being a physician. Each week, a pair of students picks the readings for class discussion from a 40-to-50-page block of material. I am eager for them to enjoy the experience of reading great literature for its own sake, but the students inevitably relate to the readings through their own experiences. I make no serious effort to clamp down on the sidebar discussions, many of which are attempts to work through the 'moral distress' they have experienced during their training. Despite the medical focus, law students find much here to which they can relate based upon experiences in the classroom, live client clinic or summer clerkships.

Literature and the Law (Morawetz 2007). After years of assembling and copying law-related readings, I have started to rely increasingly upon anthologies. Literature and the Law is my current choice, but many other equally attractive options are available. The goal for these readings is to devote as much class time to issues of legal professionalism as we do to the medical side. For example, we compare the closing arguments of the lawyers in *To Kill a Mockingbird* and Ernest J. Gaines' *A Lesson Before Dying*. Both raise important issues of race, justice and law, as well as the impact of personal morality on an attorney's duty of zealous advocacy. In an ideal world, the legal anthology would touch regularly upon medical topics as well as thorny legal issues. I have found only one book that does this (and does it brilliantly) – Norval Morris' *Brothel Boy and Other Parables of the Law* – but the students seem eventually to tire of the historical and social milieu in which the stories are set (pre-independence Burma), notwithstanding the thoroughly modern concepts and dilemmas that are delivered through Morris' pitch-perfect personification of Eric Blair (whose writings later became famous under his nom de plume, George Orwell).

Wit (Edson 1999). When I first heard of Margaret Edson's off-Broadway play about a John Donne scholar dying of metastatic ovarian cancer, I could not resist. With the help of the author (who later was awarded the Pulitzer Prize for Drama for this, her first play), I obtained the script and fell in love with the story. Eventually, the script was published in book form and, a few years ago, Mike Nichols and Emma Thompson adapted it for an HBO production. The play is useful for a number of discussion points, not all of which arise each year. End-of-life decision-making is a key plot point, of course, primarily in connection with the patient's decision to agree to a Do Not Resuscitate (DNR) order. The 'therapeutic misconception' is also relevant (and not a concept with which most law students are familiar), and that leads to a discussion of informed consent (which the play portrays in woefully inadequate terms). There are few doctrinal points beyond these, but the play still works extremely well in a course that is equally concerned with developing sensitivity to the shared experiences of patients and co-workers. In some years, we have watched the film in class and discussed it in the half-hour that remains, while in other years we have conducted a table-reading or simply discussed the moments that seemed the most salient for future professionals.

Whose Life Is It, Anyway? (Clark 1980). Brian Clark's play about a patient who has suffered a high-cervical-spine transection and wants to leave the hospital to die in peace was one of the earliest works with a 'right to die' theme at its core. It first appeared as a television play for the BBC in 1972, approximately four years before the New Jersey Supreme Court's landmark decision in the Karen Ann Quinlan case (In re Quinlan (1976)). It was later a hit on the London stage and in 1979 on

Broadway as well. It is easy to dismiss this play as a relic. The central character, Ken Harrison, would satisfy anyone's criteria for decision-making capacity, and we have long since settled the legal and ethical question of a competent patient's right to refuse even life-saving and life-sustaining treatments. Yet the play continues to serve a number of useful purposes. First, it allows the class to cover the basics of the right to die. Second, the play shows lawyers, judges, physicians and patients working through a medico-legal dilemma in their own characteristic ways. And, finally, despite all of the legal and ethical developments since 1972, the type of case represented by Ken Harrison's request to die is still one of the most difficult and perplexing encountered by hospital ethics committees. The crux of the problem is usually the worry that the patient is depressed and therefore lacks the decision-making capacity to refuse treatment. This leads to a generally useful discussion of different types of depression and the standards by which we allow patients to make certain kinds of decisions.

Limitations (Turow 2006). Scott Turow originally produced this slender novel for the *New York Times* and he was obviously aiming for something more substantial than another literary legal thriller. Although mysteries (legal and otherwise) abound, Turow offers contemplation on the subjects of lawyering, judging and the legal system, most especially on the flawed human vessels whose subjective experiences and realities inevitably shape fact-finding, doctrinal development and litigation in general.

David Kader and Michael Stanford have co-edited an excellent collection of poems about law and legal topics, *Poetry of the Law: From Chaucer to the Present* (2010). This anthology lifts the genre of law poetry considerably above the lofty-and-saccharine tradition of Law Day exhortations in which it has long been mired. Poems by some of the best writers of the past century are particularly thought-provoking.

The remainder of the readings varies rather significantly from year to year. Two recurring titles are particularly worthy of note: Raymond Carver's 'A small good thing' (Carver 2009), a short story about a couple whose child is injured by a car and eventually dies in the hospital, and an excerpt from Perri Klass' *Other Women's Children* (Klass 1990) (about the medico-legal debate over whether to write a DNR order on a five-year-old AIDS patient) in connection with our one field trip each semester: a walkabout in the paediatric Intensive Care Unit (ICU) at the Children's Medical Center. Both authors expertly describe the struggles of families and providers in extreme medical circumstances. The walkabout gives the students a chance to experience the sights, sounds and smells of the ICU first-hand, making the gravity of the work that goes on there even more immediate and real. The walkabout ends with a classroom discussion of the medical, legal, ethical, social, financial, political and emotional aspects of caring for the patients we have just visited.

Final Projects

The students are required to create a final project. They are discouraged from writing traditional research papers or, indeed, any papers at all. Instead, they are expected to create some kind of artwork. The projects have been astonishing in their range, including a French horn concerto (composed and performed) on the five stages of grief; an interpretive tap dance (also on the five stages of grief); collections of poems, short stories, and one-act plays; children's books (written and illustrated) on death and loss; a crazy quilt, with an annotated 'reader's guide' to the various design elements, appliqués and the like; oil paintings; mosaics; sculptures; and a memorable symphonic representation (recorded on a Moog synthesizer) of a myocardial infarction from the initial onset of symptoms to the patient's death after attempted resuscitation.

Final projects are presented at the class dinner, traditionally held on the evening of the last class, with readings, demonstrations and performances by the student-artistes. Some are quite remarkable, while others are a little less so. All are greeted with applause and cheers, and warm feelings abound.

The point of the final projects is obviously not to turn medical and law students into accomplished artists. Some have amazing talents, while others are dipping their toes into artistic expression for literally the first (and possibly the last) time in their lives. In any event, I am not qualified to judge the artistic merit of such a diverse collection of projects. The grading criteria have mostly to do with effort, thoughtfulness, originality and the connection to themes explored in the course. I also look for some indication that the student has respected the 'craft' elements of creation, that is, used the materials and media creatively, thoughtfully and attentively.

What Works and Why

'Law, Literature and Medicine' is of interest primarily because it joins two well-established pedagogies – 'Law and Literature' and 'Medicine and Literature' – that have not (to my knowledge) been joined before. In so doing, the course explores some of the commonalities and disjunctions between these two professions. The shared space where all of this takes place is defined by the subject of 'professionalism'. The tools are those involved in the writing and reading of narratives of many different kinds. For the most part, this is not new, except perhaps for the joinder, which was based upon the hunch that the comparisons and contrasts between the two professions would be of great interest and, it is to be hoped, of some value to both types of students. Exactly what that value is may be controversial and is certainly difficult to prove, but neither controversy nor questions of confirmability can be addressed without a theory, and I have one to propose.

At first blush, such a course would seem to cut against the grain of recent developments in American legal education. Increasingly, there are calls for movement towards a curriculum that teaches students the skills they will need in practice – memo-writing, advocacy, client interviewing and the like (American Bar Association 1992; Sullivan et al. 2007) And yet, as Professor Kristen Holmquist recently reported, the 'eminent lawyers, judges and mediators who had come together to serve as the UC Berkeley School of Law Professional Skills Advisory Board' had a distinctly different wish list:

> First, law students need to learn to recognize the complexity of their clients' stories and desired outcomes. The clients' problems may be messy, with difficult-to-determine facts, legal and nonlegal aspects, and multiple potential outcomes that may differently serve one or many of the clients' goals and aspirations. Second, law students should acquire a broad historical and contemporary sense of lawyers' varied roles in relationship to their clients, within and among institutional, and in society at large … Finally, students need to begin to develop the confidence and judgment that experience brings. (Holmquist 2012: 353–4)

'Experience' – even during the three short years of law school – goes beyond what a course like 'Law, Literature and Medicine' can realistically hope to accomplish. On the other hand, learning how to deal with clients' stories and desires, as well as developing a rich appreciation for the varied roles of lawyers within society and over time, are not just possible in a law-school literature course; they are at the heart of such a course.

An arts-based course, however, can do more. It can situate *empathy* within the tradition of professionalism in the practice of law and it can provide an opportunity for the empathic abilities of law students to develop and improve. If I am correct in this, that may explain why practising attorneys (and physicians) who are graduates of this course report back that 'Law, Literature and Medicine' was the most practical course they had in law (and medical) school. Understanding why this might be so is the burden of the remainder of this chapter.

Empathy and the Practice of Law

As Robin West has observed, empathy has recently received a bum rap (West 2011). President Barack Obama's statement that Judge Sonya Sotomayor's 'empathy' was one of the reasons he nominated her for a seat on the Supreme Court produced howls of protest that were strong enough to lead her to publicly renounce empathy as a judicial trait. Solicitor General Elena Kagan followed suit in her confirmation hearings as well (West 2011: 5). It is possible that anti-empathy senators and others equated *empathy* with *sympathy* and *sympathy* with *bias*, a distinctly unjudicial trait.

As Professor West observes, however, 'Empathy tells us, perhaps, something about what others are feeling, or at least gives us a hint of its feel. It is a source of information. Sympathy, by contrast, is the moral sentiment that aligns our interest with that of another in pain' (West 2011: 7). It is an alignment of interests that tends a judge toward bias, but that is not the result of empathy, properly understood, but of sympathy.

The utility of information provided by empathy is not limited to the judicial sphere. An empathic lawyer is one who at least attempts to see (and, one hopes, succeeds in seeing) a situation as her client does. This requires an understanding of the client's key relationships as well as his own goals, fears, understandings, misunderstandings and the like. It also requires insight into the professional relationship between lawyer and client as it is unfolding in real time. In turn, this requires that rarest of empathic skills, the ability to hear and see oneself as others do and not only as we wish ourselves to be heard and seen. The lawyer's wardrobe, demeanour, choice of words, tone of voice, timing of silences and the like all play out in a certain way and are received by different clients in different ways. These are the things that trust is built on, and they create the pathways for communication and, with luck, understanding.

Jurors, judges, opposing counsel and opposing parties all encounter a lawyer in these same ways, but the empathic turn is not limited to the courtroom. The act of writing assumes a purpose (presumably to educate and ultimately to persuade), whether the product is a brief, a memorandum of law or a term sheet for a corporate transaction. Encountering a legal document for the first time, a reader requires a frame of reference, and within that frame, the reader looks for content that, again, builds trust, educates and persuades. The legal writer who lacks the ability to see the written product as a first-time reader runs a significant risk of failure.

Similarly, the lawyer as a skilful, effective reader, no less than as a writer, summons her empathic abilities in order to situate the writing – a judicial opinion, a statute, a regulation, a contract – within a framework and, within that frame, looks for significance and for meaning. The telling detail may be the key to an argument (whether present or absent). The empathic reader finds within a particular legal rule the more general problem that the rule seeks to address, but the search for significance may not end there. What human situation gave rise to the general problem addressed by this statute or regulation? What are the circumstances that create this human situation? How general or specific are those circumstances, and how unique or repeatable?

In all of these professional settings, the lawyer is aided, even sustained, by empathy. As Professor Rosenberg has described it:

> Empathy involves some cognitive functioning, in that it requires a person to 'understand' the world in some way, but even that understanding is quite different from what we think of as the type of cognition we teach [in law school]. Empathizing with another person requires me to 'understand' the world as the other person understands it – to 'see' the world through the other's eyes and to experience the world as the other experiences it … Empathy, in other words, is

> simply the sense, emotional and cognitive, of knowing what it is like to be the other at a particular point in time. (Rosenberg 2002: 632)

Is it too much to claim that empathy, properly understood, pervades and informs every aspect of the practice of law? In doing so, I do not mean to suggest that it is the most important skill or trait that a lawyer brings to her professional activities. Nor do I maintain that empathy is either necessary or sufficient for a lawyer to function. Empathy is, however, a skill that may be necessary for a lawyer to function well or at least at the highest level of one's capabilities.

Modelling Empathy

Perhaps empathy can be taught (Rosenberg 2002; Montgomery 2008). For example, Professor Montgomery has argued forcefully that 'professionalism' needs to be reconceptualized, noting that professionalism is most commonly undermined by 'two elements, insufficient respect for others and insufficient public interest commitment.' (Montgomery 2008: 335). At the root of both problems, he argues, is 'excessive self-interest', which 'can be described by a term uncommon to law, insufficient empathy'. The cure lies in a new understanding of professionalism, one that 'include[s] empathetic understanding'. He continues: 'Stated differently, professionalism requires empathetic understanding of the interests of others, in addition to competency' (Montgomery 2008: 336). He believes quite sincerely that this new understanding of professionalism needs to be incorporated into the law school curriculum (Montgomery 2008: 352) and Professor Rosenberg makes much the same point (Rosenberg 2002: 636–52).

If Rosenberg and Montgomery are right, the question may not be whether empathy can be taught, but how. Surely Rosenberg is correct when he observes that the least effective way to teach empathy is probably the teaching methodology law schools do best: lecture, a bit of Socratic dialogue, assiduous note-taking on notebook computers and recapitulation by the students 'both that the teacher thinks empathy is important, and why the teacher thinks so' (Rosenberg 2002: 636). Rosenberg, however, 'doubt[s] that any teacher would be more successful at that than we are at convincing students generally to adopt our own values' (Rosenberg 2002: 636–7).

Lecture, then, is not enough. For the lesson to take, empathy must be modelled, first by the faculty member and then by the students. 'Modelling' is an activity that includes or crucially turns upon empathy. For example, in Professor Rosenberg's class, 'Interpersonal Dynamics for Lawyers', the modelling occurs through classroom exercises in which students engage in conversations designed to explore the emotions and interests of the other. The classroom experience is highly interactive and has as its goals '(1) learning to empathize, and (2) valuing the experience of empathizing' (Rosenberg 2002: 649).

In 'Law, Literature and Medicine', all of the participants in the room learn from one another on a dizzying array of topics, from the legal status of advance directives and in-hospital DNRs to the professional traps of representing a criminal defendant you believe to be guilty, from the law and ethics of closing arguments to legal status of abortion rights and physician-assisted suicide. All of this and much more comes as a byproduct of reading the poems, short stories, plays and novels of some of the best writers of the past 400 years. Along the way, quick points are made about the artistry and craft of a particular piece. Pieces are understood as made things that mediate and transform the space between the person behind them (the artist) and the person in front (the reader, viewer, listener, etc.).

This last point is essential. Understanding that there is a space that is meant to be transformed means that, at some level, empathy is also a byproduct of the class. All of the texts demand attention to the same sets of core questions. *Who is the speaker? Who is the intended audience? What has happened to provoke this writing (or passage or choice of word)? What was the author's response to that event? What type of reaction is the author trying to evoke in the reader?* In the first two weeks of the course, the instructors lead the discussion with these and similar questions. The students are pushed to not be content with getting at the author's meaning, at the 'take-away' of the piece, and instead are encouraged to try to dig out the human moment that lies at the heart of a particular moment in the reading. Empathy is modelled, and more empathy is the result.

As the discussions progress, the students probe their own responses to the readings, as well as those of their classmates. It's not enough to dislike a piece or to admire a particular character in a story. Sooner or later, students are expected to come to a deeper understanding of the range of reactions to a piece, including their own, and the lived experiences behind those reactions. Empathy is modelled, and more empathy is the result.

The class is a seminar, and group work makes its own demands for empathic engagement. Pairs of students select most of the anthology pieces we discuss, a process by which preferences are presented and negotiated into a set of readings for discussion that satisfies the interests and goals of each student. In-class discussion is more complex, with 15–20 students interacting for two hours. It takes an appreciation for group dynamics, including an understanding of one's own ability to contribute to the functioning of the group for the benefit of the entire class. One of my goals is to create a safe environment, but this does not mean that individual students are not challenged in many ways, both explicitly and implicitly. After a while, if the process works, students begin to learn what works and doesn't work both for them and for the group. Empathy is modelled, and more empathy is the result.

Experiencing the Arts in a Professional Context: More Empathy Results

After 14 weeks of reading non-legal, non-traditional texts, we reach the final event: final projects. As described earlier, students have considerable discretion in their choice of medium and message. The result has included musical compositions, photo-essays, dioramas, collections of poetry, short stories and novellas, one-act plays, paintings, sculptures and quilts (complete with research materials and a reader's guide to the quilt), among others.

I reserve the right to veto, which I have done only once, on advice of university legal counsel, when the student proposed a 'revealed sculpture', in which an inner sculpture would be revealed after the outer sculpture was blown up. Apparently our insurance policy did not cover intentional detonations of explosive material in or near a classroom. Generally my consultation consists of a brainstorming session with the student in order to encourage maximum creativity. The only restriction (other than the rule against pyrotechnics) is the requirement that the final project must relate to the subject matter of the course. For reasons that follow, and because of the breadth of a course that covers both medical and legal topics throughout the ages, this is no restriction at all, but rather an invitation to think deeply about what the course was about.

One of the most memorable final projects was the choreographing and performing of an interpretive tap on 'the five stages of grief'. I approved the project despite misgivings that it could possibly be done, let alone done well.

As a subject, it seemed appropriate for a law student who was exposed, possibly for the first time, to Kübler-Ross' model for grieving. We had encountered the model when we read Linda Pastan's poem 'The five stages of grief'. The medical students had helped with their discussion of current understandings and critiques of the model. All of this seemed potentially useful to future lawyers, many of whom (depending upon the nature of their practice) would have to deal with a client or other person processing their own grief.

Beyond the substantive connection to something lawyers should know about, however, I was concerned about the tap itself. On one level, I was needlessly concerned with the technical ability of the student to pull off the performance. Yet I need not have been, because the student had years of experience in a dance troupe before he started law school. On another level, I did not know if it was possible to convey the appropriate depth of meaning through a medium that I associated with vaudeville and the music of Tin Pan Alley.

My misgivings betrayed an abysmal ignorance of the nature of dance and of the way an audience responds to dance. Twyla Tharp would undoubtedly have avoided this trap, but I needed an education. My student provided that education with a brilliant performance of a dance that showed the artistic possibilities of tap and, more importantly, communicated a real depth of understanding and emotion about grief.

After the fact, the question that haunted me was, apart from the student's technical skill and creativity, *why did the dance work as well as it did?* Exploring the answer to that question informed me about how dance is experienced, how art is experienced, how art is created and how all of this promotes empathy in law students.

One key to understanding came from Maxine Sheets' *The Phenomenology of Dance* (Sheets 1966). Her description of a viewer's experience of dance rang true:

> The meaning of any dance comes alive for us only as we ourselves have a lived experience of the dance, and is not the result of either prior knowledge of dance or of any later reflective efforts. If we reflect upon the dance after it has been presented in the hope of discovering its meaning, we can only arrive at its significance from a distance. Such a meaning is akin to a lifeless fact, a second-hand piece of information, devoid of felt, lived-through experience … It is the lived experience which is of paramount significance. (Sheets 1966: 4)

Dance – motion through time and space – may be uniquely kinesthetic, but all art seems to reveal itself through an audience's 'lived experience', whether the revelatory experience unfolds through our reading of a text, listening to a musical composition or 'reading' of a supposedly static sculpture or painting. All art, it would seem, invites the same 'lived experience'. Robert Rauschenberg seemed to be getting at this when he wrote: 'Painting relates both to art and life. Neither can be made. (I try to act in that gap between the two)' (Kowal 2010: 151).

For the audience (the viewer, reader, listener, etc.), the challenge is to experience art of any type 'in the moment'. The traffic snarl on the way to the museum, the fight with the managing partner over mounting expenses in a contingent-fee case, all distractions need to be quieted. So, too, should our presuppositions about a particular medium, artist, performance or composition. Our goal should be to explore the space between art and life in which the artist has 'acted'. This is an experiential encounter, one that builds upon all of our life experiences and lessons, but it is also an encounter that transcends the search for meaning or significance by first drawing us into the world it creates.

I assume that all artists, regardless of their chosen medium, anticipate the 'lived experience' their art will provoke in their audience. They must imagine some reader or listener or viewer who encounters their creation for the first time. The piece unfolds through words, images, sounds or motion over time. The encounter will be ineluctably subjective and to that extent unpredictable, but the 'lived experience' will be common to all such encounters if the artist has successfully negotiated the gap between art and life. In short, the creation of art, no less than the experience of it, requires empathy, an appreciation of the experience of 'the other'.

Students in 'Law, Literature and Medicine' are not expected to attain the artistic heights of a Tharp or a Rauschenberg. A few students come to law school with advanced artistic skills, often rusty after three years of disuse, but most do not. For all of them, however, the challenge is the same. They need to explore Rauschenberg's gap between life as we have encountered it in class (law and medicine, life and death, rejection and desire, altruism and greed) and art. More specifically, the law students need to imagine how their classmates will approach, encounter and experience the product of their artistic efforts. The creation of a final project requires one last empathic leap into the imagined experience of others.

One last question deserves some attention: why art? Why not attempt to develop the empathic abilities of students through more professionally grounded and appropriate activities, such as brief-writing, mock trials, and negotiation and counselling exercises? My first response is that 'Law, Literature and Medicine' is not the only way, nor is it necessarily the best way, to promote the growth of empathy in law students. It is simply my way, although I believe it has certain advantages over many of the alternatives. Most, if not all, law-school activities, particularly skills courses, provide valuable opportunities for developing students' empathic skills. All law teachers should consider ways to build such opportunities into their courses. Our students and our profession would all be better for the effort.

Fiction and poetry, however, offer some unique opportunities that more traditional law-school vehicles may not. As traditionally taught and learned, law-school skills courses tend to focus primarily on technique and substantive content, with little time or effort devoted to the development of interpersonal skills. Legal clinics may be the most conspicuous exception, but only if the instructor's inclination and the time available permit the development of empathy in any focused manner. Literature, on the other hand, is all about 'lived experience' and seeing the world through the eyes of 'the other' who is represented on the page. Similarly, the final projects give the students an opportunity to try to see their own creations through the senses and reactions of an imagined 'other', their audience.

In addition, the literature we read tends to pull the students out of the familiar setting of lecture hall and courtroom and away from the traditional materials of legal education: edited cases, snippets of statutes and regulations, and condensed law review articles. The unfamiliarity of the materials in 'Law, Literature and Medicine' contributes to the success of the course. To some extent, the students' expectations in traditional law-school courses, and our expectations of them, fall into patterns and routines that seem, without extraordinary effort, to resist any suggestion of 'lived experience'. This is not universally true, of course, but the students' encounter with literature strips away those settled expectations, patterns and routines, and poses fresh challenges of reading and experiencing law-related stories of others in a new way.

The ultimate test of this approach to developing empathy through literature and other arts is whether there is a recursive effect on the students as practitioners. Does it change the way they read cases and statutes, brief cases, engage clients, judges and other counsel? In a sense, the empathic leap at the heart of this course requires a leap of faith as well. And yet there is some evidence for the success of this leap. The students are certainly energized, and their course evaluations reflect their sense that they have learned something new. More significant are the occasional reports from former students, now in practice (as well as medical practitioners), who say that 'Law, Literature and Medicine' was the most practical course they had in school. There are many reasons for a former student to say such a thing, including that they believe it. It is not a reaction I expected or even particularly sought, certainly not at the beginning of this decades-long journey. If the students gave some thought as to how their words might affect me, I will deem the course a success: empathy is modelled, and more empathy is the result.

References

American Bar Association, Section of Legal Education and Admissions to the Bar. 1992. *Legal Education and Professional Development – An Education Continuum*. Chicago: American Bar Association.

Bard, J., Mayo, T. and Tovino, S. 2009. 'Three ways of looking at a health law and literature course'. *Drexel Law Review*, 1(2), 512–72.

Carver, R. 1998. *All of Us: The Collected Poems.* New York: Knopf.

Carver, R. 2009. 'A small good thing', in *Raymond Carver: Collected Stories*. New York: Library of America, 402–25.

Charon, R. 2004. 'Narrative and medicine'. *New England Journal of Medicine*, 350(9), 862–4.

Clark, B. 1980. *Whose Life Is It, Anyway?* New York: Dramatic Publishing Co.

Collins, B. 2001. 'Introduction to poetry', in *Sailing Alone Around the Room.* New York: Random House, 16.

DeMott, B. 1991. 'English and the promise of happiness', in *Teaching – What We Do: Essays by the Amherst College Faculty.* Amherst, MA: Amherst College Press, 1–11.

Edson, M. 1999. *Wit.* New York: Dramatists Play Service, Inc.

Hamilton, N. and Monson, V. 2011. 'Answering the skeptics on fostering ethical professional formation (professionalism)'. *The Professional Lawyer*, 20(4), 3–6.

Holmquist, K. 'Challenging Carnegie'. *Journal of Legal Education*, 61(3), 353–78.

Irving, J. 1985. *The Cider House Rules*. New York: Random House.

Kader, D. and Stanford, M. (eds). 2010. *Poetry of the Law: From Chaucer to the Present*. Iowa City: University of Iowa Press.

Klass, P. 1990. *Other Women's Children.* New York: Random House.

Kowal, R. *How to Do Things with Dance: Performing Change in Postwar America.* Middletown, CT: Wesleyan University Press.

Mayo, T. 2011. 'Prospectus'. Available at: https://sites.google.com/site/tommayo2/lawlitmed_syllabus [accessed 24 August 2012].

Mayo, T. 2012a. 'Law, Literature, and Medicine, Poetry Assignment 1'. Available at: http://tom.mayo.googlepages.com/poetryassignment1.pdf [accessed 24 August 2012].

Mayo, T. 2012b. 'Law, Literature, and Medicine, Poetry Assignment 2'. Available at: http://tom.mayo.googlepages.com/poetryassignment2.pdf [accessed 24 August 2012].

Mayo, T. 2012c. 'Law, Literature, and Medicine, Essay Assignment'. Available at: http:// tom.mayo.googlepages.com/essayassignment.pdf [accessed 24 August 2012].

Montgomery, J. 2008. 'Incorporating emotional intelligence concepts into legal education: strengthening the professionalism of law students'. *University of Toledo Law Review*, 39(2), 323–52.

Morawetz, T. 2007. *Literature and the Law*. New York: Aspen.

Quill, T. 1991. 'Death and dignity – a case of individualized decision making'. *New England Journal of Medicine*, 324(10), 691–4.
Quinlan, In re [1976], 355 A.2d 647 (NJ).
Rosenberg, J. 2002. 'Teaching empathy in law school'. *University of San Francisco Law Review*, 36(4), 621–57.
Sandburg, C. 1922. 'The lawyers know too much', in T. Rosenbaum (ed.), *Law Lit: From Atticus Finch to The Practice*. New York: New Press, 171–2.
Sheets, M. 1966. *The Phenomenology of Dance*. Madison and Milwaukee, WI: University of Wisconsin Press.
Stone, J. 1980. 'The truck', in *In All This Rain*. Baton Rouge, LA: Louisiana State University Press, 14–15.
Stone, J. 2001. *On Doctoring: Stories, Poems, Essays*, edited by J. Stone et al., 3rd edn. New York: Free Press.
Sullivan, W. et al. 2007. *Educating Lawyers: Preparation for the Profession of Law*. San Francisco, CA: Jossey-Bass.
Supreme Court Historical Society. 2012. 'How the Court Works: The Justices' Conference'. Available at http://www.supremecourthistory.org/how-the-court-works/how-the-court-work/the-justices-conference/ [accessed 24 August 2012].
Tharp, T. 2003. *The Creative Habit: Learn It and Use it for Life*. New York: Simon & Schuster.
Turow, S. 2006. *Limitations*. New York: Picador.
West, R. 2011. 'The anti-empathic turn'. Available at: http://papers.ssrn.com/sol3/papers.cfm?abstract_id=1885079 [accessed 24 August 2012].
White, J. 1973. *The Legal Imagination.* Boston: Little, Brown.
White, J. 2002. 'Legal knowledge'. *Harvard Law Review*, 115(5), 1396–431.

Chapter 8
Truth in Context: Sketching a (New) Historicist Legal Pedagogy

Randy Gordon[1]

Introduction

At least as far back as Horace, humanists have postulated an interrelationship of the arts (*ut pictura poesis*).[2] But the exact nature of this interrelationship has remained a matter of dispute. Gotthold Lessing (1962: 4), for instance, stressed that the 'similarity of effect' between the visual and literary arts did not imply coincidence because 'the two arts differ both in the objects imitated as well as in the manner of imitation'. Rensselaer Lee (1967: 69), however, has more recently suggested – in apparent agreement with Sir Joshua Reynolds – that the two art forms share a deep purpose: 'the chief likeness of painting to poetry lay not in adherence to a set of precepts borrowed from the sister art, or in any imagined correspondences of form, but in "nobleness of conception"'. Despite these (and other) different ways of conceptualizing a trans-arts relationship, there remains a strong sense that textual and plastic approaches to creation and representation can each inform the other. This chapter is concerned with testing this assumption and – more particularly – considering whether a relationship between the visual, literary and performing arts extends to other disciplines, especially law (and legal texts). In the end, I hope to show that not only is there such a relationship but that the relationship can be exploited both to explain certain aspects of the law and to teach it as well. To do so, I will ask us to (re)consider a handful of cases that I have often

1 This chapter benefited from comments received from the participants in the 'Beyond Text in Legal Education' project at the University of Edinburgh. Thanks to Zenon Bańkowski and Maks Del Mar for organizing the enterprise. Thanks also to Zenon, the late Neil MacCormick and colleagues at the Dallas Institute of Humanities & Culture for helpful comments on earlier versions of some of the arguments set forth below.

2 But as with many statements that become slogans, Horace's was not a categorical statement of equivalence, as its full context reveals: 'Ut pictura poesis; erit, quae, si propius stes/Te capiat magis, et quaedam, si longius abstes' (my rough translation: 'As is painting, so is poetry; one grabs your imagination if you stand close to it, the other if you stand at a distance').

used to make theoretical or descriptive claims about the law and think here about how those cases (and the issues they raise) might be taught using extratextual tools (Gordon 2011).

Teaching Context without Text

I have taught law and literature – sometimes together, sometimes separately – for 20 years or so, and I have often remarked to myself (without doing anything about it until fairly recently) how differently I approach a doctrinal law course (like antitrust) from a literature course (like Proust or Americans in Paris). In a literature course, I have always thought it necessary not only to supplement the literary texts with non-literary texts (e.g. pairing Gertrude Stein with a dash of Whitehead and Heisenberg) but to go further and look at paintings and listen to music from the same period (e.g. considering Stein's *Autobiography of Alice B. Toklas* alongside paintings by Matisse and Picasso and music by Stravinsky, Schoenberg or Thompson). And it isn't simply a matter of intersecting biographies, interesting as those stories might be (Hemingway's *A Moveable Feast* is a particularly telling example). Nor is it just a question of expertise – I know a bit about art history but virtually nothing about music other than what my ears 'sort of' tell me (i.e. that Stravinsky sounds different from Beethoven in the same way that Stein reads differently from Fielding). So why shouldn't we do that in law courses? Ultimately, there is no good reason, and in this chapter I am going to sketch an argument for teaching at least some part of even a doctrinal law course with a contextual, beyond-textual approach.

Before doing this, though, we need to clear some underbrush to open the field of argument and dispose of an obvious objections to the proposed enterprise. To wit, one might claim a category error and note that, for example, poetry, plays, painting, novels and sculpture are all modes of expression designed to represent by different means the human condition, express states of emotion, etc. Legal texts, by contrast, are simply statements of rules (or tools to get at those rules). Thus, the fact that William Carlos Williams' poem 'The Great Figure' (1921) and Charles Demuth's painting *I Saw the Figure Five in Gold* (1928) can each cast interpretive light on the other (both are snapshots of a fire truck tearing down a wet street on the way to a fire; the poem inspired the painting) doesn't tell us anything useful about the Volstead Act (1919) from roughly the same period.[3] There is a good argument to be made that such a position is wrong, but I am not going to take up that challenge here, at least in the broadest formulation. Rather, I will assume the more modest position that – in many cases – understanding the genesis of particular laws can be conveyed most efficiently with non-textual resources. As we will soon see, this is important for two independently compelling

3 Thanks to one of my graduate students, Heather Shaw, for reminding me of this connection.

reasons. First, lawyers (including of course judges) have a duty to re-evaluate laws to make sure that they still 'fit' before applying them (Cornell 1990: 1060) (citing Derrida for the proposition that – for a decision to be just and responsible – 'it must conserve the law and also destroy it or suspend it enough to have to reinvent it in each case, rejustify it, at least reinvent it in the reaffirmation and the new and free confirmation of its principle'). Lawyers do this all the time and many, many times have later acknowledged that particular laws were created out of prejudice, ignorance or bias.[4] I hope to show that non-textual resources can help us get at that history. Second, what happens when the laws run out, when there is no clear answer to a novel legal question? Here, too, I think non-textual resources can help by inspiring moral imagination to show new perspectives and thereby identify what the right law should be. And in both cases, I believe that there is a pedagogical angle to be exploited in the classroom.

One way to ease into our discussion is to remark on the many alignments between law and narrative, both of which are historically situated. As Brook Thomas (1991a: 535) states it, laws and literature both 'grow out of a particular place and time'. This suggests that one way to examine the intersection of various narratives and laws is with the tools of historicism, whether traditional (e.g. the historical determinism of Hippolyte Taine) or 'New' (e.g. the cultural poetics of Stephen Greenblatt). For Taine, independent forces – not a summoning and exercise of personal will – compel human actors to act as they do (Taine 1965 [1864]: 254). With respect to writers, three factors are at work: race, milieu and moment. Race 'consists of those innate and hereditary dispositions which man brings with him into the world and which are generally accompanied with marked differences of temperament and of bodily structure. They vary in different nations' (Taine 1965 [1864]: 258). Milieu (environment) scoops up subfactors as diverse as climate, political events and social/religious conditions: 'man is not alone in the world; nature envelops him and other men surround him; accidental and secondary folds come and overspread the primitive and permanent fold, while physical or social circumstances derange or complete the natural groundwork surrendered to them' (Taine 1965 [1864]: 259). Moment (epoch) signifies 'the acquired momentum' at any given point in time, for '[w]hen national character and surrounding circumstances operate it is not on a tabula rasa, but on one already bearing imprints. According as this tabula is taken at one or at another moment so is the imprint different, and this suffices to render the total effect different' (Taine 1965 [1864]: 260–61).

There is much to criticize in this formulation, but it gets us to an important point – namely, that any historical artefact is situated within a causal stream. It is both producing and produced. Through reverse engineering of artefacts, then, we can learn something about how they issued and what they may have in turn influenced. With respect to literature, Taine says that a 'work is not a mere play

4 *Dred Scott v Sanford*, 60 U.S. (19 How.) 393 (1857) and *Plessy v Ferguson*, 163 U.S. 537 (1896) stand as particularly stark reminders of this proposition.

of the imagination, the isolated caprice of an excited brain, but a transcript of contemporary manners and customs and a sign of a particular state of intellect' (Taine 1965 [1864]: 254). But this isn't just a way of thinking about literature; it also applies to 'the large stiff pages of a folio volume, or the yellow leaves of a manuscript, in short, a poem, a code of laws, [or] a confession of faith' (Taine 1965 [1864]: 254). Each 'is simply a mold like a fossil shell, an imprint similar to one of those forms embedded in a stone by an animal which once lived and perished'. Thus, just as we can study a fossil to form some idea of the animal that formed it, so may we study a document to comprehend its author. Under this way of thinking, any document can be described as a momentary fix and snapshot of then-extant cultural cross-currents. Thus, contra strict textual constructionists, '[i]t is a mistake to study [a] document as if it existed alone by itself. That is treating things merely as a pedant, and you subject yourself to the illusions of a book-worm' (Taine 1965 [1864]: 255).

Historicism à la Taine as a mode of literary criticism died out in the middle of the last century in favour of text-based formalism, which found its apotheosis in New Criticism. Around 1980, though, historical criticism began a resurgence, particularly in Renaissance studies, more particularly in the work of Stephen Greenblatt (1980) and Louis Montrose (1980). The practitioners of this New Historicism are many and, in fact, there are a number of schools of influence at work, ranging from Foucault, to Marx, to Benjamin, to Bakhtin and beyond (Murfin and Ray 2003: 299). Nonetheless, there are some common approaches that I will try to quickly round up before turning to the implications that New Historicism might have for law.

New Historicist critics often assume that a literary work is not stable in the sense of self-containment. The text points outward to the world, but the world points back as well. And these referential cross-currents are not just between works of literature. Catherine Gallagher and Stephen Greenblatt (2000: 13) put it this way: 'We are intensely interested in tracking the social energies that circulate very broadly through a culture, flowing back and forth between margins and center, passing from zones designated as art to zones apparently indifferent or hostile to art, pressing up from below to transform exalted spheres and down from on high to colonize the low.' Greenblatt's technique, as Brook Thomas (1991b: 39) describes it, is to accrete historical details ('thick descriptions' in New Historicist lingo) before directly engaging a literary work: 'Starting with the analysis of a particular historical event, he then cuts to the analysis of a particular literary text. The point is not to show that the literary text reflects the historical event but to create a field of energy between the two so that we come to see the event as a social text and the literary text as a social event.' In the hands of a New Historicist, then, a Shakespearean play can be seen as a political event and royal pageantry can be read as a dramatic act (Orgel 1994: 44) (arguing that the full force of Caroline idealism is found in the masques of Inigo Jones, 'not in the promulgation of edicts, erratically obeyed, nor in military power, inadequately furnished').

The application of a New Historicist method to law 'means both that the law's supposedly prosaic, instrumental process of weighing interests and defining entitlements is a contested social process of self-definition, and that the law's literary legibility in no way implies its refinement or transcendence of venality' (Binder and Weisberg 2000: 479). Gregg Crane (1997: 772) offers a useful way of approaching the task: 'Instead of theorizing an essential barrier between [legal and literary] discourses, one might situate these discourses in the historical moment (for example, the proximity of each to state power, the various roles that each has played in reproducing or challenging dominant notions of the social order, the types of institutional and material support each has received, and the effects on each of commercial or professional development).' The point would be to 'trace the patterns of influence between law and literature' by 'analyzing their points of thematic and figural intersection'. To fix these abstractions somewhat and to show how the interplay of incongruent or hidden social discourses can influence legal outcomes and rules, I want us to consider two well-known cases: *Peevyhouse v Garland Coal & Mining Co.* and *Life Ins. Co. of New York v Hillmon.* I picked these cases because they are often taught in law school (and excerpted in casebooks) and – for very different reasons – each has intersected with my own experiences in one way or another.[5]

Although *Peevyhouse* is interesting for a number of reasons, I want us to focus here principally on one aspect. But first, let me recap the facts and the holding. In the mid-1950s, Willie and Lucille Peevyhouse leased their farm for five years to Garland Coal for the purpose of strip-mining coal. In addition to standard lease provisions, the Peevyhouses bargained for and obtained Garland's agreement to remediate the land at the end of the lease. But when term of the lease expired, Garland refused to perform the promised restoration, which would have cost nearly $30,000, yet – if performed – would have increased the market value of the land by only $300. Ultimately, the Oklahoma Supreme Court held that the Peevyhouses were entitled to only the lesser amount (not the $5,000 that they had won at trial) and announced the rule that 'where the economic benefit which would result to the lessor by full performance of the work is grossly disproportionate to the cost of performance, the damages which lessor may recover are limited to the diminution in value resulting to the premises because of the non-performance.

In casebooks and classrooms, *Peevyhouse* is often paired with *Groves v John Wunder Co.*, a case standing for the opposite proposition and one that *Peevyhouse* itself is at some pains to discount and distinguish. To teach and understand *Peevyhouse*, then, one strategy would be to undertake a fresh comparison of the two cases, retrace the comparative analysis taken in *Peevyhouse* and then discuss whether one rule is right and the other is wrong, or whether the rules can peacefully coexist because they are getting at fundamentally different deep issues.

---

5 Throughout this piece, from time to time I draw distinctions between personal (e.g. ontological) and higher-order (e.g. public) narrative forms. In doing so, I am drawing on work done by, among others, Margaret Somers (1994).

But that only gets us so far. So what else might we do? To suggest a partial answer, I need to step back into my own personal narrative for a moment.

When I was practising law in a large Oklahoma City law firm many years ago, one of the perennial rights of passage for a new lawyer (especially one, like me, who had been trained out of state) was for the new lawyer to endure an interrogation that went something like this:

> SENIOR PARTNER: I've been going over the memorandum you prepared on [subject x]. I see that you've relied almost exclusively on *Smith v Jones*. Is that good law?
>
> HAPLESS ASSOCIATE: Uh … I think so … I Shepardized it and it has never been overruled … so … uh … yeah – I mean yes – it's good law.
>
> SENIOR PARTNER: Hmmmm … In what year was that case decided?
>
> HAPLESS ASSOCIATE: Uh … [shuffling through papers] … Nineteen … Fifty … No Sixty … Here it is [proudly] – 1962!
>
> SENIOR PARTNER: Are you aware of the Oklahoma Supreme Court scandal?
>
> HAPLESS ASSOCIATE: Uh … well … um … No.
>
> SENIOR PARTNER (tossing reading glasses on top of memorandum and leaning back in chair): In 1964, there was a big bribery scandal involving several Justices on the Supreme Court. Some of the specifics came out as part of the investigations and trials, but nobody knows for sure exactly which cases from the late '50s and early '60s were involved. Just the same, though, they are all suspect to one degree or another. So any lawyer worth his salt will back up citations to cases from back then with additional authority. Think maybe you can do that?
>
> HAPLESS ASSOCIATE (slowly backing out of corner office): Uh … yes, sir … will get right on it.

Peevyhouse is one of the cases often suspected to have resulted from a bribe. Judith Maute (1994–1995), in an engaging and thorough investigation and analysis of the case, ultimately concludes that the case is tainted, but probably from a mixture of much bad lawyering and some judicial bias (one of the Justices had a cosy relationship with the defence counsel) rather than bribery (because the case didn't involve enough money). Nonetheless, the naked text of the opinion bears no trace of taint or scandal – it certainly looks like a 'legal' text and its reasoning – though pro-business – is still recognizable as 'legal' reasoning, and it is not the only case to hold that 'diminution in value' is a proper way to monetize injury to real estate.

How, then, does a teacher get to the non-obvious problems with *Peevyhouse*? The answer is that the teacher needs to get beyond the casebook text. And Maute has done just that. Her article brims with photographs, charts, maps and even a ballad – as well, of course, with documents and textual analysis. The point here is that she effectively assembles textual and non-textual materials in a way that allows students to see *Peevyhouse* in its historical context and judge its central holding in light of that context. It may be that some students, lawyers and judges will hew to the case's stated holding, but they will be doing so from a vantage point superior to that offered by the case opinion alone.

Interesting and helpful as Maute's approach may be, it still gets us only part of the way 'beyond text'. To take us further into the beyond, I want us to (re)consider a hoary evidence case, *Mutual Life Ins. Co. of New York v Hillmon* (1892), that fits neatly with my own ontological narrative as well as a couple of others. The case begins, as do I, on the Great Plains of Kansas, only a few years before my grandfather (who lived until the late 1980s) arrived in Kansas in a covered wagon with his parents and siblings. To keep the length of this story manageable, I will have to compress and condense considerably, but Marianne Wesson has written at great length about the case as part of an investigation that is ongoing, and her efforts are readily available to round out the story for the curious (2006, 2007).[6]

Towards the end of 1878, John W. Hillmon purchased $25,000 of life insurance (a considerable sum in those days) before setting out from Lawrence, Kansas for points west. The ostensible purpose of his trip was to meet up with a friend, John H. Brown, who would accompany him on an expedition to find and purchase land for a ranching operation. Brown and Hillmon connected in Wichita sometime in February 1879 and on around 5 March headed southwest towards Medicine Lodge, where they stayed for a few days before decamping for a relatively unpopulated area called Crooked Creek. There, tragedy befell Hillmon: Brown's rifle discharged as he was unloading it from a wagon and a bullet struck Hillmon in the head. The verdict after two coroner's inquests was 'accidental death'. That probably would have been that had not Hillmon's wife of six months, Sallie, made a claim on the insurance policies, setting in motion a litigation of *Bleak Housian* proportions, spawning six trials (and two trips to the Supreme Court) and spanning the turn of a new century. Only one of those trials, the third, will be our object of study.

Sallie Hillmon's claim bore obvious indicia of fraud: Hillmon was of relatively modest means (compared to the amount of insurance), a relative had paid part of the insurance premiums, the couple had been married only a short time and Hillmon's 'death' came right on the heels of the multi-policy purchase. Unsurprisingly, given these circumstances and a general proliferation of insurance fraud in the late nineteenth century, the insurance companies refused to pay voluntarily and

6 Wearing her novelist hat, Professor Wesson is working on a fictionalized account of the case. The factual account that I am reciting is based on the Supreme Court opinion cited above, fleshed out here and there by Wesson's investigatory findings.

litigation ensued. In 1888, after two trials had already resulted in hung juries, the third trial came on as a consolidation of three separate actions (one against each insurance company).

At trial, Sallie's case rested on evidence supporting the gun-fell-out-of-the-wagon story that I have just described. However, the defendants 'introduced evidence tending to show that the body found in the camp at Crooked creek on the night of March 18th was not the body of Hillmon, but the body of one Frederick Adolph Walters' (1892: 287). There was 'much conflicting evidence' on the point, but in the defendants' telling 'Walters left his home at Ft. Madison, in the state of Iowa, in March, 1878, and was afterwards in Kansas in 1878, and in January and February, 1879; that during that time his family frequently received letters from him, the last of which was written from Wichita; and that he had not been heard from since March, 1879'. To tie Walters to the corpse at Crooked Creek, the defendants tried to introduce two letters from Walters, one written to his sister and one to his fiancée. The sister's letter had been lost, but the fiancée's letter was available. The trial court refused to allow the sister to testify as to the contents of her letter or to allow the contents of the fiancée's letter to be read to the jury. For the Supreme Court's purposes, the two letters contained evidence of the same operative fact, so I will focus on the letter that was physically available.

The fiancée, Alvina D. Kasten, testified that she was 21 years of age, a resident of Ft. Madison and was engaged to Walters, whom she last saw in March 1878. After Walters left, she corresponded regularly with him, receiving a letter from him about every two weeks until 3 March 1879, which was the date on which she received his final letter. That letter was dated at Wichita, 1 March 1879 and was signed by Walters; the envelope was postmarked 'Wichita, Kansas, March 2, 1879'. Here's what it said:

> Dearest Alvina: Your kind and ever welcome letter was received yesterday afternoon about an hour before I left Emporia. I will stay here until the fore part of next week, and then will leave here to see a part of the country that I never expected to see when I left home, as I am going with a man by the name of Hillmon, who intends to start a sheep ranch, and, as he promised me more wages than I could make at anything else, I concluded to take it, for a while at least, until I strike something better. There is so many folks in this country that have got the Leadville fever, and if I could not of got the situation that I have now I would have went there myself; but as it is at present I get to see the best part of Kansas, Indian Territory, Colorado, and Mexico. The route that we intend to take would cost a man to travel from $150 to $200, but it would not cost me a cent; besides, I get good wages. I will drop you a letter occasionally until I get settled down. Then I want you to answer it. (1892: 288–9)

The trial court ruled that this letter (and the one to Walters' sister) was inadmissible hearsay. So, when Sallie prevailed at trial, the defendants included this evidentiary ruling as a point of error on appeal.

In the Court's view, '[t]he matter chiefly contested at the trial was the death of John W. Hillmon' – i.e. 'whether the body found at Crooked creek on the night of March 18, 1879, was his body or the body of one Walters'. The defendants introduced evidence tending to show that Walters was at Wichita in early March, that he had not been heard from since, that his body had been found at Crooked Creek, and that he went to Crooked Creek between early March and 18 March. Thus, '[e]vidence that just before March 5th he had the intention of leaving Wichita with Hillmon would tend to corroborate the evidence already admitted, and to show that he went from Wichita to Crooked Creek with Hillmon. Letters from him to his family and to his betrothed were the natural, if not the only attainable, evidence of his intention'. And 'whenever the intention is of itself a distinct and material fact in a chain of circumstances, it may be proved by contemporaneous oral or written declarations of the party' (1892: 294–5).

Thus is born the modern 'statement of intention' exception to the hearsay rule. This exception has been much criticized, and it does seem overbroad. (Could a statement that 'I'm going to do my homework' be used later as collateral proof that the dog did eat it?) So why did the Court (largely) invent this exception? Wesson makes a good structuralist (without using that term) argument that 'narrative exigencies' rather than 'policy views' drove the Court's decision (2006: 350).[7] Specifically, she argues that the Court was compelled to read the story before it as a 'romance', into which the 'Dearest Alvina' letter (in its very artlessness) fits perfectly as a signifier of truth. Without disagreeing with this assessment, I would offer something different, tied back to the idea of cultural context.

In *The Frontier in American History*, a book that influenced more than a generation of American historians and literary critics, Frederick Jackson Turner (1893) equated the frontier with lawlessness: 'I have refrained from dwelling on the lawless characteristics of the frontier, because they are sufficiently well known. The gambler and desperado, the regulators of the Carolinas and the vigilantes of California are types of that line of scum that the waves of advancing civilization bore before them, and of the growth of spontaneous organs of authority where legal authority was absent.'[8] When Jackson says that the lawlessness of the frontier was 'sufficiently well known', I think he is simply identifying the public narrative that had grown up to both describe and define life on the frontier (especially to

7 For a very good application of structuralist principles to legal fact-finding via narrative, see Jackson 1988: 61–88 (discussing Bennett and Feldman's theory of fact-finding at trial: 'People carry around with them a stock of socially-constructed narratives, acquired through the whole range of their social experience (including their education). A significant factor affecting the plausibility of a newly-communicated story is the degree to which it fits a narrative which already exists within this stock of social knowledge').

8 Turner's positions have been qualified and debunked over the years, so I don't offer them for the truth of the matter – maybe as a 'state of the American mind' exception to hearsay.

those not living there).[9] If that is right, then the Supreme Court was in some sense constrained to read the facts of the *Hillmon* case in light of that narrative. In other words, the Court created a rule of evidence that would allow the construction of a better, more truthful story – one in which John Hillmon was a murdering, thieving desperado who preyed on a hapless young adventurer out to 'strike something better' on the frontier. But, as Wesson shows, that is probably not the case: the 'Dearest Alvina' letter is either an outright fake or at best is full of lies.[10] In either case, it is probably an invention of the insurance companies.

The *Hillmon* opinion, like a work of art, is a historical product, which is to say that it is a product of a multiplicity of discourses – of narratives. Its authors (I will assume more than one hand in the opinion) therefore could not stand outside that narrative stream as 'objective' observers of the evidence. Rather, they read the evidence in light of (among other things) a stock public narrative of the lawless frontier. In that light, the 'Dearest Alvina' letter made it easier to find 'facts' that fit into a story that coordinated with that public narrative. In other words, the letter had to be admissible. And so it was.

Now, the question becomes: 'How best to teach the historical point of a case like *Hillmon*?' Plainly, one could effectively create context by pairing the Supreme Court opinion with other readings – perhaps one of Wesson's articles and one of Turner's essays. These items would most certainly lay an ample predicate for a discussion focused on the idea of a public narrative that served as a lens through which the Justices would have viewed the facts of the case. But I think a more economical – and perhaps more effective – approach would be to show students a few dime-novel covers (see Figure 8.1).

To my mind, these novel covers convey the then-current attitudes about the West every bit as effectively as does Jackson's prose. Even more important, the cover paintings force observers to make the types of connections that Wesson is making for them – i.e. they are being offered clues upon which to build an analysis rather than being handed that analysis fully cooked. And *that* is a valuable lawyerly skill – far more valuable, in fact, than being able to recite the statement-of-intention exception to the hearsay rule.

9 The image of places like Dodge City and Tombstone as pits of teeming lawlessness were exaggerated (as were the legends that grew up around Bat Masterson, the Earps, Bill Cody and others) and were fuelled by an endless supply of dime-novel Westerns and ludicrous newspaper reports (Jones 1978). Those images persist to some degree today, even though the academic literature (and the literature-literature) has moved off this flat-footed position since Turner's time (Shepard 1981; Reid 1996).

10 Wesson's conclusion is based on several factors. At one point, she was convinced that the letter was a simple forgery, but she came around to the view that Walters probably did write the letter – just not when and where stated. She found persuasive evidence that Walters was alive well after he was supposedly killed, that the insurance companies had fabricated other evidence and – based on modern forensic tests – that Hillmon probably was the person killed at Crooked Creek.

Figure 8.1 Dime novels
Source: Nebraska State Historical Society.

Before leaving this point, it's worth noting how well it squares with aspects of recent critiques of contemporary legal education. For example, the *Carnegie Report* notes that '[a]ctual legal practice is heavily dependent on expertise in narrative modes of reasoning' (Sullivan et al. 2007: 97). This is so because abstract legal principles remain largely unintelligible, absent narrative frameworks to give them concrete, cognizable form. But we must remember that the narrative contained in any particular legal text is highly distilled and that knowing how to place that distilled narrative back into its larger context can reveal analytical flaws, biases and the like that are obscured after the distillation process is finished. In practising the art of recontextualizing and supplementing narratives (like *Hillmon*), students gain a skill critical to the practice of law, namely, actively building narratives both comprehensively and contextually, rather than passively accepting what a client or witness claims to be 'what really happened'. And this skill, when yoked to the type of detached analytical thinking encouraged by traditional legal education, is, I think, one way to bridge the gap between what the *Carnegie Report* identifies as, on the one hand, 'thinking like a lawyer' and actual 'lawyering' on the other. I will return to this theme in a bit.

Provoking Moral Imagination without Text

In a pair of poems in the *Lyrical Ballads*, 'Expostulation and Reply' and 'The Tables Turned', William Wordsworth neatly stakes the bounds of what I think of as the textual and non-textual educational camps.[11] In both these short poems, 'William' and 'Matthew' debate the efficacy of two principal ways of learning. Matthew gets the first word, exhorting William to get up off 'that old grey stone' upon which he is 'dream[ing his] time away'. For Matthew, there is a surer path to knowledge and insight:

> 'Where are your books? – that light bequeathed
> To Beings else forlorn and blind!
> Up! up! And drink the spirit breathed
> From dead men to their kind.
> You look round on your Mother Earth,
> As if she for no purpose bore you;
> As if you were her first-born birth,
> And none had lived before you!'

William suggests that Matthew's books lead down too narrow a path and – as a better alternative – 'That we can feed this mind of ours/In a wise passiveness'. In the companion poem, William leaves no doubt as to what this passiveness entails

11 Thanks to my fellow Dallas Institute Fellow Willard Spiegelman for suggesting Wordsworth and Shelley as sources of commentary on the idea of moral imagination.

and, paradoxically, how passiveness can lead ('to lead' is the fossilized metaphor in the word 'education') one further than 'book learning' (traditional education):

> Up! up! my Friend, and quit your books;
> Or surely you'll grow double;
> Up! up! my Friend, and clear your looks;
> Why all this toil and trouble.
> ***
> Books! 'tis a dull and endless strife:
> Come, hear the woodland linnet,
> How sweet his music! on my life,
> There's more of wisdom in it.

Not only is nature a superior teacher, but cultural wisdom is actually perverted once it is ossified in texts and cut off from experiential modes of learning (and thereby substitutes cold intellect for imagination):

> One impulse from a vernal wood
> May teach you more of man
> Of moral evil and of good,
> Than all the sages can.
> Sweet is the lore which Nature brings;
> Our meddling intellect
> Mis-shapes the beauteous forms of things: –
> We murder to dissect.
> Enough of Science and of Art;
> Close up those barren leaves;
> Come forth, and bring with you a heart
> That watches and receives.

To show how this debate might inform what we do in a modern law school classroom, I want to sketch out the facts and holdings of a pair of so-called 'battered spouse' cases and then suggest a non-textual way of getting behind those cases to show why they arose when they did. In the first case, *State v Hundley* (1985), the Kansas Supreme Court was presented with a homicide conviction involving a defendant who had failed in her effort to mount a defence based on proof that she suffered from what is now generally referred to as 'battered person syndrome'. There was no factual dispute that the Carl and Betty Hundley had a hellish marriage or that Carl physically and psychologically abused Betty. In the course of their 10-year marriage, 'He had knocked out several of her teeth, broken her nose at least five times, and threatened to cut her eyeballs out and her head off. Carl had kicked Betty down the stairs on numerous occasions and had repeatedly broken her ribs' (1985: 475).

Betty finally ran and moved into a motel in Topeka, Kansas. Carl found her, though, and tried to pick up where he had left off:

> On January 13, 1983, the day of the shooting, Betty had seen Carl early in the day, at which time Carl told Betty he was going to come over and kill her. That night she heard a thumping on her motel door while she was in the bathroom. By the time Betty got out of the bathroom Carl had broken the door lock and entered the room. His entry was followed by violence [which the Court recounts in graphic detail] … Even after that, Carl continued to threaten Betty. She was sobbing and afraid. He pounded a beer bottle on the night stand and threw a dollar bill toward the window, demanding she get him some cigarettes. Betty testified Carl had hit her with beer bottles many times in the past. Therefore, feeling threatened by the beer bottle, she went to her purse, pulled out the gun and demanded Carl leave. When he saw the gun, Carl laughed tauntingly and said, 'You are dead, bitch, now!' As he reached for the beer bottle, Betty shut her eyes and fired her gun. She fired it again and again. There were five spent shells in the gun when it was seized. At the time of the shooting the deceased had his back to Betty and was paying attention to the beer bottle. She was not physically blocked from going to the door. (1985: 476)

None of this was disputed: the only issue on appeal was whether the trial court improperly instructed the jury as to the elements of self-defence.

In Betty's case, the trial court had used the then-standard instruction on self-defence, which read:

> The defendant has claimed his conduct was justified as (self-defense) (the defense of another person). A person is justified in the use of force against an aggressor when and to the extent it appears to him and he reasonably believes that such conduct is necessary to defend himself or another against such aggressor's immediate use of unlawful force. Such justification requires both a belief on the part of defendant and the existence of facts that would persuade a reasonable person to that belief. (1985: 477)

On appeal, Betty's counsel argued that the use of the word 'immediate' in the jury instruction (rather than 'imminent', as stated in the statute) prevented the jury from considering (even though it had been copiously presented at trial) the evidence concerning the long-term violence that Betty suffered at the hands of Carl. For the Court, then, the question became 'what instruction should accompany this evidence in order to charge the jury with the proper manner in which such evidence should be considered?' (1985: 477). In other words, the Court wanted to ensure that Betty's status as a battered woman figured into the self-defence equation. And to do so, it undertook a somewhat strained, dictionary-based analysis of the difference between 'immediate' and 'imminent'. Despite the appeal to semantics, the Court was up to something different. It wanted to make room in its jurisprudence for an issue that had remained hidden (in plain sight) for centuries:

> The issue is dramatized by the nature of this case. This is a textbook case of the battered wife, which is psychologically similar to hostage and prisoner of war cases. Betty Hundley had survived her husband's brutal beatings for ten years. Her bones had been broken, her teeth knocked out and repeated bruises inflicted, but she did not leave him. She called the police occasionally but would continue to stay with Carl Hundley. The mystery, as in all battered wife cases, is why she remained after the beatings. The answer to that question can only be gleaned from the compiled case histories of this malady. It is not a new phenomenon, having been recognized and justified since Old Testament times. It goes largely unreported, but is well documented. It is extremely widespread, estimated to affect between four and forty million women. (1985: 477)

From this, the Court concluded that: 'Battered women are terror-stricken people whose mental state is distorted and bears a marked resemblance to that of a hostage or a prisoner of war … They become disturbed persons from the torture' (1985: 477). It is unnecessary for us to spend much time with *how* the Court technically tied Betty's situation to the law of provocation, but it made room for the situation in which there has been a 'buildup of terror and fear … systematically created over a long period of time' (1985: 477).

In the wake of *Hundley*, courts began to give broad, 'battered-woman' self-defence instructions and juries began to acquit defendants on that basis. The limits of this line of defence were tested when the first 'burning-bed' case (i.e. a case in which an abused spouse kills her husband while he is sleeping) arrived at the Kansas Supreme Court. That case, *State v Stewart* (1988), arose from a context much like *Hundley*: a marriage troubled from the outset, a cruel, unpredictable and physically abusive husband, attempted flights by the battered wife – and a gun. At trial, the Court gave the jury a standard self-defence instruction (duly modified to reflect the *Hundley* holding that imminence rather than immediacy was the proper standard for judging temporal proximity), but the judge also added what we might call a *Hundley* tag: 'You must determine, from the viewpoint of the defendant's mental state, whether the defendant's belief in the need to defend herself was reasonable in light of her subjective impressions and the facts and circumstances known to her.' So, once again, the Court undertook to make a broad policy determination using jury-instruction language as the vehicle.

The Court did this by asking two related questions: first, whether a person in Stewart's shoes should be entitled to a self-defence instruction *at all* and, second, whether the *Hundley* tag was an appropriate statement of the law of self-defence. It answered these questions by turn, holding first that:

> In order to instruct a jury on self-defense, there must be some showing of an imminent threat or a confrontational circumstance involving an overt act by an aggressor. There is no exception to this requirement where the defendant has suffered long-term domestic abuse and the victim is the abuser. In such cases, the issue is not whether the defendant believes homicide is the solution to past or future problems with the batterer, but rather whether circumstances surrounding the killing were sufficient to create a reasonable belief in the defendant that the use of deadly force was necessary. (1988: 577 and Syl. § 4)

Given this holding, it was probably superfluous to consider the form and content of the jury instruction given, but the Court did so anyway, apparently to emphasize two key points: viz, that 'battered woman's syndrome' is not in itself a defence to murder (rather, evidence of the syndrome may be introduced in support of a defence of self-defence) and that the defence of self-defence has both objective and subjective elements (1988: 579). This turn to objectivity is troublesome, especially because notions of objective reasonableness depend on notions of common sense. But as *Hundley*, *Stewart* and a host of other cases make clear, there is no 'common sense' when it comes to battered women – they exist in a condition outside the ordinary juror's ability to know. Justice Herd (the author of the *Hundley* opinion) explicitly makes that point in dissenting from the *Stewart* majority (1988: 582).

Hundley and *Stewart* thus stand in support of the proposition that legal standards are recalibrated on a case-by-case basis. But why is this so? And how do we explain this process to students, especially the question of 'why *this* rule at *this* time?'. I have found it useful to turn to an iconic work of early modern feminism, Susan Glaspell's one-act play *Trifles* (1996) (also published as a short story, 'A Jury of Her Peers'). The play opens in the gloomy and disordered kitchen of a Nebraska farmhouse of a century ago. The owner of the farm, John Wright, has been murdered – strangled – and his wife has been taken into custody. Five characters occupy the stage as the curtain rises: County Attorney Henderson, Sheriff Peters and his wife, and two neighbours, Mr and Mrs Hale. Mr Hale had stopped by the farmhouse the day before and found Mrs Wright sitting in the kitchen looking 'queer'. She told him that Mr Wright had 'died of a rope around his neck' and that she didn't know who did it because – although she slept in the same bed – she 'sleep[s] sound'. Because of that story's incredibility, Mrs Wright was arrested and held for murder. From the opening lines, though, we sense that this will be a story less about murder than about gender. Glaspell first puts this in spatial terms, showing how the men set about to discover clues upon which they can construct a story of Mrs Wright's guilt: 'what was needed for the case was a motive; something to show anger, or – sudden feeling'. But they take up this task from a decidedly masculine point of view, looking only at the immediate crime scene and masculine spaces like the barn:

COUNTY ATTORNEY: [*Looking around*] I guess we'll go upstairs first – and then out to the barn and around there. [*To the Sheriff*] You're convinced that there was nothing important here – nothing that would point to any motive.

SHERIFF: Nothing here but kitchen things. (Glaspell 1996: 154)

The men denigrate everything feminine, unable to see feminine artefacts as anything other than 'trifles'. But these 'trifles' hold the key to the mystery, to the *narrative*:

MRS PETERS: She was piecing a quilt.

MRS HALE: … I wonder if she was goin' to quilt it or just knot it?

SHERIFF: They wonder if she was going to quilt it or just knot it!

[*The men laugh, the women look abashed.*]

MRS HALE: [*resentfully*] I don't know as there's anything so strange, our takin' up our time with little things while we're waiting for them to get the evidence. I don't see as it's anything to laugh about. … Mrs Peters, look at this one. Here, this is the one she was working on, and look at the sewing! All the rest of it has been so nice and even. And look at this! It's all over the place! Why, it looks as if she didn't know what she was about!

[*After she has said this, they look at each other, then start to glance back at the door. After an instant Mrs Hale has pulled at a knot and ripped the sewing.*]

MRS PETERS: Oh, what are you doing, Mrs Hale?

MRS HALE: Just pulling out a stitch or two that's not sewed very good. [*Threading a needle*]. Bad sewing always made me fidgety.

***

MRS PETERS: Why, here's a birdcage. Did she have a bird, Mrs Hale?

MRS HALE: Why, I don't know whether she did or not – I've not been here for so long. There was a man around last year selling canaries cheap, but I don't know as she took one; maybe she did. She used to sing real pretty herself.

MRS PETERS: Seems funny to think of a bird here. But she must have had one, or why should she have a cage? I wonder what happened to it?

MRS HALE: I s'pose maybe the cat got it.

MRS PETERS: No, she didn't have a cat. She's got that feeling some people have about cats – being afraid of them. My cat got in her room, and she was real upset and asked me to take it out. … Why, look at this door. It's broke. One hinge is pulled apart.

MRS HALE: Looks as if someone must have been rough with it.

The women next discuss Mr Wright's character. Mrs Hale describes him as honest, but 'hard' and just passing time with him was like 'a raw wind that gets to the bone'. They then decide to take the quilt to Minnie to help her pass the time in jail and they set about finding her sewing materials:

[*They look in the sewing basket.*]

MRS HALE: Here's some red. I expect this has got sewing things in it (*Brings out a fancy box.*) What a pretty box. Looks like something somebody would give you. Maybe her scissors are in here. [*Opens box. Suddenly puts her hand to her nose.*] Why – [MRS PETERS *bends nearer, then turns her face away.*] There's something wrapped up in this piece of silk. … Oh, Mrs Peters – it's –

MRS PETERS: It's the bird.

MRS HALE: But, Mrs Peters – look at it. Its neck! Look at its neck! It's all – other side to.

MRS PETERS: Somebody – wrung – its neck.

[*Their eyes meet. A look of growing comprehension of horror. Steps are heard outside. Mrs Hale slips box under quilt pieces, and sinks into her chair.*]

MRS HALE: She liked the bird. She was going to bury it in that pretty box.

MRS PETERS: When I was a girl – my kitten – there was a boy took a hatchet, and before my eyes – and before I could get there – If they hadn't held me back, I would have – [*Catches herself, looks upstairs, where steps are heard, falters weakly.*] – hurt him.

MRS HALE: I wonder how it would seem never to have had any children around. No, Wright wouldn't like the bird – a thing that sang. She used to sing. He killed that, too.

MRS PETERS: We don't know who killed the bird.

MRS HALE: I knew John Wright …

MRS PETERS: We don't know who killed him. We don't *know*.

MRS HALE: If there'd been years and years of nothing, then a bird to sing to you, it would be awful – still, after the bird was still …

MRS PETERS: My, it's a good thing the men couldn't hear us. Wouldn't they just laugh! Getting all stirred up over a little thing like a – dead canary. As if that could have anything to do with – with – wouldn't they laugh!

MRS HALE: Maybe they would – maybe they wouldn't. [*Mrs Hale soon hides the canary and its box*.] (Glaspell 1996: 157–63)

The men end the play as they began it: literally and figuratively clueless. They are so trapped within their masculinity that they cannot read the signs that are so obvious to the women. In other words, they cannot construct a text – a coherent narrative – that will make sense of the crime. As a result, the murderer will likely go free, as the County Attorney predicts: 'No, Peters, it's all perfectly clear except a reason for doing it. But you know juries when it comes to women. If there was some definite thing. Something to show – something to make a story about – a thing that would connect up with this strange way of doing it' (Glaspell 1996: 163). The women, on the other hand, have not only solved the murder but have justified it to their own satisfaction as well. In other words, as the play's final line ironically suggests, they have tied up all the loose ends:

COUNTY ATTORNEY: [*Facetiously*] Well, Henry, at least we found out that she was not going to quilt it. She was going to – what is it you call it, ladies!

MRS HALE: [*Her hand against her pocket*] We call it – knot it, Mr Henderson. (Glaspell 1996: 164)

At this point, one may ask what it is that students can learn from the play that they couldn't get straight from the cases. My answer comes in two parts, one having to do with how reading cases can have a stultifying effect on the imagination and the other having to do with how the play is used in the classroom setting.

A recurring theme in much recent criticism of legal pedagogy is the heavy reliance placed (especially in first-year courses) on the case method. There are a variety of ways to frame this issue, but one that has particular resonance for me is the notion that the case method exalts a text-bound 'analytical' mode of thinking over a context-sensitive 'narrative' mode. As the *Carnegie Report* puts it:

> In the narrative mode of thought, things and events are given significance through being placed within a story, an ongoing context of meaningful interaction. The narrative is a mode of thinking that integrates experience through metaphor and analogy. It is employed in the arts and also in practical situations, including professional work. Meaning and value have their origins here. (Sullivan et al. 2007: 83)

Thus conceived, the narrative mode of thinking is essential to moral reasoning, deliberation and conduct. Steven Fesmire (2003: 4), following on John Dewey's heels, helpfully suggests that there are three interrelated ideas at work here: '(1) Moral character, belief, and reasoning are inherently social, embodied and historically situated; (2) Moral deliberation is fundamentally imaginative and takes the form of a dramatic rehearsal; (3) Moral conduct is helpfully conceived on the model of aesthetic perception and artistic creation.' All this squares with Percy Shelley's conception of Reason and Imagination:

> Reason is the enumeration of quantities already known; imagination is the perception of the value of those quantities, both separately and as a whole. Reason respects the differences, and imagination the similitudes of things. Reason is to Imagination as the instrument is to the agent, as the body to the spirit, as the shadow to the substance. (Shelley 1977: 480)

Imagination thus ties to morality in a fundamental, empathetical way:

> The great secret of morals is Love; or a going out of our own nature, and an identification of ourselves with the beautiful which exists in thought, action, or person, not our own. A man, to be greatly good, must imagine intensely and comprehensively; he must put himself in the place of another and of many others; the pains and pleasures of his species must become his own. The great instrument of moral good is the imagination … (Shelley 1977: 487–8)

In yoking empathetic imagining to morality, Shelley stands in a line of thinkers as diverse as Adam Smith, Dewey and – more recently – Neil MacCormick, who have posited that one must step outside oneself (via imagination) to assess the morality of a proposed act. Dewey, for instance, proposes that imaginative empathy is 'the animating mold of moral judgment'. Fesmire takes this to mean that '[t]aking the attitudes of others stirs us beyond numbness so we pause to sort through others' aspirations, interests, and worries as our own' (2003: 65). Smith offers, as MacCormick (2008: 64) describes it, 'the model of an ideal and impartial spectator. Right and wrong are matters of which we judge, by filtering immediate responses of the sentiments by reference to the sentiments we think imputable to somebody situated as we are but possessed of perfect impartiality and complete knowledge'. MacCormick states his own version of empathy-through-imagination by grafting Kant's categorical imperative onto Smith's 'impartial spectator':

> Enter as fully as you can into the feelings of everyone directly involved in or affected by an incident or relationship, and impartially form a maxim of judgement about what is right that all could accept if they were committed to maintaining mutual beliefs setting a common standard of approval and disapproval among themselves. (2008: 64)

Inherent in these conceptions of moral deliberation is a sense of drama, a coupling of imagination and observation. It is not surprising, then, that some have made the link express: Dewey, for example, goes so far as to call moral deliberation 'dramatic rehearsal', a metaphor that Alasdair MacIntyre extends into a conceit:

> we are never more (and sometimes less) than the co-authors of our own narratives. Only in fantasy do we live what story we please. In life, as both Aristotle and Engels noted, we are always under certain constraints. We enter upon a stage which we did not design and we find ourselves part of an action that was not of our making. Each of us being a main character in his own drama plays subordinate parts in the dramas of others, and each drama constrains the others. (2007: 213)

From this – in agreement with Martha Nussbaum – Fesmire (2003: 112) concludes that '[t]o discover how others' life-dramas can develop coordinately with one's own requires attention to the constraints imposed and possibilities made available by other dramas enacted on the same stage'.

All this suggests links among drama, imagination and moral growth. Shelley draws attention to these links with the suggestion that great drama offers a sure spur to imaginative growth and moral strength:

> The tragedies of the Athenian poets are as mirrors in which the spectator beholds himself, under a thin disguise of circumstance, stripped of all but that ideal perfection and energy which every one feels to be the internal type of all that he loves, admires, and would become. The imagination is enlarged by a sympathy with pains and passions so mighty, that they distend in their conception the capacity of that by which they are conceived; the good affections are strengthened by pity, indignation, terror and sorrow; and an exalted calm is prolonged from the satiety of this high exercise of them into the tumult of familiar life; even crime is disarmed of half its horror and all its contagion by being represented as the fatal consequence of the unfathomable agencies of nature; error is thus divested of its wilfulness; men can no longer cherish it as the creation of their choice. In a drama of the highest order there is little food for censure or hatred; it teaches rather self-knowledge and self-respect. Neither the eye nor the mind can see itself, unless reflected upon that which it resembles. The drama, so long as it continues to express poetry, is as a prismatic and many-sided mirror, which collects the brightest rays of human nature and divides and reproduces them from the simplicity of these elementary forms, and touches

> them with majesty and beauty, and multiplies all that it reflects, and endows it with the power of propagating its like wherever it may fall. (1977: 490–91)

Is there a teaching angle here? I think so, for at least two related reasons. First, as Fesmire (2003: 114) argues, Aristotelian 'flexible practical wisdom, not unthinking subjugation to law, is the ideal for citizens, legislators, and judges' and – more important – practical wisdom can be *taught*, as Nussbaum explains:

> Aristotelian education is aimed at producing citizens who are perceivers. It begins with the confident belief that each member of the heterogeneous citizenry is a potential person of practical wisdom, with the basic (that is, as yet undeveloped) ability to cultivate practical perception and use it on behalf of the entire group. It aims at bringing these basic abilities to full actuality. (Quoted in Fesmire 2003: 114)

Second, Dewey's thinking dovetails nicely on this point and emphasizes the central role that imagination plays in meaningful education: '[a]n adequate recognition of the play of imagination as the medium of realization of every kind of thing which lies beyond the scope of direct physical response is the sole way of escape from mechanical methods in teaching' (Dewey 1916: 237). This is so because 'imagination is as much a normal and integral part of human activity as is muscular movement'. But this is not the most interesting part of his theory for our purposes. He goes on to suggest that drama (or acts that approximate drama) is the catalyst for transforming a mere act into representative knowledge:

> The educative value of manual activities and of laboratory exercises, as well as of play, depends upon the extent in which they aid in bringing about a sensing of the meaning of what is going on. In effect, if not in name, they are dramatizations. Their utilitarian value in forming habits of skill to be used for tangible results is important, but not when isolated from the appreciative side. (Dewey 1916: 237)

Dewey's overarching point here is that playacting offers an important mode of learning. This logic can easily be extended to include the observation of playacting. Indeed, J.M. Balkin and Sanford Levinson have persuasively argued that the performative aspects of the law are more important than the textual ones: 'Law, like music or drama, is best understood as performance – the acting out of texts rather than the texts themselves' (1999: 729). Their rationale is that legal texts no more constitute the social practice of law than sheet music or scripts constitute the social practice of music or drama. For them, then, law-as-performance is a more useful analogy than the more familiar law-as-literature comparison because the latter obscures important features of legal practice. Most important for our purposes is their observation that legal practice is built on a triangular relationship among law-creating institutions, law-interpreting institutions and persons affected by law interpretations. Performing arts share this structure in the form of author, performer and audience. Merely reading a text collapses the roles of interpreter and audience, and thereby diminishes the public aspect of a social practice. Even more problematically, we can find ourselves – like Kafka's man from the country – perpetually separated from the law, which, as Derrida describes it, trapped in an infinite loop of textual self-referentiality:

> The story *Before the Law* does not tell or describe anything but itself as text. It does only this or does also this. Not within an assured specular reflection of some self-referential transparency – and I must stress this point – but in the unreadability of the text, if one understands by this the impossibility of acceding to its proper significance and its possibly inconsistent content, which it jealously keeps back. The text guards itself, maintains itself – like the law, speaking only of itself, that is to say, of its non-identity with itself. It neither arrives nor lets anyone arrive. It is the law, makes the law and leaves the reader before the law. (1992: 210–11)

It is for the reason that texts can become self-isolating, among others, that – to illuminate *Hundley*, *Stewart* and their historical context and even deeper background – I have students act out in class the various roles in *Trifles*, rather than have them just read and discuss Glaspell's short-story version of the same basic narrative, 'A Jury of Her Peers'. As a teaching tool, the play – in ways that the story cannot – emphasizes the performative aspects of the law, invokes different senses (and attendant learning paths) and draws attention to the non-verbal aspects of legal performance. It also, in my experience, generates a richer discussion than does a straight-on comparison of *Hundley* and *Stewart*. By this I mean that – without the benefit of *Trifles* – it is easy for students to draw a legal rule amounting to this: 'If you want to claim self-defense, make sure he's awake when you kill him.' *Trifles* shows that the moral issues that surround and penetrate the law of provocation are not so neatly drawn – or, as Gillian Calder more generally suggests elsewhere in this collection, '[i]n being asked to put their bodies into the action of their learning, … those who study and practice law gain access to the means of constituting and transforming a basic rethinking of the power of law itself'. All this is designed to cast off, if even for a few moments, the tyranny of habit and free students to see things anew, to see familiar legal rules bobbing in a sea of moral complexity and to rejudge those rules before blindly applying them.

Conclusion

Law school and law practice are, as Philip Kissam (2003) has argued, akin to a Foucauldian discipline. What he means is that law students traditionally learn (and lawyers traditionally come to practise) in a narrowly instrumental way. This is not, all in all, a bad thing. Law students must learn to understand how to read cases and thereby understand how courts articulate rules in the context of factual determinations. And much of what lawyers do in the workaday world is routine. All this is to say that law schools and legal institutions benefit greatly by the efficiencies associated with repetition and habitual practices. Nonetheless, these efficiencies come with a high associated cost: a valorization of rules and familiar forms of legal narrative that – in some cases – proves insufficient. What the 'Beyond Text' project aims to do is demonstrate how a process of defamiliarizing received legal forms can cultivate in students and practitioners alike a rounder imagination, one that – especially in novel and hard cases – offers new ways out of the legal thicket. Teaching and learning law with contextual-historicist tools is perhaps one such way.

References

Balkin, J.M. and Levinson, S. 1999 'Law as performance', in M. Freeman and A.D.E. Lewis (eds), *Law and Literature*. Oxford: Oxford University Press, 729–51.

Binder, G. and Weisberg, R. 2000. *Literary Criticisms of Law.* Princeton, NJ: Princeton University Press.

Cornell, D. 1990. 'The violence of the masquerade: law dressed up as justice'. *Cardozo Law Review*, 11, 1047–64.

Crane, G.D. 1997. 'The path of law and literature'. *American Literary History*, 9, 758–75.

Derrida, J. 1992. *Acts of Literature*, edited by D. Attridge. New York: Routledge.

Dewey, J. 1916. *Democracy and Education.* New York: Free Press.

Fesmire, S. 2003. *John Dewey & Moral Imagination: Pragmatism in Ethics.* Bloomington, IN: Indiana University Press.

Gallagher, C. and Greenblatt, S. 2000. *Practicing New Historicism.* Chicago: University of Chicago Press.

Glaspell, S. 1996. *Trifles*, in L. Ledwon (ed.), *Law and Literature: Text and Theory*. New York: Garland, 151–64.

Gordon, R.D. 2011. *Rehumanizing Law: A Theory of Law and Democracy.* Toronto: University of Toronto Press.

Greenblatt, S. 1980. *Renaissance Self-Fashioning: From More to Shakespeare.* Chicago: University of Chicago Press.

Jackson, B.S. 1988. *Law, Fact and Narrative Coherence*. Roby, Merseyside: Deborah Charles.

Jones, D. 1978. *The Dime Novel Western.* Bowling Green, OH: Bowling Green State University Popular Press.

Kissam, P.C. 2003. *The Discipline of Law Schools: The Making of Modern Lawyers.* Durham, NC: Carolina Academic Press.

Lee, R.W. 1967. *Ut Pictura Poesis: The Humanistic Theory of Painting.* New York: Norton.

Lessing, G.E. 1962. *Laocoon*, translated by E. Allen. Indianapolis: Bobbs.

MacCormick, N. 2008. *Practical Reason in Law and Morality.* Oxford: Oxford University Press.
MacIntyre, A. 2007. *After Virtue*, 3rd edn. Notre Dame, IN: Notre Dame University Press.
Male, E. 1958. *The Gothic Image: Religious Art in France of the Thirteenth Century*, translated by D. Nussey. New York: Harper.
Maute, J.L. 1994–1995. 'Peevyhouse v. Garland Coal & Mining Co. Revisited: the Ballad of Willie and Lucille'. *Northwestern University Law Review*, 89, 1341–486.
Montrose, L.A. 1980. 'The purpose of playing: reflections on a Shakespearean anthropology'. *Helios*, 32, 51–74.
Murfin, R. and Ray, S.M. 2003. *The Bedford Glossary of Critical and Literary Terms*, 2nd edn. Boston: Bedford/St Martin's.
Orgel, S. 1994. 'The role of king', in H.A. Veeser (ed.), *The New Historicism Reader*. New York: Routledge, 35–45.
Praz, M. 1970. *Mnemosyne: The Parallel Between Literature and the Visual Arts.* Princeton, NJ: Princeton University Press.
Reid, J.P. 1996. *Law for the Elephant: Property and Social Behavior on the Overland Trail*. San Marino: Huntington Library Press.
Shelley, P. 1977. 'A defence of poetry', in D.H. Reiman and S.B. Powers (eds), *Shelley's Poetry and Prose*. New York: Norton.
Shepard, S. 1981. *True West.* New York: Samuel French.
Somers, M. 'The Narrative Constitution of Identity: A Relational and Network Approach'. *Theory & Society*, 23, 605–49.
Sullivan, W.M. et al. 2007. *Educating Lawyers: Preparation for the Profession of Law.* San Francisco: Jossey-Bass (this work is popularly known as *The Carnegie Report*).
Sypher, W. 1955. *Four Stages of Renaissance Style: Transformations in Art and Literature 1400–1700.* Garden City, NY: Doubleday.
Taine, H. 1965 [1864]. 'History of English literature', in R. Ellman and C. Feidelson, Jr. (eds), *The Modern Tradition: Backgrounds of Modern Literature.* New York: Oxford University Press.
Thomas, B. 1991a. 'Reflections on the law and literature revival'. *Critical Inquiry*, 17, 510–39.
Thomas, B. 1991b. *The New Historicism and Other Old-Fashioned Topics.* Princeton, NJ: Princeton University Press.
Turner, F.J. 1893. *The Frontier in American History*. New York: Holt.
Wesson, M. 2006. 'Particular intentions: the Hillmon case and the Supreme Court'. *Law & Literature*, 18, 343–401.
Wesson, M. 2007. '"Remarkable stratagems and conspiracies": how unscrupulous lawyers and credulous judges created an exception to the hearsay rule'. *Fordham Law Review*, 76, 1675–706.

Cases

Groves v John Wunder Co. [1939] 286 N.W. 235.
Life Ins. Co. of New York v Hillmon [1892] 145 U.S. 285.
Mutual Life Ins. Co. of New York v Hillmon [1892] 145 U.S. 909.
Peevyhouse v Garland Coal & Mining Co. [1962] 382 P.2d 109.
State v Hundley [1985] 693 P.2d 475.
State v Stewart [1988] 763 P.2d 572.

Chapter 9

Performance, Pedagogy and Law: Theatre of the Oppressed in the Law School Classroom[1]

Gillian Calder

Theatre, Pedagogy, Ethics and Law

> Theatre of the Oppressed is about acting rather than talking, questioning rather than giving answers, analysing rather than accepting. This is … for all those who are interested in theatre as a force for change. (Jackson 2002: xxvii)

There is an uneasy sense out there in the ethos that there is a crisis of legal ethics and professionalism in Canada and that this crisis is tied in some measure to legal education.[2] This uneasy sense has recently been exacerbated by two fairly high-profile events. The first was an address made by the Governor General of Canada, David Johnston, to an annual meeting of the Canadian Bar Association (CBA). Garnering considerable media attention,[3] the address called on the profession to craft a new definition of the lawyer as professional. Pointing to several relationships of tension for the legal profession in Canada – including the relationship between the Bar and the academy – he appealed to members of the CBA to imagine themselves as oysters, embracing the irritation of those relationships like sand that may ultimately produce a pearl. In so doing, he echoed a call that resonates

1 This chapter was first published as 'Embodied Law: Theatre of the Oppressed in the Law School Classroom' (2009) 1 *Masks: The Online Journal of Law and Theatre* 1–35 and is archived here: http://masksjournal.com/issues/Masks-Issue1-February2009.pdf [accessed 28 August 2012]. I am very grateful to the editors for their permission to republish with revisions.

2 For discussion and contestation of this notion of crisis, see, for example, Mackenzie 1995; DeCoste 2001; Macdonald 2001; and Dodek 2008. My gratitude to Allan Wu for bringing these articles to my attention.

3 The complete speech is archived here: http://www.cba.org/CBA/news/2011_Releases/2011-07-14-CLC-eng.aspx [accessed 28 August 2012]. See commentary on the speech at: http://www.theglobeandmail.com/news/opinions/editorials/david-johnstons-welcome-words-to-lawyers/article2132725/ and http://business.financialpost.com/2011/08/24/david-johnstons-speech-to-cba-gets-noticed/ [accessed 28 August 2012].

at present through Canadian law for a 'broad and extensive focus on ethics in law school' to help aspiring lawyers develop a greater understanding of the ethical implications of a proposed course of action.[4]

The second event highlighting current unease about legal ethics and professionalism is the release of the 'Final Report' authored by the Canadian Federation of Law Societies Task Force on the Canadian Common Law Degree (hereinafter the 'Task Force').[5] This document was the final of a series of reports drafted by the Task Force over a two-year period, all with the aim of recommending to provincial law societies that they develop a national 'approved' law degree as a prerequisite for admission to the profession of law. Although the Final Report addressed the criticisms and concerns arising from previous drafts of their recommendations, the Final Report (as adopted) mandates that all law schools in Canada require students to take a stand-alone course in legal ethics, with a detailed list of what such a course should address.[6]

The aspects of legal education that I view as fundamental – empathy, creativity and a nuanced understanding of equality – rarely appear on any detailed list of what a course in legal ethics should address. Indeed, one of the things that we need to bring to the fore in legal education in Canada is our capacity to enhance the ethical imagination of the legal advocate through the creative, the embodied, the visual and the performative. The development of ethical sensibility is critical for the practice of law, and yet there is still a sense that all we need to do to ensure the ethical sensibility of students is to train them to be lawyers (Del Mar 2010: 991). It is not enough. While we are chastised by professional bodies who assert that not enough attention is being paid to questions of legal ethics in law schools, the realities of trying to keep pace with the changing demographics of law students, including diversities of gender, class, language, ethnicity, culture, religious backgrounds, age, sexuality and Indigeneity, as well as the diverse ways in which students in the twenty-first century learn and communicate, are not addressed.

The sense that there is a crisis in how law schools and the legal profession are addressing issues of legal ethics and professionalism in Canada seems to be widely shared. What we don't all share, however, is a common understanding of 'ethics' and 'professionalism'.[7] Nor, with very few exceptions, do we share

---

4 This call was supported, unfortunately, with an 'old boy's network' story from the Governor General's own law teaching days.

5 http://www.flsc.ca/_documents/Common-Law-Degree-Report-C.pdf [accessed 28 August 2012]. The Federation of Law Societies is the national coordinating body for Canada's 14 provincial and territorial law societies.

6 http://www.ccld-cdfdc.ca/documents/LSUCletterNov2009.pdf [accessed 28 August 2012].

7 As Constance Backhouse writes, 'the history of the legal profession illustrates that concepts such as professionalism, civility, community, and collegiality have been imbued with discriminatory intent and practice. These are, indeed, ideas that have been pressed

a sense of what kind of legal pedagogy is best suited for enhancing the ethical sensibilities of law students in Canada. These questions have been the central and driving force behind the 'Beyond Text in Legal Education' project hosted at the University of Edinburgh with particular focus on how the exclusive emphasis on textual resources, on languages and their manipulation, carries with it significant dangers. Such an exclusive focus can be restrictive in that it can result in law students and legal professionals never acquiring the skill of coming to see and recognize the ethical complexity of any given situation; it places at risk their ability to overcome the limitation of the categories with which they are working, particularly when the particular situation itself puts into question the categories that are supposed to deal with it. Coping with this limit requires the exercise of the ethical imagination. Such an exercise enables the person to respond to the complexity and particularity of the situation, and to come up with just and imaginative ways of going forward.[8]

On the most fundamental of levels, much of law involves embodied concepts,[9] yet rarely do we ask our students to put their bodies into the theoretical learning of law. In other words, we teach our students primarily by talking to them. And then we evaluate them by asking them to put into action what they have learned, usually in a three-hour, sit-down exam, and we are surprised when many of them do not do well, and some of them fail. Building on my own work in trying to move beyond text, the aim of this chapter is to offer another set of questions to ongoing discussions about the teaching of law in Canadian law schools. This project's central aim is to rethink the way in which we approach legal teaching and learning as a predominantly intellectual pursuit where the teachers are the sole experts (Macfarlane 1996: 72). Drawing on the work of educational theorists, I explore Augusto Boal's observation 'that the whole body thinks – not just the brain' (Boal 2002: 49) and, through the use of theatrical games and techniques in the classroom, open up embodied possibilities for law students and law teachers to reconceptualize their understandings of law and its power.

---

into service to allow the most privileged of lawyers and judges to exercise power and promulgate exclusion based on gender, race, class and religion' (Backhouse 2003: 2–25). See also Pue 1991 and 2009.

8 This is taken from the 'rationale and research context' description of the 'Beyond Text in Legal Education' project on its website: http://www.law.ed.ac.uk/beyondtext [accessed 28 August 2012]. Although hosted at Edinburgh, this project had a diversity of jurisdictions represented in its members, including Canada.

9 For example, my primary research has been focused on law's engagement with the pregnant body, primarily through the delivery of maternity and parental leave benefits in Canadian law: Calder 2007: 135–41. Traditional modes of communication can marginalize embodied forms in many ways: Adjin-Tettey et al. 2008: 8.

Research Questions

This chapter sets out to provide the theoretical and practical context that informs a component designed and delivered in the first-year orientation curriculum at the University of Victoria's Faculty of Law (UVic Law) described below. The exercises are drawn from the work of Augusto Boal, as it has been taught to me by several practitioners of Theatre of the Oppressed, including Boal himself, and adapted particularly for the unique setting of the law school environment.[10]

This curricular component is one piece of a larger project that I am pursuing: a commitment that aims to explore the transformative potential of engaged experiential learning, drawing on non-textual (or 'Beyond Text')[11] resources, as a means of understanding the power of law.[12] By probing the theoretical integrity

10 I have been trained to be a facilitator of workshops employing the theatre techniques of *Theatre of the Oppressed*. This training primarily began in September 2006 when I was selected to be one of six facilitators trained by the Puente Theatre, pursuant to a federal government grant, to deliver 'Act Now Against Racism' workshops in their respective communities. It included the development and implementation of *Theatre of the Oppressed* techniques in two law school courses (Family Law 322 and Civil Liberties 359), workshops in two law school courses (Equality Law 378 and Racism and the Law 358), workshops for two student groups (the Dean's Advisory Committee on Ethnicity and Culture and the UVic Association of Women and the Law), a workshop at the UVic Faculty Retreat 2007 in Cowichan Bay, BC, and presentations at four legal conferences: the Canadian Association of Law Teachers, Saskatoon, SK, May 2007; Gender Unbound, Keele, England, July 2007; Law and Society Annual Meetings, Berlin, Germany, July 2007; and the Canadian Initiative in Law, Culture and the Humanities, Ottawa, ON, October 2007. This training was augmented in June 2007 when I was chosen to train with Augusto Boal at an 'Aesthetics of the Oppressed' workshop in New York, 4–7 June 2007, and in December 2007 and January 2008 when I trained with Sanjoy Ganguly and Jana Sanskriti, in Badu, India. Since then I have also presented this work at the University of Victoria (February 2008), UBC Law (May and June 2008), at the Law and Society meetings in Montreal, QC (June 2008) at Carleton University (October 2008), at the University of Alberta (November 2008), at the University of Edinburgh (June 2009), at the University of Oregon (May 2010), at UVic's Teaching and Learning Centre (November 2010) and in Limerick (March 2011).

11 I am fortunate to have been a participant at a 'Beyond Text in Legal Education' conference at the University of Edinburgh in June 2009.

12 I was first introduced to the potential of these kinds of materials, and primarily the work of Augusto Boal, in a collaborative project with seven colleagues at the law school in the spring of 2005. This work led to presentations at several international conferences, employing a performance-based approach to law: *Performing Apology: Being/Saying/Feeling/Hearing/Knowing Sorry* (NAISA, Sacramento, California, May 2011) (with Miranda Johnson, Kirsty Gover and Emily Snyder); *Marriage, Polygamy, Monogamy: Coded Words, Embodied Silence* (CILCH, Ottawa, Ontario, October 2010); *The Card Game* (Barbados, June 2010) (with Sharon Cowan); *The Jane Doe Coffee Table Book about Rape – Reflections on Rebellious Writing and Teaching* (Law, Culture and the Humanities, Boston, MA, April 2009) (with Rebecca Johnson); *Reimagining Equality: Dancing with*

of this work, I aim to explore solutions to the kinds of challenges first-year law students face entering legal education in early twenty-first-century Canada. Of concern here is the continued marginalization in the study and practice of law experienced by students on the basis of their lived diversities.[13] Ultimately, I aim to bring three underexplored aspects of the relationship between performance and law into the law school classroom. These three concepts are briefly discussed below as a means through which to situate the theory and the practice that informs the curricular component developed and delivered as part of UVic Law's orientation curriculum.

The first aspect is the hierarchical way in which law is taught. Here, the focus is on dialogic techniques drawn from *Theatre of the Oppressed* to see what they can offer communities who face exclusion and discrimination in the law, law school and the legal profession. During my first few years of teaching law at two Canadian universities, I was struck and surprised by experiences in the law school classroom impacting the dynamics of the law school environment as a place of engaged pedagogy and learning. Some are experiential, some are speculative and some result from my involvement in a research project investigating student course choices at seven law schools in Canada (Bakht et al. 2007). In particular, this part of the larger project will look at the use of embodied exercises as a means to explore dialogue as a solution to each of the following observations: the way in which the pressure to find work as a lawyer is imposed upon law students from the first semester of the first year;[14] the way in which electronic media create a barrier

Dichotomies (Law, Culture and the Humanities, Washington, DC, March 2007) (with Sharon Cowan); *Postcards from the Edge (of Empire)* (Why and How? Theoretical and Methodological Directions in Law, Feminism, Gender and Sexuality Workshop, University of British Columbia, August 2006) (with Elizabeth Adjin-Tettey, Hester Lessard, Angela Cameron, Margot Young and Maneesha Deckha); *Reimagining Equality: Dancing with Dichotomies* (Revisiting Equality Workshop, Onati, Spain, July 2006) (with Sharon Cowan); *Reimagining Equality: Dancing with Dichotomies* (Up Against the Nation-States of Feminist Legal Theory, Kent, England, June 2006) (with Sharon Cowan); and *Roundtable: Postcards from the Edge (of Empire)* (CLSA, Harrison Hot Springs, BC, June 2005) (with Elizabeth Adjin-Tettey, Angela Cameron, Maneesha Deckha, Rebecca Johnson, Hester Lessard, Maureen Maloney and Margot Young).

13 I have also seen in my time at four different law schools in Canada that there is an overt hostility experienced by, amongst others, students of colour, female students, queer students and Aboriginal students. Despite curricula that offer a diversity of choices, commitments to equity and diversity by faculties, cultural and academic supports in the law schools themselves and admissions policies that respect life experience as a criteria for law school success, students often articulate that they feel silenced in the classroom: Bakht et al. 2007: 686–92.

14 My first reflection is on the way in which job searches have become something that first-year students do from the moment that they arrive at law school. Before they even know what it is that they are embarking upon, they are inundated with student seminars, workshops and firm-based 'wine and cheeses' focusing their attention on the work they will

between the student and the professor, and between students and each other;[15] the strongly articulated critique that the views of privileged students are not valued in the law school classroom;[16] and finally difficulties experienced by students of colour, women, queer students, students with disabilities and Indigenous students, despite increased numbers and attention to diversity in the curriculum (see footnote 13 above).

The second aspect of this larger curricular project is critical reflection on the role of image in our understanding of what constitutes law. As Alison Young argues, the institutions of law often disavow connection to the aesthetic and the imaginary despite law's reliance on regimes of images to found its authority (2005: 13). Thinking about law *as* art offers to both students and teachers an opportunity to stand in a different place with respect to interpretation. The diverse group of scholars, artists, activists and lawyers working on the 'Beyond Text in Legal Education' project have through their divergent projects argued for a reconceptualization of the kinds of tools that we use in legal education to enhance the ethical imaginations of our students.

Arguably, the exercise that I describe below is text-based, in the sense that all the scenes that the students are called upon to act out begin with a scripted text. However, I will argue that the exercise challenges the students to think with their bodies, to place themselves into the action that the scene provokes and to try to identify what is problematic in the scene through the implications of their actions. It also asks them to centre how the scene they watch makes them feel, where there is discomfort for them, and to envision embodied strategies for change. It is the image of law, relationships, justice and fairness that is presented before them and the interpretive lens that they bring to bear on that image that drives this exercise.

By pushing ourselves and our students to consider the affective dimension of law *as* art, we reinforce the role that both play in mediating the social imaginary (Buchanan and Johnson 2009: 38). In this sense, the project will explore the

do when they leave law school as opposed to the work they will do while they are there. My experience is of a sense of anxiety and urgency that is generated, in some cases, before they even arrive. There is no question that law schools in Canada are becoming more expensive places to study: Bakht et al. 2007. And, as tuition rises, so does the student debt level, leaving students with a greater sense of urgency to secure employment at the completion of their studies.

15 My second reflection flows from the use of laptops in classrooms. As someone who now thinks with her fingers, I am not surprised by the rise in their use, a faster, more efficient way to take notes in class. However, what does surprise me is how an attempt to transcribe what the teacher says word for word replaces engaged dynamics in class, and how surfing the net, social media, instant messaging and other forms of disengagement often characterize the classroom.

16 My third reflection is of a form of backlash in the classroom. This manifests itself in several ways, but includes a form of complaint by students of privilege that there is no place for their views at law school. It also manifests itself in active resistance and disengagement in classrooms in which alternative approaches to teaching law are employed.

relationship between teacher, student and community, with attention to the transformative potential of this particular theatrical technique. In particular, this part of the project will allow students to engage in revisioning law; identifying little examined spaces that law inhabits, particularly spaces where the relationship between government action, local participation and citizen engagement has been fractured.[17] One of the goals of Theatre of the Oppressed is 'profoundly to disrupt existing authority structures, in the first instance by disrupting the space of conventional theatre' (Pratt and Johnston 2007: 106). My goal is to do the same to the law school classroom and, through that disruption, to engage students and teachers more explicitly in the study and practice of law.

The third aspect of the larger project flows from the conceptualization of lawyers as actors. Here the dual meaning of the verb 'to act' (acting is both performing and taking action) becomes relevant. I will highlight the way in which theatre techniques can be employed to train future lawyers for the work they will do acting on behalf of clients, and advocating for those clients in the theatrical venue of the courtroom and other spaces of power. In a concrete and experiential way, this aspect of the project uses theatrical games and exercises to strengthen student confidence, to work with issues of presence and ultimately to bring more of a sense of joy into the way in which they learn to be legal advocates while being mindful of the incredible power of law.

With attention to how each of these reflections contributes to developing the skills of empathy, creativity and imagination, my goal is to query whether there is something about the primarily top-down way in which we teach and learn law in Canada that could withstand some scrutiny. My hope is that the law school is not just a place in which the status quo of privilege is enhanced, but a place in which true ethical dialogue exists and expands.[18]

In the next part of this chapter I will do two things. The first is to begin to explore the theoretical underpinnings of an approach to teaching and learning law that centres dialogue in the relationship between the teachers and learners of law. The second is to explore different methodologies of teaching and learning that can put this approach to pedagogy in place. This exploration is preliminary and introductory, and is not meant as a panacea to the problems raised above. Instead, the goal here is to develop and implement different teaching exercises, drawing on a particular set of theatrical traditions, as one way to begin a rethinking of the role of the body in the development of the ethical legal professional.

---

17 A good example of an attempt to put this work into action in Canada is Headline Theatre's 2004 project using Legislative Theatre to engage with social welfare cuts in the city of Vancouver, entitled 'Practicing Democracy'. Information about the project can be found at: http://www.headlinestheatre.com/past_work/pd/how/index.html [accessed 22 August 2012].

18 The relationship between monologue and dialogue is key to this argument and to the work of Paulo Freire, Augusto Boal and those who applied and modified their techniques over the years.

Paulo Freire and *Pedagogy of the Oppressed*

In 1970, Paulo Freire published his influential text *Pedagogy of the Oppressed*, in which he set out a revolutionary approach to education. He envisioned that the ontological vocation of human beings is to be subjects who act upon and transform their own worlds. For Freire, every human being, no matter where they are situated, is capable of looking critically at the world in a dialogical encounter with others (Schaull 1996: 14), exchanges in which both student and teacher learn, question, reflect and participate in meaning-making (Freire 1996: 60–62). Articulated primarily as a means to promote education through action for the illiterate of his own country, Brazil, Freire's *Pedagogy of the Oppressed* has translated into an effective means of overcoming other 'cultures of silence',[19] including those of advanced technological societies (Hooks 1994: 45–58). The text and its arguments, although subject to some strong critical commentary over the years (Freire 2003: 54–6), have been and continue to be employed in many educational contexts throughout the world.

Freire's approach to pedagogy is probably best understood as a critique of what he called the 'banking' concept of education. He writes:

> Narration (with the teacher as narrator) leads the students to memorize mechanically the narrated content. Worse yet, it turns them into 'containers,' into 'receptacles' to be 'filled' by the teacher. The more completely she fills the receptacles, the better a teacher she is. The more meekly the receptacles permit themselves to be filled, the better students they are. Education thus becomes an act of depositing, in which the students are the depositories and the teacher is the depositor. Instead of communicating, the teacher issues communiqués and makes deposits which the students patiently receive, memorize and repeat. This is the 'banking' concept of education, in which the scope of action allowed to the students extends only so far as receiving, filing and storing the deposits. (Freire 1996: 52–3)

Freire argued that formal education was an instrument of oppression rather than liberation and that banking education acted as a pillar in maintaining that social order. The more time that students spend with rote pedagogy, 'the less they develop the critical consciousness which would result from their intervention in the world as transformers of the world' (Freire 1996: 54).

In Freire's approach to pedagogy, learners do have opportunities that arise from being collectors and cataloguers of the things they store. However, knowledge only comes through invention and reinvention 'through the restless, impatient, continuing, hopeful inquiry human beings pursue in the world, with the world

---

19 Freire's pedagogy is in many ways centrally a response to his concern for citizens whose silence in the face of their own oppressions resulted from systems of economic, social and political domination that often made critical awareness and political engagement impossible: Schaull 1996: 12.

and with each other' (Freire 1996: 53). He thus calls on educators to reject the banking approach in favour of problem-posing, that is, the posing of the problems of human beings in relation with the world. Although this approach to education might not seem particularly revolutionary, what makes it problem solving and not problematization is its dialogical construction. Through dialogue, 'the teacher is no longer merely the-one-who-teaches, but one who is himself taught in dialogue with the students, who in turn while being taught also teach[es] … The students, no longer docile listeners – are now critical investigators in dialogue with the teacher' (Friere 1996: 61–2).

In Friere's theoretical approach to education, what matters most is that human beings have the capacity for creative thinking and, by engaging in dialogue, have the capacity to transform rather than merely to adapt to reality (Blackburn 2000: 5). A constant and dynamic process, Freire does not envisage a future just society, but sees the process of liberation and of humanization as an ongoing process. Central to this aspect of Freire's theory is what he calls 'conscientisation', that is, the process by which human beings become more aware of the sources of their oppression. But this is not purely an intellectual process. This approach sees education as being constantly remade in a cycle of action-reflection-action. As compared to an approach to education that emphasizes permanence and reaction, problem-posing education 'roots itself in the dynamic present and becomes revolutionary' (Freire 1996: 65). It is only through action and reflection as a dynamic and dialectical process that education can be truly achieved.

Freire's method sees the role of the educator as catalyst, or animator, a facilitator who creates space for dialogue and for those facing oppression to become creative subjects of the learning process rather than passive objects (Blackburn 2000: 8–9). For Freire, the challenge was illiteracy and he put his practice into action in an effective way for peasants in rural communities near his own, as well as in many other similar contexts. For teachers and learners of law, the challenge seems entirely different. Thus, the next part of this chapter looks at how this particular approach to pedagogy can be translated into a context, in this case a Canadian law school, in which the idea of oppression translates in different and complicated ways (Thornton 1998: 376).

Augusto Boal and Theatre of the Oppressed

In the Theatre of the Oppressed, oppression is defined, in part, as a power dynamic based on monologue rather than dialogue; a relation of domination and command that prohibits the oppressed from being who they are and from exercising their basic human rights.[20]

20 This quote is often used without attribution to describe what lies at the heart of Theatre of the Oppressed. See, for example, http://www.pepol.info/docs/casestudies/RO%20-%20Forum%20Theatre.pdf at 19 [accessed 28 August 2012].

In 1974, Augusto Boal wrote his influential text *Theatre of the Oppressed* based upon his work both as Artistic Director of the Arena Theatre in Sao Paulo from 1956 to 1971 and as a Workers' Party activist over the same period of time. Inspired by fellow Brazilian Paulo Freire, Theatre of the Oppressed's techniques are based on the Freirean principles of dialogue, interaction, problem-posing, reflection and conscientization and are designed to activate spectators (or, as Boal calls them, 'spect-actors') to take control of situations, rather than being passive subjects of action (Singhal 2004: 143–52). Theatre of the Oppressed is thus a means of putting Freire's pedagogy of the oppressed into action and particularly, seeing theatre as a political vehicle of liberation.

The main objective of Boal's practice was 'to change the people – "spectators", passive beings in the theatrical phenomenon – into subjects, into actors, transformers of the dramatic action' (Boal 1985: 122). Through a series of exercises, games and techniques, Boal proposes a method that transforms the notion of theatre from one in which the spectator no longer delegates power to characters on stage to think or act in their place, but is freed to think and act for themselves. The theatrical act is thus experienced as conscious intervention, as a rehearsal for social action rooted in a collective analysis of shared problems.[21] It is in this manner – theatre as a rehearsal for transformation – that the relationship between equity, law and performance begins to emerge.[22]

For Boal, theatre is a language that is capable of being utilized by any person, with or without artistic talent, and a language whose first word is the human body (Boal 1985: 121, 125–6). To begin to use this language, participants must therefore know their own bodies and learn to express themselves using their bodies. Once this is experienced, spectators can move towards becoming actors, changing from objects to subjects, from witnesses to protagonists in the exercise and then in their own lives (Boal 1985: 121, 125–6). The method has several stages: first, 'a series of exercises by which one gets to know one's own body'; second, 'a series of games by which one begins to express one's self through body, abandoning other, more common and habitual forms of expression';[23] third, the practice of theatre as

21 See descriptions of Theatre of the Oppressed at: http://brechtforum.org/abouttop [accessed 28 August 2012].

22 Some important work has been done using the techniques of Theatre of the Oppressed in the Canadian context. One example is the work of David Diamond and the Headlines Theatre in Vancouver, BC. Diamond's work draws on systems theory to reconceptualize the techniques of Theatre of the Oppressed away from the clear boundaries of oppressor and oppressed and more towards viewing the issues of contemporary Canadian society as a living organism. As Diamond writes, 'in order to get to the root causes of a problem, *Theatre for Living* investigates the oppressed, but also makes space to investigate the fears, desires and motivations of the oppressor' (Diamond 2007: 38).

23 Many of the games and exercises are detailed in *Games for Actors and Non-Actors*. This is an invaluable text for the work of Theatre of the Oppressed in any educational setting. Many other texts also detail the kinds of games and exercises that ground this work, for example, *Theatre for Living*.

language through Image Theatre, in which spectators speak through images made with actors' bodies, and forum theatre where the 'spectators intervene directly in the dramatic action and act'; and finally through 'simple forms in which the spectator-actor creates "spectacles" according to his [or her] need to discuss certain themes or rehearse certain actions' (Boal 1985: 125–55). The goal of the process is to free the audience for action.

With Image Theatre and Forum Theatre at the heart of the work, Theatre of the Oppressed becomes one way of putting Freire's pedagogical principles into action (Boal 2006: 4–7). The goal of both is to provide a stimulant for participants to transform their own worlds. The theory is that overcoming the challenges presented in theatrical form makes participants better qualified to overcome the same challenges in reality when the situation arises (Boal 2002: 241–52). The translator's introduction to the first edition of *Games for Actors and Non-Actors* provides a good description of these two fundamental techniques:

> Image Theatre is a series of exercises and games designed to uncover essential thoughts about societies and cultures without resort, in the first instance, to spoken language – through this may be added in the various 'dynamisations' of the images. The participants in Image Theatre make still images of their lives, feeling and experiences, oppressions; groups suggest titles or themes, and then individuals 'sculpt' three-dimensional images under these titles, using their own and others' bodies as the 'clay.' However, the image work never remains static – as with all of Theatre of the Oppressed, the frozen image is simply the starting point for or prelude to the action, which is revealed in the dynamisation process, the bringing to life of the images and the discovery of whatever direction or intention that is innate in them. (Jackson 2002: xxii; Adjin-Tettey et al. 2008)

And:

> Forum Theatre is a theatrical game in which a problem is shown in an unsolved form, to which the audience, again spectactors, is invited to suggest and enact solutions. The problem is always the symptom of oppression, and generally involves visible oppressors and a protagonist who is oppressed. In its purest form, both actors and spectactors will be people who are victims of the oppression under consideration; that is why they are able to offer alternative solutions, because they themselves are personally acquainted with the oppression. After one showing of the scene, which is known as 'the model' (it can be a full-length play), it is shown again slightly speeded up, and follows exactly the same course until a member of the audience shouts 'Stop!' takes the place of the protagonist and tries to defeat the oppressors.
>
> The game is a form of contest between spectactors trying to bring the play to a different end (in which the cycle of oppression is broken) and actors ostensibly making every possible effort to bring it to its original end (in which the oppressed

> is beaten and the oppressors are triumphant). The proceedings are presided over by a [facilitator], whose function it is to ensure the smooth running of the game and teach the audience the rules … Many different solutions are enacted in the course of a single forum – the result is the pooling of knowledge, tactics and experience, and at the same time what Boal calls a 'rehearsal for reality'. (Jackson 2002: xxiv)

The techniques that ground Boal's *Theatre of the Oppressed* have been applied and practised throughout the world in a variety of contexts; educational, social and theatrical.[24] They have rarely so been, however, in legal education.[25]

Boal himself drew the direct connection between his theatrical work and the power of law when elected as a Vereador (city councillor) for Rio de Janeiro in 1993. There he used his lifelong body of work to create 'legislative theatre', a set of processes which mix his theatrical techniques with 'the conventional rituals of a parliamentary chamber or assembly, with the objective of arriving at the formulation of coherent and viable bills of law' (Boal 2006: 6). Detailed in his 1998 text *Legislative Theatre*, Boal shows the relationship between theatre, democracy and law, and in the process demonstrates how at the heart of his work is the word 'to act' in all of its various meanings.

An attempt to explain how this dynamic operates might enable a more critical reflective approach to legal education. I now foreground the performative nature of the work undertaken at UVic by looking at how the concept of performativity is of importance to scholars and theorists of gender.[26]

---

24 See www.theatreoftheoppressed.org [accessed 28 August 2012]. Practitioners of Theatre of the Oppressed, however, often address legal issues. For example, Headlines Theatre in Vancouver has undertaken several projects addressing legal issues facing, particularly, Canadians living in poverty: Diamond 2007: 209–80. Similarly, Jana Sanskriti, a theatre company practising Theatre of the Oppressed in West Bengal, India, has been addressing issues of domestic violence, land expropriation and food policies, amongst other issues through theatre since the mid-1980s: Ganguly 2004: 220–57.

25 There is little written in the academic literature on using *Theatre of the Oppressed* in teaching law. I am aware, however, of several colleagues who have drawn on this work in their teaching. I am grateful to Maureen Maloney whose work with Forum Theatre at UVic Law was the impetus for my own work. I am also aware of the work of Lani Guinier using Democratic Theater at Harvard Law School.

26 An interesting challenge of this work was how to present on it, particularly at legal conferences. It seemed problematic, or even ironic, to talk about an exercise that was about doing. As a result, my first presentations on this work at the University of Kent and in Berlin were comprised of theatrical exercises with the audience as opposed to a formal presentation. I have not detailed that work in this piece, but have co-written elsewhere on the power of the performative in legal conference spaces: Adjin-Tettey et al. 2008; Calder and Cowan 2008.

Performativity, Gender and Law

In the methodology of Theatre of the Oppressed, there is no being, only becoming. One isn't restricted from writing a poem because one isn't a poet, but in the process of writing a poem, one becomes a poet (Boal 2006: 85). This aspect of the work, one that requires some attention to the distinction between performance and performativity, is strongly evocative of Judith Butler's work on gender and on the idea of gender as performed. She writes:

> Gender is the repeated stylization of the body, as a set of repeated acts within a highly rigid regulatory frame that congeal over time to produce the appearance of substance, a natural sort of being. A political genealogy of gender ontologies, if it is successful, will deconstruct the substantive appearance of gender into its constitutive acts and locate and account for those acts within the compulsory frames set by the various forces that police the social appearance of gender. (Butler 1990: 45)

It is in this sense, Butler's understanding of gender not as a noun but always as a doing (1990: 34), that the potential of Theatre of the Oppressed as a methodology for students, teachers and others learning about law and its power is revealed. In being asked to put their bodies into the action of their learning and to respond to the polysemic (Boal 2002: 139 and 175) in the images that surround and confront them, those who study and practise law gain access to the means of constituting and transforming a basic rethinking of the power of law itself (Smart 1989: 4–25).

This also resonates with Butler's later work and, in particular, with her re-engagement with performativity. Responding directly to criticism of the definition of performativity noted above, Butler argued that 'performance is not about taking on the garb of a particular elected gender at whichever moment one chooses – in fact it is not really about choice at all, since the range of garments and the language and tools of gender available to us are already prescribed within society' (Cowan 2001). On one level, the use of theatre in the learning of law offers a way of analysing how identity is not at any given time concrete, stable and immutable. On another level, however, Theatre of the Oppressed is a means of illuminating the systemic factors that place strictures of constraint on law's engagement with these very notions of identity.

Probing further the relationship between feminist theory, performativity and law is in this way a means to rethink our own understandings of what constitutes law. Here the work of Julie Lassonde is particularly instructive, as she investigates the ways in which daily performances transform the law that we live in and that surrounds us. Through an analysis of disruptions of seemingly routine interactions, Lassonde develops an argument of how we can learn law by participating in it, 'paying attention to how we act in daily life … helps understand how we create legal norms' (Lassonde 2006: 7). This sort of analysis, broadening the idea of law, also enables a challenge to law's authority as something held only by the professional, as 'people, legally trained or not, have embodied knowledge they can draw on to solve legal problems' (quoted in Lassonde 2006: 10–11). Approaching the learning of law from this more destabilized place offers an otherwise little-examined view of legal norms.

With reference to Butler, Lassonde ultimately argues that 'law is a way for us to develop a series of narratives that simultaneously create norms and give them meaning. Norms, like identities, are not fixed. They depend on the way we build and interpret them through our daily life gestures' (Lassonde 2006: 3). This kind of interpretation relies not just on the written word, but expands our understanding of law to the image, the corporeal, the embodied and the daily, and demonstrates how performing law in everyday life is an effective means of engaging with and transforming the legal world. Explorations such as these illuminate the 'troubled relationship between outsider voices and the dominant racist, classist and gendered conventions surrounding academic practice, including the valorisation of text over non-text' (Bouclin, Calder and Cowan 2012).

The transformative potential of performance, particularly for those who are marginalized through law, is a contentious issue (Schutzman and Cohen-Cruz 1994; Alexander, Anderson and Gallegos 2005; Cohen-Cruz and Schutzman 2006; Diamond 2007). Ann Elizabeth Armstrong takes up this argument and returns the focus to gender. She argues that as a site where liberatory theory and practice intermingle, Theatre of the Oppressed has strong resonance with feminist theory (2006: 178). This is particularly so, she asserts, for feminists who are simultaneously formulating theoretical positions that incorporate multiple categories of difference and advocating positive strategies for change and for understanding the often unstable, transitive and fluid relationship between oppressor and oppressed. Here Armstrong asserts:

> Feminist epistemology frequently challenges the distinction between subject and object, revaluing the position of those that frequently serve as embodied objects (gendered or racialized 'Others') to knowing subjects ('universal' white men). Similarly, [Theatre of the Oppressed] values the particularity of embodied experiences, activates the sensate body, and acknowledges the mind-in-the-body … Instead of denying the existence of cultural boundaries, Theatre of the Oppressed focuses on displacing and reconfiguring the boundaries between subject and object, mind and body. … The body is a critical site in both Theatre of the Oppressed and feminism through which to explore identity politics, locating experience within the particularities of physical and social contradictions.
>
> As one means of approaching issues of oppression, so central to the perpetuation of law's power, the value of these embodied techniques includes their capacity to unearth the importance of positionality in the very understanding of what constitutes oppression. (Armstrong 2006: 179)

Using the role that performance offers law, particularly as a way to understand the complicated interactions of identity, the body and oppression, the next section details the development and implementation of an orientation component, based on Theatre of the Oppressed, designed for and by the students of UVic Law.

Workshops in the Law School

> Theatre is a form of knowledge; it should and can also be a means of transforming society. Theatre can help us build our future, instead of just waiting for it. (Boal 2002: 16)

This project included the development and implementation of a workshop series delivered at UVic Law. The workshops were designed to involve law students in telling stories about their own experiences at law school, with an eye to transformative change both of the learning and of the practice of law through the presentation of Forum Theatre. The broad goal of the work was to involve the first-year class in a larger-scale version of what these smaller workshops had done. The following describes that process and the ultimate delivery of Forum Theatre in UVic Law's orientation, first in the fall of 2007 and then each fall since.[27]

The Design

The project began as a response to concerns, primarily articulated by equity-seeking groups within the law school, but also by colleagues, of ongoing and persistent issues of classroom climate, discrimination and voice – issues that remain prominent at most law schools across the country.[28] The result was student interest in the design and delivery of a component of the Legal Process curriculum (Law 106) for incoming students: a session addressing equity norms and practice in the classroom.

Legal Process is a mandatory, two-week introductory course at UVic, with all first-year students involved in small group exercises and large group lectures for the first two weeks in September followed by a series of seminars over the course of the fall, and where possible a further interactive week at the outset of the spring term. The incoming class is divided into five sections of 21 or 22 students, with

27 This component of Legal Process has, at the time of publication, been delivered in the 2007–2008, 2008–2009, 2009–2010, 2010–2011 and 2011–2012 academic years.

28 A recent example of how these issues often manifest themselves is a newsletter circulated in the fall of 2007 anonymously to students at the University of British Columbia's Faculty of Law that contained racist, sexist and homophobic comments, cloaked in a satirical format. See a discussion of this particular incident in the local Vancouver media: http://www.canada.com/story_print.html?id=7b3cd5ff-115b-4a98-ac2c-3dd35376ce0b&sponsor [accessed 28 August 2012].

three instructors assigned to each of the five groups. The goals of Legal Process are primarily to introduce basic concepts of law, to instill community values and to provide a social forum to students to ease themselves into law school.[29] Based on a series of workshops that had been designed and delivered in the law school over the course of the 2006–2007 school year, and in consultation with the student body and legal process instructors, it was decided that a process drawing on the theatrical traditions of Theatre of the Oppressed with the goal of a student-designed and delivered component for that fall's Legal Process was the best format to pursue.

The Format

The work involves four stages. First, a series of workshops, specifically designed for delivery at the law school, were offered to the whole student body. The primary goal of the workshops was to enable students through Image Theatre and Forum Theatre to engage with personal challenges they have experienced inside and outside the law classroom.[30] A secondary goal of the workshops was for the students to translate their experiences into script form, with each script portraying an actual moment of challenge at law school, constructed as an anti-model, in the tradition of Forum Theatre. The scripts were written to show a moment or intersecting moments of challenge or oppression, with no solution to the challenge explicit in the text.[31] The scripts portrayed scenes both inside and outside of the classroom involving moments of power-imbalance from relatively benign but uncomfortable student interactions to moments of racism, sexism and homophobia.

The second stage consisted of working with the scripts and ultimately selecting the ones that would form the basis of the exercise. In the first year, this aspect of the process drew on the work and experience of senior practitioners of Theatre of the Oppressed in the community, primarily Lina de Guevara of the Puente Theatre and River Chandler of TheatreWorks Consulting, as well as professors within the law school who were working on the redesign of the Legal Process curriculum. In subsequent years, the students themselves have been the final arbiters of which scripts should be delivered in the fall session.

The third stage is the production of the plays. For the success of this component, it is necessary to recruit students from the upper years who perform the scripts, and to give them some training with the requirements of acting a scene in Theatre of the Oppressed. Given the need to have the scripts enacted in each of

---

29 The materials introduce the objectives of the Legal Process course as being organized around two themes: first, that the legal system is not static and must be viewed as a dynamic process; and, second, that the primary responsibility of legal education rests with the students (University of Victoria 2011: *Processes* 1-1).

30 Agendas from the workshops delivered in the summer of 2011 are attached in Appendix 9.1.

31 The six scripts used in the fall of 2010 are attached in Appendix 9.2. Used with permission of the student authors.

the five legal process classrooms, each year we have to recruit at least 25 student actors. The originating vision was that the actors in each of the five Legal Process sections would be representative of the student body broadly, so that the work of performing the scripts did not fall solely onto the shoulders of the students who had written them. With the assistance of the law student's society each year, we have been able to recruit a group of students who are a snapshot of the student body generally, including members of the student government, students of colour, Indigenous students, students of diverse sexualities, ages and from both the second and third years.

The final stage is the delivery of the exercise. For this component to be successful, it is key to have five trained theatre professionals who can facilitate the Theatre of the Oppressed exercise. This was accomplished through connection to Victoria's Puente Theatre,[32] the Act Now Against Racism workshop group,[33] Victoria's TheatreWorks consulting[34] and through the broader UVic community.[35] Similarly, it is crucial that the audience of the plays have some preparation. As such, prior to the exercise, the first-year students had been given a preface to one of Augusto Boal's books explaining Image Theatre and Forum Theatre (Jackson 2002: xii–xxvii), and two academic readings about classroom climate, one by Brenna Bhandar paying attention to the effects of systemic racism on the law school classroom and one by Patricia Monture-Angus focusing on law itself as a locus of harm in the lived realities of Indigenous peoples. Legal Process has also been modified to include other embodied exercises (see, for example, Bouclin, Calder and Cowan 2012) and the instructors spend some time in the afternoon before the exercise setting up what exactly the students can expect the following morning.

The Delivery

The day then unfolds like this: the facilitators spend about half an hour warming up the class, including some introduction to the theory and practice of political theatre and where possible some exercises to get the audience out of their heads and into their bodies. Then, each of the scripts is acted out by the upper-year students, one at a time. At the end of each scene, the facilitator engages the audience in a process of identifying their concerns with the various sites of challenge and oppression in

32 http://www.puentetheatre.ca/ [accessed 28 August 2012]. Thank you to Lina de Guevara, the Puente Theatre's founding Artistic Director and tour de force.

33 The Puente Theatre offered an intensive 'Act Now Against Racism' workshop in September 2006 to train six facilitators in the Victoria area to do Theatre of the Oppressed in their own communities. Particular thanks are due to Anna Escher.

34 http://www.theatreworksbc.ca/ [accessed 28 August 2012]. Thank you to River Chandler, founder of Theatre Works.

35 Thank you to Catherine Etmanski from the Faculty of Education and the Office of Community Based Research for her ongoing support and critical engagement.

the play, asking the audience to think about what they want to change about what they have seen and why. The actors then began the scene again.

In Forum Theatre generally,[36] the goal of the actors is to stay in character and to take the scene to its natural uncomfortable conclusion, no matter what occurs. In contrast, the goal of the audience is to prevent the play from ending as scripted through active intervention. With the help of the facilitator, members of the audience – or 'spect-actors' in Boal's vernacular – yell 'stop' when they want to try to change the oppression that characters in the scene are facing. They then go into the scene and either add a character or replace a character and try to shift the play's outcome, with the actors instructed to stay in character and respond as truthfully as they can in character to each intervention. The facilitator allows the intervention and the response to it by the actors to carry on for a while, and then works with the actors and the audience to assess the intervention. This is usually done by asking the audience and the actors: what can we learn about the central moments in the play from this intervention? What can we learn about the sexism, racism, homophobia or other oppression in the scene by what intervention was attempted and what that intervention ultimately shifted or reinforced?

The actors then continue and the audience is given the chance to try again to keep the scene from arriving at its scripted conclusion. The presentation of the scenes, the interventions they prompt and the facilitation around them enables a conversation, for the most part, between the upper-year student actors and the first-year student audience about law school, UVic Law in particular and the kind of classrooms they collectively want to have. Although some students remain sceptical about the exercise, the upper-year students offer their reflections about the real moments underlying the scripts and the analogous moments of difficulty they may experience themselves.

In each of the rooms between four and six of the scripts are usually performed, with time for a break. At the end of this period, the student actors and the facilitator leave, enabling the Legal Process instructors, who up to that point have been spectactors themselves, to engage in a debriefing session for the final half-hour. This debrief focuses primarily on asking the students to talk about what they had learned through the exercise. The time is also used to connect the students back to their experiences that brought them to law school, through the time they have spent together in law school to this point, and ahead to what they could expect as they move into their substantive courses the following week, and at some point down the road, into the legal profession.

36 It is important to note that Forum Theatre has evolved in the various places in the world in which it has been developed and implemented. For example, in Boal's description of Forum Theatre, the audience can only replace the protagonist to the oppression (Boal 2002: 242–5). In contrast, in David Diamond's *Theatre for Living*, he consciously adapts this part of Boal's work to enable the replacement of other characters in the play. Our version here is more closely related to Diamond's adaptation, while retaining the significance of the use of the word 'oppression'.

The Results

The success of this project is difficult to quantify, but has been evident on many levels to those of us involved.[37] That first pivotal year, the facilitators and faculty participants were quite pleased by what they saw in the classrooms, from the work of the upper-year students, in the quality and challenge of the scripts, and from the interventions attempted by the first-year students.[38] Upper-year students who acted in the plays gave overwhelmingly positive feedback, with an expressed longing for the opportunity to experience something similar in their own years. And the feedback in the form of anonymous journal entries from the first-year students also marked this exercise – risky as it was – as one of the most powerful experiences of their Legal Process course.[39]

For many of my colleagues, I say somewhat hesitantly that the success of this exercise is measured by the fact that it is not a complete disaster. Not surprisingly, as its biggest supporter, I am also its greatest critic. My own gauge of success is not that it was a feel good exercise in the moment, but that it gives students skills to confront these moments during their time at law school and beyond, and that it contributes to the development of their ethical imaginations for whatever work they may choose to do with their legal educations.

---

37 Each year the students provide anonymous feedback on each aspect of Legal Process in journal form. In the fall of 2007, for example, the anonymous feedback from all 108 students in the first-year class was compiled and roughly tabulated, giving some subjective assessment of the kinds of feedback given. Students were asked to evaluate each of the components of Legal Process. The Forum Theatre component was 'very highly rated' with 71 positive comments, 29 general comments and 8 critical or not so positive comments. Of the 14 components of Legal Process, only 5 were evaluated more positively. Summary of comments on file with the author.

38 One faculty member provided the following reflection following the workshop and circulated to the faculty as a whole: 'I attended one of the groups this morning and am still processing what I witnessed today: courage and leadership from the upper-year actors [names omitted] and our facilitator [name omitted]; care, intelligence, creativity, openness, and support from the first-years; guidance, wisdom, and understanding from faculty members [names omitted]. This was an excellent opportunity for building the kind of community (and world) we aspire to and I look forward to seeing how we can continue this initiative.' Email on file with the author, used with permission.

39 For example, one student writes: 'I believe that this theatre exercise was excellent. It was hard to see these hard situations, especially because they were real student's experiences. This exercise, I think, forces people to be more empathetic towards everyone especially to people in disadvantage. It made it easier to imagine how the person discriminated against might have felt then, and how isolated they can be. It also illustrated how one "insensitive" comment might terribly affect someone else's feelings. It showed me how *active* against discrimination and racism one should be in order to help create a more positive environment.' Taken from anonymous comments compiled by the research assistant to the Director of Legal Process and held on file.

In March 2008, the law school experienced, in a more public and collective way, a 'Forum Theatre moment'. At a school 'Skit Night', a guest performer sang a song that left many in the audience extremely uncomfortable. Intended to be satirical, the song mocked some of the admission policies at a school like UVic Law, policies that recognize some life circumstances to be considered alongside a student's marks and LSAT scores. In my view, the 'success' of introducing Forum Theatre in Legal Process can best be assessed at a moment like this, where students, faculty and staff put up their hands, actually and metaphorically, and yelled 'stop'. They may not have had solutions readily to hand, but they knew that they needed to interrupt.

In this way, what continues to be of interest, as the students' law school experience progresses, is the effect this early critical dialogic engagement with classroom climate has on each class' engagement with the law and each other.[40] At the end of the day, it is clear that there are levels of discomfort experienced in the learning of law in Canada – what this project continues to explore is whether a model of learning law utilizing theatre as one of its tools will reach differently situated students.

Continued Presence at the Law School: Connecting Performance, Performativity and Law

A project of this nature cannot be a one-off attempt. Nor is it a panacea for the difficulties inherent in the learning and practice of law. And although the project attempts to de-centre text in its goal of getting students to act with their bodies, it still has text as part of its delivery.[41] Thus, the goal is to continue to develop and redevelop critical pedagogy for delivery at the law school to explore the various ways in which the relationship between performance, pedagogy and law offers opportunities for law students to further their skills as law students, future legal actors and engaged members of the legal profession working with diverse and equality-seeking communities. Alongside this work, however, is the much-needed work of integrating some of these performative exercises more centrally into substantive course work and furthering the development of a curriculum

40 One important aspect of this project is scheduling an hour in which all of the students can come together after the exercise to talk about the work. This can elicit the critical feedback that is necessary to ensure that the work's goals are being met, and it can also provide an opportunity for student participants and actors to learn from the work done in the other classrooms. In the fall of 2008, for example, the large group session enabled several students critical of the exercise to voice that criticism and for other participants to learn not only from the successes in their own rooms but from the challenges in others.

41 My point here is that despite having a textual component, this kind of exercise primarily de-centres text as the central mode of learning.

for legal ethics and professionalism which challenges the accepted definitions of those terms.

It is envisioned that this kind of course work, either integrated or standing alone, will be grounded in a methodology that aims to disrupt the notion of learning law as banking education; an opportunity to use non-text-based media as a means of rethinking the relationship between lawyers, legislators and citizens; and a series of games and exercises that develop the performative skills of students who will in some capacity act on behalf of others in their legal careers. The introduction of this work in Legal Process is thus one step in the larger project, described earlier, of integrating the transformative potential of pedagogical tools that de-centre our reliance on text and promote engaged experiential learning into Canadian legal education.

The relationship between performance, pedagogy and law in legal education is rarely theorized or studied.[42] The gift that the 'Beyond Text' project offers legal educators is thus immeasurable. The goal of my use of Forum Theatre as legal pedagogy is to disrupt the law school classroom using as a model the way in which Augusto Boal and many others have disrupted the relationship between audience and actors in the theatre, and the way in which Paulo Freire and others have disrupted our understanding of education for people living in poverty. The full potential of this work is, however, yet to be uncovered. Learning law is a privilege. The more conscious and analytical students are of that privilege and its potential, the more open are the possibilities for the active use of law as a transformative tool of social change.

Conclusions: More Beginnings

> In truth, a session of Theatre of the Oppressed has no end, because everything which happens in it must extend into life. Theatre shall have no end! Theatre of the Oppressed is located precisely on the frontier between fiction and reality – and the border must be crossed. If the show starts in fiction, its objective is to become integrated into reality, into life. (Boal 2002: 276)

The fall of 2011 will be the fifth year that this project has been delivered at UVic Law. Each year, the discoveries build on the last. In the summer of 2011, for example, I had the largest ever response to my call for actors. To have upper-year students willing to take time out of their studies to take part in an exercise that is difficult and vulnerable work reminds me both that it is their project and that it matters. From my perspective, what this project aims to explore is whether a model of learning law that utilizes theatre as one of its tools will ensure that enhancing

42 Julie Lassonde's work is a notable exception. See her LLM thesis, *Performing Law*, available online at: http://law.uvic.ca/lassonde [accessed 28 August 2012]. This volume and the work of all involved with 'Beyond Text' will be pivotal in addressing this concern.

the ethical imagination of students is placed at the centre of legal education. Early on in the project, it seemed to me that the answer rested in creating more space for dialogue. Oppression is used in Theatre of the Oppressed to denote a power dynamic based on monologue rather than dialogue. As the work has continued, however, alongside other projects like 'Beyond Text', I have come to embrace the notion that the potential of understanding law as art has much broader and deeper ramifications. It is a means, as Del Mar argues, for 'lingering in the dark, the silent, the ephemeral and opaque, the anxious, the inarticulate … to make ourselves vulnerable … and to thereby become more responsive to the infinite variety and depth of suffering and vulnerability around us' (2010: 992–3). Using a theory of education based on a pedagogy of the oppressed and a methodology based on bringing the creative, the embodied, the visual and the performative into our curricula, this project queries whether this kind of experiential legal education will enable a more ethical practice of law.

Acknowledgements

Thank you to Sharon Cowan, Suzanne Bouclin, Alison Latimer, Qian Mou, Sharon Fox, Allan Wu, Jenni Campbell, Rebecca Johnson, Hester Lessard, Maneesha Deckha, Elizabeth Adjin-Tettey, Maureen Maloney, Andrew Petter, Maxine Matilpi, Catherine Etmanski, Anna Escher, River Chandler and Lina de Guevara for their critical reflection and unwavering support. I have also had the good fortune to present this work at several domestic and international conferences, and by invitation to other law schools in Canada. My thanks to all the spectactors involved in those venues. I am also grateful to the journal editors at *Masks: The Online Journal of Law and Theatre* and to all the participants at the 'Beyond Text in Legal Education' project, with particular thanks to Maksymilian Del Mar, Zenon Bańkowski and Paul Maharg. Ultimately, my gratitude is most due to the students at UVic Law for their honesty, courage and trust. This chapter is dedicated to Emily Goodbrand.

References

Adjin-Tettey, E., Calder, G., Cameron, A., Deckha, M., Johnson, R., Lessard, H., Maloney, M. and Young, M. 2008. 'Postcards from the edge (of empire)'. *Social and Legal Studies*, 17(1), 5–38.

Alexander, B.K., Anderson, G.L. and Gallegos, B.P. (eds). 2005. *Performance Theories in Education: Power, Pedagogy, and the Politics of Identity.* Mahwah, NJ: Lawrence Elrbaum Associates.

Armstrong, A.E. 2006. 'Negotiating feminist identities and Theatre of the Oppressed', in J. Cohen-Cruz and M. Schutzman (eds), *A Boal Companion: Dialogues on Theatre and Cultural Politics*. New York and London: Routledge, 173–84.

Backhouse, C. 2003. *Gender and Race in the Construction of 'Legal Professionalism': Historical Perspectives*, First Colloquium on the Legal Profession, Faculty of Law, University of Western Ontario, London, Ontario, 20 October. Available at: http://www.lsuc.on.ca/media/constance_backhouse_gender_and_race.pdf [accessed 28 August 2012].

Bakht, N., Brooks, K., Calder, G., Koshan, J., Lawrence, S., Mathen, C. and Parkes, D. 2007. 'Counting outsiders: a critical exploration of outsider course enrolment in Canadian legal education'. *Osgoode Hall Law Journal*, 45(4), 667–732.

Bhandar, B. 2002. 'Always on the defence: the myth of universality and the persistence of privilege in legal education'. *Canadian Journal of Women and the Law*, 14(2), 341–7.

Blackburn, J. 2000. 'Understanding Paulo Freire: reflections on the origins, concepts, and possible pitfalls of his educational approach'. *Community Development Journal*, 35(1), 3–15.

Boal, A. 1985. *Theatre of the Oppressed.* New York: Theatre Communications Group.

Boal, A. 2002. *Games for Actors and Non-Actors*, 2nd edn. London: Routledge.

Boal, A. 2006. *The Aesthetics of the Oppressed.* London and New York: Routledge.

Bouclin, S., Calder, G. and Cowan, S. 2012. 'Playing games with law', in Z. Bańkowski, M. Del Mar and P. Maharg (eds), *The Arts and the Legal Academy*. Aldershot: Ashgate.

Buchanan, R. and Johnson, R. 2009. 'Strange encounters: exploring law and film in the affective register'. *Studies in Law, Politics and Society*, 46, 33–60.

Butler, J. 1990. *Gender Trouble: Feminism and the Subversion of Identity*. London: Routledge.

Calder, G. 2007. 'The personal *is* economic: unearthing the rhetoric of choice in the Canadian Maternity and Parental Leave Benefit debates', in S. Cowan and R. Hunter (eds), *Choice and Consent: Feminist Engagements with Law and Subjectivity*. London: Cavendish Publishing, 125–41.

Calder, G. and Cowan, S. 2008. 'Re-imagining equality: meaning and movement'. *Australian Feminist Law Journal*, 29, 109–30.

Cohen-Cruz, J. and Schutzman, M. 2006. *A Boal Companion: Dialogues on Theatre and Cultural Politics.* New York and London: Routledge.

Cowan, S. 2001. 'Identity, community difference: feminist and queer perspectives on the legal regulation of sexuality', PhD thesis. London: Brunel University (unpublished).

DeCoste, F.C. 2001. 'Towards a comprehensive theory of professional responsibility'. *University of New Brunswick Law Journal*, 50, 109–24.

Del Mar, M. 2010. 'Beyond text in legal education: art, ethics and the Carnegie Report'. *Loyola Law Review*, 56(4), 955–94.
Diamond, D. 2007. *Theatre for Living: The Art and Science of Community Based Dialogue*. Victoria: Trafford Publishing.
Dodek, A. 2008. 'Canadian legal ethics: ready for the twenty-first century at last'. *Osgoode Hall Law Journal*, 46, 1–49.
Freire, P. 1996. *Pedagogy of the Oppressed.* London: Penguin.
Freire, P. 2006. *Pedagogy of Hope.* London: Continuum.
Ganguly, S. 2004. 'Theatre – a space for empowerment: celebrating Jana Sanskriti's experience in India', in R. Boon and J. Plastow (eds), *Theatre and Empowerment: Community Drama on the World Stage*. Cambridge: Cambridge University Press, 220–57.
Hooks, B. 1994. *Teaching to Transgress: Education as the Practice of Freedom*. New York and London: Routledge.
Jackson, A. 2002. Translator's introduction to the first edition, in *Games for Actors and Non-Actors*, 2nd edn, by A. Boal. London: Routledge, xxii–xvii.
Lassonde, J. 2006. *Performing Law*, LLM thesis. Victoria: University of Victoria. Available at: http://law.uvic.ca/lassonde [accessed 28 August 2012].
Macdonald, R.A. 2001. 'Let our future not be behind us: the legal profession in changing times'. *Saskatchewan Law Review*, 64, 1–27.
Macfarlane, J. 1996. 'Teacher power in the law school classroom'. *Dalhousie Law Journal*, 19, 72.
Mackenzie, G. 1995. 'The Valentine's card in the operating room: codes of ethics and the failing ideals of the legal profession'. *Alberta Law Review*, 33, 859–73.
Monture, P.A. 1990. 'Now that the door is open: first nations and the law school experience'. *Queen's Law Journal*, 15(1), 179–207.
Pratt, G. and Johnston, C. 2007. 'Turning theatre into law, and other spaces of politics'. *Cultural Geographies*, 14, 92–113.
Pue, W.W. 1991. 'Becoming "ethical": lawyers' professional ethics in early twentieth century Canada'. *Manitoba Law Journal*, 20, 237–77.
Pue, W.W. 2009. 'Introduction', in W.W. Pue and C. Backhouse (eds), *The Promise and Perils of Law: Lawyers in Canadian History*. Toronto: Irwin Law Inc., 1–11.
Schaull, R. 1996. 'Foreword', in P. Freire, *Pedagogy of the Oppressed.* London: Penguin, 11–16.
Schutzman, M. and Cohen-Cruz, J. 1994. *Playing Boal: Theatre, Therapy, Activism.* London: Routledge.
Singhal, A. 2004. 'Empowering the oppressed through participatory theatre'. *Investigación y Dessarollo*, 12(1), 138–63.
Smart, C. 1989. *Feminism and the Power of Law.* London: Routledge.
Thornton, M. 1998. 'Technocentrism in the law school: why the gender and colour of law remain the same'. *Osgoode Hall Law Journal*, 36(2), 369–98.

University of Victoria, Faculty of Law. 2011. *Legal Process Coursebook, Law 106*. Victoria: University of Victoria.

Young, A. 2005. *Judging the Image: Art, Value, Law*. London and New York: Routledge.

Appendix 9.1

Legal Process Workshop, 30 July 2011

Agenda: The Ethical Imagination

Objectives

- Develop self-expression in order to reimagine individual and group challenges in the law school environment.
- Analyse structures, systems and relations of power.
- Practise transformation through non-verbal and verbal dialogue techniques.
- Recognize that what we create and what others will see may be different things.
- Develop cooperation, collaboration and trust-building skills.
- Learn movement exercises, group integration games and narrative techniques that can be used to democratize groups and organizations.

I. Introduction (10:00–10:15)

Goals: convey basic information about the project, my work in the project and Theatre of the Oppressed, set an enthusiastic tone for the workshop, and ensure that guidelines for the workshop are in place.

1. The Envelope
2. Introduction to 'Theatre of the Oppressed'
3. Agenda
4. Guidelines

II. Warm-up Games (10:15–11:00)

Goals: I anticipate the room will be anxious; need good, fun, ice-breaking games to get us warmed up with each other, but also to get us thinking with our bodies; developing trust for the work that we need to do; infused with fun.

1. Warm-up: Walking in the Space
2. Games
    a. Pulling and Pushing
    b. The Knot
    c. Columbian Hypnosis

   d. Driving the Car
   e. Boxing Match
   f. The Lying Game
   g. Bird, Cat, Tree

In the poetics of *Theatre of the Oppressed*, Boal uses exercises and games to develop better awareness of the body and its mechanisms, and to deal with the expressivity of the body as emitter and receiver of messages. The games are dialogue; they require an interlocutor. They are extroversion. Like chess players who physically train before a match, the games are to reinforce that the whole body thinks, not just the brain (Boal 2002: 48–9).

III. Image Theatre: Creating Images of Law School Challenges (11:00–12:15)

Goals: introduce the notion of image creation, demonstrate the key techniques and enable participants to engage with the techniques; use one-on-one interviews to engage the questions of conflict in the classroom.

1. Images and What those Images Provoke
   a. Walking in the Space
   b. Images in the Space
   c. Complete the Image

2. Introduction to Image Creation
3. Creation of Images in Pairs
4. Groups of Four Images
5. Interviews

IV. Lunch (12:15–12:45)

V. Images and Activation (12:45–1:45)

Goals: building on the discussions, goals are to enable image creation from those interviews; enable a discussion on the power of image work; use images as a means of creating and telling stories primarily without words.

VI. Debrief and Next Steps (1:45–2:00)

Goals: conclude the workshop with positive energy and releasing energy; create a mechanism to give gifts; create space for debriefing and discussion of next steps.

1. Debrief
2. Giving Gifts

<u>Legal Process Workshop, 20 August 2011</u>

Agenda: Second Session: Forum Theatre

Objectives:

- Develop self-expression in order to discuss individual and group challenges in the law school environment.
- Analyse structures, systems and relations of power between the audience and the actors.
- Practice transformation through engaged interaction.
- Develop cooperation, collaboration and trust-building skills.
- Learn movement exercises, group integration games and narrative techniques that can be used to democratize groups and organizations.

Goal of Forum Theatre: to transform the spectator into the protagonist of the theatrical action and, by this transformation, to try to change society rather than contenting ourselves with merely interpreting it (Boal 2002: 253).

I. Introduction (10:00–10:45)

Goals: reconnect to the previous session; reharness the playful energy; focus the group on the goals and agenda for the day.

1. Welcome
2. Warm-up Games
   a. Walking in the Room
   b. Blind Knot
   c. Mirroring in Twos
   d. Emily's Morph
   e. Glass Cobra

3. Debrief the Games

II. Forum Theatre (10:45–12:00)

Goals: connect Forum Theatre to Image Theatre; use the medium to enable a discussion and interaction on solutions to racism, focus on the practical and the creative; create awareness of the spect-actors and the bystanders; demonstrate the power of theatre as a form of political action.

1. Introduction to Forum Theatre
2. The 'Rules'
3. Workshopping a Scene
4. Acting out the Scene
5. Interventions
6. Discussion
7. Repeat with other Scenes

In Forum Theatre, in contrast to classic form of theatre, it is the spect-actor, the audience, that takes the heroic stance, not the character or the act … 'And in so doing within the fiction of the play, [we are] preparing [ourselves] to do it in reality as well. [We] come face to face with reality (fictitiously). [We] become acquainted with the difficulties which [we] will meet later – fear of unemployment, [our] fellow workers' arguments, etc. – and if [we] manage to overcome all these things in Forum Theatre, [we] will be better qualified to overcome them in reality when the situation arises. Forum Theatre does not produce catharsis: it produces a stimulant for our desire to change the world' (Boal 2002: 251).

III. Lunch (12:00–12:45)

IV. Workshop: Forum Theatre Scenes (12:45–1:45)

V. Conclusion (1:45–2:00)

Goals: conclude the workshop with positive energy and releasing energy; create a mechanism for evaluation.

1. Concluding Exercise

This is theatre of the oppressed, not the depressed, so the goal of any and all workshops is to end with optimism; we are often good at identifying our oppression but not at identifying our dreams.

2. Feedback

> 'In truth, a session of Theatre of the Oppressed has no end, because everything which happens in it must extend into life. Theatre shall have no end! Theatre of the Oppressed is located precisely on the frontier between fiction and reality – and the border must be crossed. If the show starts in fiction, its objective is to become integrated into reality, into life' (Boal 2002: 276).

Appendix 9.2

Equity Norms and Practices: Legal Process 2010–2011

Script #1

Setting:	**The Student Lounge**
Characters:	**Four students (S1, S2, S3 and S4)**
Context:	***A female student of colour has attended a wine and cheese evening put on by the firms and had a difficult comment made to her. She is struggling with what to do about it and seeks counsel from other students.***

S1: (*Approaches S2 who is sitting and reading*)

S2: Hey – how are you?

S1: (*Visibly upset*) I just was at an orientation to law firms yesterday, and some of the things they said that would qualify you for a position did not sound right …

S2: What do you mean, what kind of things?

S1: Well nobody else in the room seemed to notice … and I was the only one there who is truly … you know.

S2: Can you remember what they said exactly, because maybe they shouldn't be saying that …

S1: Well, basically it's what they implied by talking about the kinds of extra-curricular things you do. Essentially, if you weren't *Western* or *white* enough then they didn't want you and you wouldn't fit properly into firm culture. I think I am going to write a letter, will you edit it for me?

S2: Sure, definitely.

S3 and S4 enter.

S3: Hi, what are you writing there?

S1: It's a letter to one of the law firms at the orientation thing I went to last night. I want them to know how alienated I felt listening to a pitch that was clearly not aimed at students like me.

S4: That's what happens here, what did you expect? We are surrounded by racism! Can't blame people for becoming *white washed* …

S3: (*Rubs S1's shoulder*) But don't worry, it's no big deal, you will find a position.

S4: I'd totally think twice about writing that letter, though – you need to think carefully about your career, even now. Don't want to get *black listed* …

S3: Yes, you know that people will not want to hire you if you try to make trouble!

S1: Oh, I never thought of that.

S3 and S4 leave together.

S2: Hey you – how's the draft coming?

S1: Actually, I've changed my mind about writing the letter. I can't risk it.

S2: What do you mean!? … But it's not right! If you don't take this on – who will?

S1: Just forget about it, you don't know what it's like.

S2: Okay, I'm sorry. Let's meet for coffee after your exam then, kay? (*Walks away – starts shaking head side to side when further from S1 and nods it once downwards in dismay*).

***

Equity Norms and Practices: Legal Process 2010–2011

Script #2

Setting: **The Student Lounge**
Characters: **Four students (S1, S2, S3 and S4). Other students within earshot can be drawn from the audience**
Context: ***A student from Northern British Columbia is introduced to three students in the first week of law school.***

S1: I think you are really going to enjoy it here at UVic.

S2: Thanks, I hope so. I keep hearing about the 'UVic difference', where everyone is so nice and welcoming. I won't lie though, I miss all my friends and my home. It's gonna be a hard adjustment coming from such a close-knit community up North.

S1: I totally understand. Let me introduce you to a couple of my friends. (*Introduces S2 to S3 and S4*) Hey guys meet Sam, he's from up North!

S3: Very nice to meet you when did you move to Victoria?

S2: Just last week.

S4: Cool, where are you from?

S2: Fort St John.

S3: (*Dismissively*) Oh … (*Suddenly looks uninterested*).

S4: I can't believe you actually made it all the way down to Victoria to come to school!

S3: I've heard that barely anyone gets an education up there. Isn't that one of those places where people who get out never want to go back!

S1, S3 and S4 all laugh together.

S2: (*Sheepishly*) well, not really …

S4: (*Cuts off S2*) Wait! Isn't Fort St John the town where the pulp mill is ruining the river, and there's all that clear-cutting going on?

S2: Well, there has been some debate on how to try to make logging more environmentally friendly, but …

S4: Anyone who works at a mill is so selfish! All they care about is getting more money so they can build a bigger house and get a second vehicle. They don't even understand how much damage they are causing to future generations.

S2: (*Clearly intimidated*) Actually, both my parents work at the mill as well as quite a few of the guys I went to high school with. I don't know what we would do if it weren't there. It would be devastating to the …

S3: (*Cuts off S2*) They should totally close that mill. Communities like that just aren't sustainable.

S4: Ya, I think you made a great decision to come to the coast! Got out that trap buddy!

S2: (*Is now looking really uncomfortable*) Thanks …

S3: Ya, it's a good thing you decided to come to UVic.

S3 and S4 walk away.

S1: Hey, it sounds like you have a pretty conservative attitude.
You probably want to tone that down while you're here. Especially during our environmental law class.

End Scene

***

Equity Norms and Practices: Legal Process 2010–2011

Script #3

Setting: **The Student Lounge**
Characters: **Two female students (W1 and W2) and two male students (M1 and M2)**
Context: ***Two male students and two female students are discussing their family law class and their differing views on what the professor has taught them about the enforcement of child support. One of the female students is a single parent.***

Two women are sitting in the lounge talking. Two men are sitting within earshot.

W1: Our family class was pretty hard today.

W2: Why, what happened?

W1: Well, our prof was talking about deadbeat dads, mostly statistical stuff about child poverty and the relationship to non-payment of support. Some of the guys were getting pretty defensive.

W2: Huh. What'd they say?

W1: Well, most of it was sort of mutterings, but one guy did challenge the prof on her use of statistics, and asked a question about a recent case involving a woman denying her ex access to the kids by using a false accusation of abuse.

The two guys turn towards the two women to interrupt.

M1: What, are you taking about that family class thing?

M2: Yeah, that was brutal.

W1: Well, I don't think that was …

M1: I mean, it's clear what side she's on. Why do we have to listen to that?

W1: But the point isn't to …

M2: Men get blamed for this stuff that doesn't even happen, and if we speak our minds about it in class, we're going to get ripped apart.

W2: (*To M2*) You do have a point there.

W1: (*To W2*) What?! (*To the two men*) It's not like she …

M1: (*Mockingly*) And I bet there's someone in the class that's experienced exactly what she's talking about.

W1: Hey man, I'm a single parent, and I can't stand it when people talk about stuff in class they don't know anything about.

M1: See! That's what I'm saying! How are we supposed to talk about this stuff with you in there?

The two men get up and start to walk away.

M2: We shouldn't have to deal with this – that class sucks anyway, it's all theory and no law.

***

Equity Norms and Practices: Legal Process 2010–2011

Script #4

Setting:	**A Law School party**
Characters:	**Three female students (W1, W2 and W3) and one male student (M1)**
Context:	***The students are at a party, W1 is an Indigenous student, something that is not known by the other students in the scene.***

A single table in a living room at a party. Two women are sitting at the table, drinking.

W1: I'm so exhausted. I think this is the first time I've been out of my house in a week.

W2: Wow, you're working really hard.

W1: I'm so behind. I feel like everyone else is miles ahead of me. I've been going through a lot this year with my family.

W2: Oh, I'm sorry to hear that. Is there anything I can do to help?

W1: No. Thanks though. My band is in the middle of a title dispute right now over some land that my people have been using forever. My parents are really involved, and it's been so hard on them.

W2: Oh, are you Native?

W1: Yeah. Yeah, I am. I know I don't really look it.

W2: Oh no, I didn't mean it that way. I just didn't know. I'm sorry to hear about the dispute, that must be hard.

W1: It's okay. You get used to it, I guess.

W2: I'd like to talk about this more, but I really need a drink. Can I get you something while I'm up?

W1: Just some water would be great, thanks.

W2: Sure.

W2 walks off. W1 sits alone, looking uncomfortable for a moment until M1 and W3 walk in and join her.

M1: Hey, how's it going?

W1: I'm alright. School is getting me down. It's nice to have a break.

W3: Tell me about it. Constitutional is kicking my ass.

W1: Really? It's one of the only classes I like.

W2 re-enters with drinks, hands W1 a glass and sits back down.

W3: Uh, I can't stand it. We've been doing 'Native rights' for the past week and it is just so much bullshit.

M1: Why do you say that?

W3: Oh God, I am so sick and tired of hearing people complain about 'Aboriginal rights'. Honestly, I think they've got more rights than I do. I mean, most people can't just go up to a piece of land they think is valuable, start protesting and then be taken seriously at court by claiming they have some sort of ancient ancestral connection.

M1: Hey, Aboriginal people are the poorest people in the country.

W3: So that means they should get favourable treatment by the government? That's racism. I mean, that goes against the *Charter* itself. It violates my s. 15 equality rights. There should be absolutely no benefits or rights based on race. It doesn't make sense.

M1: But c'mon, think about what you're saying. What about history?

W3: What about history? Exactly. Why can't everyone just accept that they are a conquered people and get on with things?

M1: Would you be saying that if Michael was here? You know his parents were in the residential schools.

W3: Well, sometimes I feel like I should be politically correct, but that doesn't mean it's what I really think. I should be able to say what's on my mind with just my friends around.

W1 stands up to leave.

M1: Hey, where are you going?

W1: Oh, just for a walk. I just need some air.

***

Equity Norms and Practices: Legal Process 2010–2011

Script #5

Setting: **Law School classroom, five minutes before the exam**
Characters: **Four students preparing for exam (S1, S2, S3 and S4) and a professor (P) who enters for the start of the exam**
Context: ***Four students are getting ready to sit an exam. S3 is a Muslim student, a fact that is known to one of the other students in the scene, but not all the students. S3 is also a student of colour, while the other students in the scene are white.***

Students are getting ready for an exam which is set to start in five minutes. They are arranging their pens, outlines, etc. On the board is an announcement about an upcoming talk on Terrorism and the Criminal Law.

S2: (*Talking to S3 and gesturing towards writing on the board*) Are you going to that talk on terrorism and the criminal law?

S1: (*Enters the room laughing, stops next to two students who are already seated*) Terrorism, you've got to be kidding!

S3: I'm so curious to see what a talk like that will be about.

S1: Terrorism is all about a bunch of Muslims who are pissed off. (*Laughs at his own comment and sits down to write his exam*).

S3: (*Feeling shocked and upset but trying to contain her anger at the offensive comment*) It is much more complex than that.

S2: (*Turning to S1*) You're so irritating, this is why no one likes you. You just think you know everything right? Racist and narrow-minded white people like you are so offensive and should not be allowed to share your ignorant comments.

S4: (*Turns to S2*) Hey, c'mon generalizations about white people don't help either. I'm white and I certainly don't think like him (*pointing at S1*). Right? (*This final comment is directed at S3*)

S3: Well, you know… (*struggles to find words, looks like she might cry, leaves the room*).

Just then the professor enters the room.

P: Quiet everyone. Does everyone have their exam papers? Turn them over and begin.

The room goes quiet for about a minute and students begin to write furiously. S3 re-enters the room looking visibly distressed.

S3: Sorry, I couldn't find my notes.

P: Well, get started.

***

Equity Norms and Practices: Legal Process 2010–2011

Script #6

Setting: **A First-Year Criminal Law classroom**
Characters: **Professor (P), six students in the classroom (S1–S6), plus additional students to be drawn from the audience**
Context: ***Students are awkwardly asking questions in a Criminal Law class. This is causing varying levels of distress for the other students in the room.***

P: OK, now with the few minutes we have remaining in today's class, let's turn to talking about consent in assault and sexual assault. OK, for the purposes of sexual activity, no consent is obtained if the complainant expresses a lack of agreement to continue … Yes, a question in the second row.

S1: Do you have to ask for consent at every … base? Isn't it awkward if you have to keeping getting consent?

Other students look surprised or baffled.

P: Well, why can't giving consent be sexy? So, consent can be revoked at any time during sexual activity, and anything beyond that revocation moves us into the realm of assault … Another question, from the back. Yes?

S2: *(Hesitantly)* I don't understand. Once two people have consented, aren't they supposed to be able to, um, finish?

S1 giggles.

P: What does the statute say? No consent is obtained where a complainant who has given consent shows a lack of agreement to continue.

S2: But … one person can't just stop consenting right in the middle of things, can they? I mean, c'mon ... (*turns and starts talking to S6 and keeps the conversation going, although now privately*).

Students 3 and 4 glare at S2, Student 5 puts head down on desk.

P: I see from the clock that our time is up – that's an unfortunate place to leave things, so we'll take this up at the start of next class.

S1: (*To S4*) I'm really confused, I really just don't understand.

Students 3 and 4 get up and begin to leave the room.

S3: Can you believe the question that guy asked? Was he asking if it was against the law to … keep going even after a partner asks to stop?

S4: I wanted to say something, but I didn't know what. I feel horrible.

Index

Figures and Tables indexed in **bold**.

For Product Safety Concerns and Information please contact our EU representative GPSR@taylorandfrancis.com
Taylor & Francis Verlag GmbH, Kaufingerstraße 24, 80331 München, Germany

www.ingramcontent.com/pod-product-compliance
Ingram Content Group UK Ltd.
Pitfield, Milton Keynes, MK11 3LW, UK
UKHW020014200926
475702UK00014B/1878
9781138272576